"McKay and West have developed a brief, practical, and p
become more skillful with their critically important emo
evidence, they offer a structured program rich with usefu
examples, and guidance for specific issues. This is an extr
ized, and thorough book—useful for clinicians at any leve

—**Rick Hanson, PhD**, author of *Buddha's Brain* and 1 ̣̣̣̣̣̣̣̣̣̣̣̣ ̣̣̣̣̣̣̣̣̣̣̣̣ *Happiness*

"This book is a must read for any therapist who wants to work with emotionally dysregulated clients in a time-effective fashion. The brief, structured, highly practical emotion efficacy therapy (EET) approach is clearly described—step by step—and integrates mindfulness, acceptance, and emotion processing strategies drawn from different therapy models in a masterful way. Each facet of EET is demonstrated via therapist-client dialogues, which make the concept come alive clinically. There are tons of patient handouts, worksheets, and other useful clinical tools. This book is so well organized that any clinician could use it off the shelf to deliver a highly effective emotion regulation treatment!"

—**Kirk Strosahl, PhD**, cofounder of acceptance and commitment therapy (ACT), and coauthor of *Inside This Moment*

"In this excellent text, McKay and West present EET, a well-crafted treatment protocol that combines techniques from effective, emotion-focused, and transdiagnostic treatments. This well-written eight-week program gives concrete guidelines for the therapist to help their clients enhance their emotional awareness, utilize mindful acceptance and coping strategies to regulate emotions, and choose adaptive and value-based actions. Using concrete examples, monitoring forms, and summary points, this valuable book will provide clinicians with a powerful and much-needed clinical tool. It will help countless clients suffering from emotional distress. It is a must-read."

—**Stefan G. Hofmann, PhD**, professor of psychology at Boston University, and author of *Emotion in Therapy*

"I learned a ton of super-helpful things from reading this book! Written by truly brilliant clinicians, it provides an easy-to-use set of concepts and tools. I love the progress monitoring scales, the transcripts of delivering the interventions, and especially the description of emotion exposure procedures. We often tell our patients to 'sit with' their painful emotions. I've frequently wondered what that meant and how to do that exactly. This book's description of the skills of emotion surfing gives me the information I've been seeking. This book is a gift to me—and to my patients."

—**Jacqueline B. Persons, PhD**, director of the Cognitive Behavior Therapy and Science Center in Oakland, CA; and clinical professor in the department of psychology at the University of California, Berkeley

"Based on sound, evidence-based principles, this book presents a straightforward approach to helping individuals who struggle with intense emotions with few resources or skills to manage them. I highly recommend this book."

—**Michael A. Tompkins, PhD**, licensed psychologist; codirector of the San Francisco Bay Area Center for Cognitive Therapy; assistant clinical professor at the University of California, Berkeley; diplomate and founding fellow of the Academy of Cognitive Therapy; and author of *Anxiety and Avoidance*

"This highly practical and timely treatment flows naturally from the transdiagnostic literature, and offers therapists a clear, step-by-step guide to helping clients improve their awareness of and ability to cope with strong emotions—an important aspect of successful therapy outcomes. Every page is clear, concise, and to-the-point, allowing clinicians to quickly grasp the treatment rationale and master the protocol. The illustrative dialogues and accompanying worksheets reflect the authors' expertise in translating techniques into practice with actual clients, which is supported by the robust initial outcome data. A 'must' for therapists, supervisors, and trainees attempting to treat multiple problems simultaneously using a transdiagnostic approach."

—**Rochelle I. Frank, PhD**, assistant clinical professor of psychology at the University of California, Berkeley

"This is a refreshingly straightforward and practical resource for clinicians seeking to integrate components from acceptance and commitment therapy (ACT), dialectical behavior therapy (DBT), and cognitive behavioral therapy (CBT) to target specific transdiagnostic mechanisms underlying problems with emotion regulation. Instructive handouts and sample therapist-client dialogues bring treatment components to life. Clinicians now have a resource that strategically guides them when helping clients increase awareness and acceptance of emotions, choose value-based actions, and practice distress tolerance skills, all within an exposure-based model. This is the book that clinicians have been waiting for!"

—**Joan Davidson, PhD**, codirector of the San Francisco Bay Area Center for Cognitive Therapy; assistant clinical professor in the clinical science program at the University of California, Berkeley; coauthor of *The Transdiagnostic Road Map to Case Formulation and Treatment Planning*; and author of *Daring to Challenge OCD*

"EET combines strategies from several proven approaches for dealing with distressing emotions. The strategies laid out in this well-written, accessible, and practical guide will show clients how to experience a full range of emotions while reducing their pain and suffering. Each chapter is filled with illustrative case examples and practical worksheets that make it easy to deliver the program."

—**Martin M. Antony, PhD, ABPP**, professor of psychology at Ryerson University in Toronto, ON, Canada; and coauthor of *The Shyness and Social Anxiety Workbook* and *The Anti-Anxiety Workbook*

EMOTION EFFICACY THERAPY

A BRIEF, EXPOSURE-BASED TREATMENT FOR EMOTION REGULATION INTEGRATING ACT & DBT

MATTHEW McKAY, PhD

APRILIA WEST, PsyD, MT

CONTEXT PRESS

An Imprint of New Harbinger Publications, Inc.

Publisher's Note

Distributed in Canada by Raincoast Books

Cover design by Sara Christian
Acquired by Catharine Meyers
Edited by Marisa Solís
Indexed by James Minkin

Library of Congress Cataloging-in-Publication Data on file

18   17   16

10   9   8   7   6   5   4   3   2   1   First Printing

For my dear friend, Jeff Wood, PsyD.
—Matt

For my parents, Robert and Peggye.
—April

Contents

1   Emotion Efficacy Therapy   1

2   Emotion Awareness   13

3   Mindful Acceptance   29

4   Emotion Surfing   43

5   Values-Based Action, Part 1   59

6   Values-Based Action, Part 2   75

7   Relaxation and Self-Soothing   89

8   Coping Thoughts and Radical Acceptance   103

9   Distraction and Time-Out   123

10   Pulling It All Together   139

     Appendix A: Outcome Measures for Assessment   149

     Appendix B: Research and Results   159

     Appendix C: EET Eight-Session Protocol   165

     EET References   261

     Index   267

CHAPTER 1

Emotion Efficacy Therapy

Emotion efficacy is defined as how effectively a person can experience and respond to a full range of emotions in a contextually adaptive, values-consistent manner. As such, emotion efficacy encompasses both the beliefs people have about their ability to navigate their emotional life as well as their ability to do so. The more people can effectively experience difficult emotions, regulate their emotions through coping, and express their values, the higher their emotion efficacy.

In conceptualizing *emotion efficacy therapy* (EET), we reviewed the full range of factors that make up a person's relationship with his or her emotions, and we identified key factors implicated in emotion efficacy. We concluded that *low emotion efficacy* is likely to be the result of key vulnerabilities or patterns of *maladaptive behavioral responses*—behaviors enacted in response to emotional pain, or the desire to avoid pain, which fuel and maintain psychopathological processes. Some common vulnerabilities and patterns may take the form of one of more of the following:

- Biological predisposition or sensitivity that leads to high levels of reactivity

- Significant levels of *emotion avoidance* (sometimes also called *experiential avoidance*)—efforts to avoid experiencing uncomfortable sensations, emotions, and cognitions triggered by internal or external cues

- Significant levels of *distress intolerance*—the perception or the belief that one cannot tolerate aversive emotions

- Significant lack of emotion-shifting skills to downregulate emotion

- Consistent and significant socially invalidating environments

Individuals with these vulnerabilities often develop significant emotion problems. They may also lack understanding of their emotional experience and the clarity or tools to either tolerate difficult emotions, make values-consistent choices, or regulate their emotions. Over time, these vulnerabilities and life-long patterns of maladaptive behaviors can result in chronic *emotion dysregulation* and its downstream symptoms of depression, anxiety, and stress. In fact, these maladaptive patterns become so ingrained that they are all but hard-wired and very difficult to change, leaving individuals feeling trapped, stuck, and hopeless.

In EET, we define emotion dysregulation as the full range of thoughts, feelings, somatic sensations, and behavioral urges that are contextually maladaptive. Emotion dysregulation is also problematic in that it frequently leads to *behavior dysregulation*—acting on emotion in contextually maladaptive ways. In this way, emotion dysregulation and behavior dysregulation lead to low emotion efficacy.

The impact of low emotion efficacy is wide and far reaching. Some data suggest that low emotion efficacy creates and maintains tremendous suffering for the more than 75 percent of people who seek psychotherapy across multiple diagnostic categories (Kring & Sloan, 2010). In addition, pervasive emotion problems can significantly impact clients across multiple domains including interpersonal, work, school, and legal. Low emotion efficacy can significantly impair quality of life, and, in more extreme cases, it can be life interfering.

For example, research shows emotion dysregulation has been correlated with higher levels of depression, anxiety, impulsivity, and suicide (Garnefski & Kraaij, 2007; Carver, Johnson, & Joormann, 2008; Kleiman & Riskind, 2012); reduced quality of life; increased distress and restricted life functioning; increased suffering and pain; impaired memory and problem solving; and diminished contact with meaningful and valued life activities (Richards & Gross, 2000; McCracken, Spertus, Janeck, Sinclair, & Wetzel, 1999; Marx & Sloan, 2002; Hayes, Luoma, Bond, Masuda, & Lillis, 2006). Additionally, emotion dysregulation has been linked to lower social skill functioning, substance abuse, low lifetime achievement, and low sense of self-efficacy (Berking et al., 2011; Eisenberg, Fabes, Guthrie, & Reiser, 2000; Caprara et al., 2008).

Why Emotion Efficacy Therapy?

Despite the prevalence of emotion-regulation problems, available treatments often treat just the symptoms and fail to identify and target the underlying drivers of the problem. In addition, treatments may teach clients how to use skills but can lack the experiential component essential to accelerate learning new ways of relating to and responding to difficult emotions. Even current evidence-based treatments show only modest treatment effects for improving emotion regulation and its downstream symptoms (Kliem, Kroger, & Kosfelder, 2010). Emotion efficacy therapy attempts to provide a more effective, portable, universal protocol for emotion problems.

The underlying philosophical premise of EET is that while pain is unavoidable, suffering is not. Suffering comes, in part, from not knowing how to enact values that bring meaning to life. More often, it comes from the unwillingness to experience difficult emotions, which then fuels distress and leads to more suffering. Moreover, suffering is maintained and even increased when clients try to avoid or control their pain through maladaptive behavioral responses. To the extent that clients can learn how to powerfully navigate the space between being emotionally triggered and their response, they can be empowered to create lives that are increasingly values-consistent and fulfilling.

We believe EET stands to help millions of people increase their emotion efficacy through increasing their ability to regulate their emotions and make choices that are consistent with their values and intentions. Ultimately, *high emotion efficacy*—the ability to experience a full range of emotions and respond with mindful acceptance, values-based action, and mindful coping—means a world where more people create lives that are more authentic, powerful, and conscious.

Emotion Efficacy Therapy: Foundational Elements

EET was conceived as a transdiagnostic, theoretically driven, contextually based treatment integrating findings from affect science, traditional and third-wave cognitive behavioral therapies, and learning theory. As such, EET is an outgrowth of several cognitive behavioral therapies, integrating components of acceptance and commitment therapy (ACT) and dialectical behavior therapy (DBT) into an exposure-based treatment. ACT is a mindfulness-based therapy developed by Steven Hayes, Kelly Wilson, and Kirk Strosahl that teaches clients to accept distress instead of trying to control it, and to commit to action that originates from client values (Hayes, Strosahl, & Wilson, 1999). DBT was developed by Dr. Marsha Linehan and is used in treating severe and complex mental disorders involving serious emotion dysregulation (Linehan, 1993).

The rationale for EET is based on research that supports foundational ideas for its treatment structure and content:

Transdiagnostic Treatment to Treat Low Emotion Efficacy

Data suggests there are more commonalities than differences across diagnostic disorders, which further underscores the need for transdiagnostic approaches to treatment (McEvoy, Nathan, & Norton, 2009). Instead of focusing on reducing symptoms, as in diagnostic treatment, transdiagnostic formulation identifies and targets the mechanisms driving the symptoms as a focus of intervention. From a philosophical perspective, transdiagnostic formulation posits that suffering is not a result of a disorder and its originating pain but rather of the vulnerabilities and maladaptive behavioral responses to the pain.

Further, research suggests that treatment that targets transdiagnostic, or underlying, drivers is more effective than categorical diagnostic formulation (McEvoy et al., 2009; Frank & Davidson, 2014). Transdiagnostic approaches not only address the drivers of problems, they also allow for a single therapy for clients who present with a wide range of symptoms. In fact, a meta-analysis by McEvoy and colleagues (2009) found that unified (transdiagnostic) treatments for emotion disorders are correlated with symptom improvement, perform better overall than wait-list control groups, are associated with improvements in comorbid disorders, and may compare well with diagnostic-specific protocols.

Emotion efficacy therapy targets the transdiagnostic drivers of low emotion efficacy. Instead of focusing on the reduction of emotion dysregulation and its downstream symptoms of anxiety, depression, stress, and impulsivity, EET skills focus on increasing distress tolerance and decreasing emotion avoidance. Using five components—*emotion awareness, mindful acceptance, values-based action, mindful coping,* and *exposure-based skills practice*—clients learn to expand their choices in the face of difficult emotions. Instead of reacting with ineffective, contextually maladaptive responses, they learn tools that allow them to develop a new relationship with their emotions.

Since clients don't often fit into one diagnostic category, or may fit into multiple categories, we believe it is imperative for treatment to identify and target the actual mechanisms that create and maintain suffering. EET targets two transdiagnostic drivers implicated in low emotion efficacy: *distress intolerance*—the perception or belief that one cannot experience distressing emotions—and *emotional avoidance*—attempts to avoid or change aversive emotional experiences. By teaching clients to tolerate distress instead of avoiding their emotional experience, they are empowered to choose to effectively respond to their emotions in a contextually adaptive, values-consistent manner.

Transemotional Learning as the Key to Change

Based on affect science, we know that patterns of behavior are the result of a confluence of factors that work on neural pathways both hardwired from birth (e.g., flight, fight, freeze) and created over time, making up experiences or preferences (Hanson, 2009). These pathways are created and maintained by learning and memory (e.g., when the dog growls at me, he is unpredictable, and I should avoid him; when mommy smiles she is open to hugs and giggles). After learning occurs, these pathways become reactivated in response to internal cues (cognitive, somatic, or affective) and external cues (in the environment) that are appraised as being "like" other events, so the emotional response is automatic. When the learned responses are maladaptive—meaning they fail to motivate effective values-consistent choices—they can cause suffering and play an etiological role across psychopathological disorders and processes (Tryon, 2005).

Research shows that new learning is the key to change and is transemotional, including cognitive, affective, somatic, and behavioral components (Tryon, 2005; Lauterbach & Gloster, 2007). This means that in order to facilitate new responses to painful or feared experiences, new learning must take place. Because learning and memory are created through the encoding of experiences, it follows that utilizing all sensory and perceptual components (cognitive, somatic, and affective) is essential for new learning. In EET, transemotional learning occurs through the activation of all emotional components—thoughts, sensations, feelings, and urges—that build neural pathways around new behaviors.

Exposure-Based Skills Practice to Improve Learning, Retention, and Recall

Grounded in theory and research that support the effectiveness of exposure therapy and state-dependent learning, exposure-based skills practice is the application of skills in an activated state of distress to facilitate transemotional learning (Szymanski & O'Donahue, 1995). In the last twenty-five years, exposure therapy has been increasingly recognized as one of the most effective therapy interventions for the treatment of anxiety. It's also considered to be the gold-standard treatment for panic disorder.

State-dependent learning is the concept that whatever state a person is in when learning occurs becomes encoded and paired with the stimuli. This has several implications for the use of emotion in therapy. For instance, some research suggests that, in studies, participants had superior recall when the same affective state was induced at both exposure and retrieval, compared to those whose affective state was different between learning (exposure) and recall (retrieval) (Szymanski & O'Donahue, 1995). In addition, some studies show that mood may increase access to the neuronal networks that are online and paired with specific affect states (Persons & Miranda, 1992).

EET leverages state-dependent learning through exposure, which facilitates new learning in emotionally activated states by increasing learning, retention, and recall of EET skills. Clients are guided using both emotion and imaginal exposure to face difficult internal and external emotional experiences while applying EET skills to enact contextually adaptive, values-consistent behavioral responses.

Emotion Efficacy Therapy Protocol

EET uses psychoeducation, skills practice, and experiential activities to increase emotion efficacy. By integrating the components of emotion awareness, mindful acceptance, values-based action, and mindful coping within exposure-based skills practice, clients learn to tolerate their distress, downregulate emotions when necessary, and make choices that are consistent with their values.

The Five Components of EET

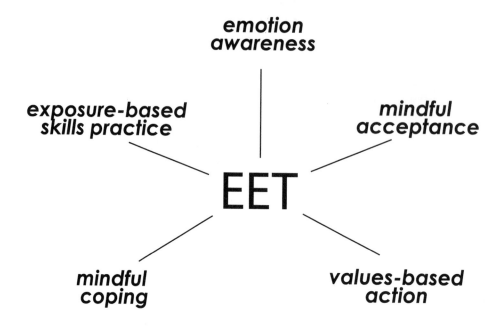

Each session focuses on one or more of five treatment components that build on each other as follows:

Emotion Awareness

Emotion awareness is the ability to make present-moment contact with emotion. Emotion is experienced through its four components, and clients learn to recognize how it manifests through thoughts, feelings, sensations, and urges. Often clients know they are feeling an emotion, but they're not sure what it is. Or they may know the emotion but not realize how it is manifesting in the components of emotion. Emotion awareness also entails understanding the origin or trigger of the emotion as well as the typical lifespan of an emotion wave. Having an awareness of one's emotional experience is the first step toward increasing emotion efficacy.

Mindful Acceptance

Building on emotion awareness, mindful acceptance is the practice of nonjudgmentally and nonreactively observing one's emotional experience and allowing (accepting) each of the components of an emotion: thoughts, feelings, sensations, and urges. Clients learn to tolerate a distressing emotion by learning to experience the emotion—and each of its components—without trying to alter it. Together, emotion awareness and mindful acceptance offer an alternative to emotion avoidance, giving clients concrete skills to practice in place of attempts to avoid or alter their emotional experience.

Research suggests that both emotion awareness and mindful acceptance are components of effective transdiagnostic interventions for emotion dysregulation (Ruiz, 2010; Wilamoska et al., 2010). In fact, observing and accepting experience appears to enhance emotion regulation (Ruiz, 2010). These two core components form the foundation for emotion efficacy therapy. Emotion awareness and mindful acceptance position clients to identify the *moment of choice*—the space between an emotional trigger and a response—when they are able to choose how they respond to their pain. More specifically, clients learn to locate the moment of choice even in the face of difficult or aversive emotions. In this moment, they can choose to just "surf" the emotion wave instead of reacting to it or acting on it.

Values-Based Action (VBA)

VBA is the practice of mindfully enacting a valued intention in the moment of choice. Having increased distress tolerance through emotion awareness and mindful acceptance, clients are now positioned to recognize a moment of choice and make values-consistent choices in the face of aversive emotions. With values-based action, clients first identify what their core values are in a variety of contexts, such as work, home, community, family, and so on. By naming what they value in each of these contexts, clients can then identify specific values-based actions that allow them to express themselves—in the moment of choice—in a manner consistent with their values. As with all the EET skills, clients practice choosing values-based actions in an activated state through exposure-based skills training.

Some research shows that the enactment of values is correlated with psychological well-being and an increase in quality of life (Hayes, Strosahl, & Wilson, 1999; Ruiz, 2010). Because EET seeks not only to increase distress tolerance and emotion regulation but also quality of life, values-based action is a core EET skill. Further, VBA is essential to increasing emotion efficacy, as it enhances motivation to commit to new behavioral responses that are difficult. By choosing values-based action instead of reacting through maladaptive emotion-driven behaviors, clients further increase their distress tolerance as well as the quality of their life.

Mindful Coping

Mindful coping is developed through the practice of using mindful acceptance to recognize a moment of choice, and then utilizing coping skills to downregulate emotion.

Sometimes individuals can become so overwhelmed by difficult emotions that they aren't able to practice mindful acceptance and surf the emotion wave until it resolves, much less choose values-based action in the moment of choice. In these situations, they need strategies for regulating emotion to keep from making a bad situation worse (Linehan, 1993). When clients' capacities to observe, accept, and/or choose values-based action are exceeded by emotional pain, they can choose mindful coping skills to downregulate emotion.

While coping has been typically conceptualized as an attempt to change and alter emotional experience, mindful coping uses mindful acceptance as a portal to choosing emotion-regulation skills. Mindful coping begins with mindful acceptance—the practice of observing and accepting the emotion and its components. It follows with recognizing a moment of choice and choosing a coping skill as a way to downregulate emotion.

The concept of mindful coping is new with EET and represents an attempt to give clients essential emotion-regulation skills in crisis situations, while also encouraging them to choose coping only as a last resort—after first practicing mindful acceptance. Instead of choosing coping skills to avoid or change aversive emotion, mindful coping is chosen with the intention of expanding choices and to help clients recover so they can choose values-based action.

Exposure-Based Skills Practice

This practice refers to the use of EET skills in an activated state using both emotion and imaginal exposure (also called imagery-based exposure). In *emotion exposure*, clients learn to intentionally activate themselves as a way to practice mindful acceptance and mindful coping. In addition, clients learn to use *imaginal exposure*—using imagery from a situation to become emotionally activated, and then visualizing enacting values-based action. As previously discussed, practicing skills in an activated state improves learning, retention, and recall; creates new neural pathways; and makes it easier to enact effective choices in the face of distressing emotions.

How Is Emotion Efficacy Therapy Unique?

By teaching individuals that pain can be faced—that it will not destroy or overwhelm them, and that it doesn't have to lead to more suffering or destructive behaviors—their motivation to tolerate distress will increase, opening the door to expanded choices for action. Through psychoeducation and skills training in an activated state, clients learn new ways of responding to difficult emotions.

In the moment of choice, clients are able to choose to mindfully accept the present emotional experience, enact a values-based action, and/or downregulate their emotions.

Using EET skills, clients are able to effectively experience difficult emotions, recover more quickly from being emotionally dysregulated, break out of patterns of responding that are maladaptive, and express what they value in the face of distress—moment to moment.

As clients practice EET skills when they get triggered by painful emotions, new choices become easier and easier. In a brief time, they can develop a new relationship with their emotions, giving them increased emotion efficacy in significant ways:

- Power to experience themselves as distinct from their emotions

- Power to experience intense emotions, instead of reacting and avoiding

- Power to choose values-based action, even when emotionally triggered

- Power to choose strategies to downregulate emotion and keep from making difficult situations worse

While emotion efficacy therapy integrates components from acceptance and commitment therapy, dialectical behavioral therapy, and exposure therapy, several characteristics distinguish it from current treatments for emotion problems:

- **EET is a unique hybrid.** Emotion efficacy therapy combines emotion awareness, mindful acceptance, values-based action, and mindful coping to provide a range of tools for clients at all levels of emotion efficacy.

- **EET uses exposure-based skills training.** Emotion efficacy therapy uses both emotion and imaginal exposure to accelerate new learning and improve retention and recall.

- **EET incorporates mindful coping.** Rather than just offering coping skills to downregulate emotion, emotion efficacy therapy combines mindful acceptance with select coping skills, allowing clients to first accept their emotional experience, identify the moment of choice, and then choose to intentionally and mindfully shift their emotion.

- **EET is brief and portable.** Unlike some treatments for emotion problems, emotion efficacy therapy can be administered in eight weeks and can be adapted for either a group or individual format.

To date, EET has been shown to dramatically decrease emotion dysregulation ($d = -1.21$), increase efficacy with negative emotions ($d = 1.38$), increase distress tolerance ($d = 1.34$), and decrease experiential avoidance ($d = -0.81$). (For details, see Appendix B.) EET is brief, cost efficient, and available in both individual and group formats.

How to Use This Book

In this book we lay out how to use EET in both individual and group therapy format. Chapters 2 through 10 cover each of the EET processes, including psychoeducation on each of the treatment concepts, examples of therapist-client dialogues, handouts and worksheets you can use with your clients, and scripts for experiential exercises to teach and implement the new skills.

In chapter 2, we cover the first EET skill, emotion awareness: the ability to identify and observe the four components of an emotional response. In chapter 3, we introduce the second EET component, mindful acceptance: to nonreactively and nonjudgmentally observe and accept emotions while emotionally triggered. Chapter 4 covers emotion surfing, which builds on the core skills of emotion awareness and mindful acceptance, applying them to the life cycle of an emotion, and recognizing a moment of choice. Chapter 5 introduces values and values clarification to help clients identify values-based action. Chapter 6 covers using values-based action in the moment of choice. Chapter 7 introduces mindful coping and covers the use of mindful acceptance with relaxation and self-soothing coping skills. Chapter 8 covers the use of mindful coping through mindful acceptance and coping thoughts. Chapter 9 uses mindful coping through mindful acceptance and distraction. Chapter 10 maps out how to help your clients pull all of this together to develop customized emotion efficacy plans; it also offers tips for common issues that may arise in treatment.

This book also has three appendices. Appendix A contains some outcome measures you may find helpful for assessing clients' emotion efficacy before, during, and after treatment. Appendix B features research results from a quantitative outcome trial for EET. Appendix C provides single-page versions of the handouts and worksheets that you can photocopy, and outlines the eight-session protocol for using EET in a group therapy format.

In addition, every handout and worksheet in this book is also available for download at http://www.newharbinger.com/34039.

For each EET therapy session, you'll follow a structured format to allow clients to practice skills, understand the rationale behind them, and do problem solving around any challenges. At the end of each session, you'll review the skills practice assignments to be completed as homework between sessions and recorded on the Skills Practice Record.

Following is the basic session structure for EET:

- Mindful acceptance practice

- Skills practice review and troubleshooting problems with homework

- Review of previous week's skill(s)

- Psychoeducation on the new skill for the coming week

- Practice new skill(s) using exposure

- Homework via the Skills Practice Record

We hope you find EET helpful for working with clients struggling with low emotion efficacy. We believe that when people experience increased choice about how they respond to life, they will find more freedom and power to express the best of themselves. With more freedom and power, they have a chance at a better, more meaningful life.

Summary

Following is a synopsis of content covered in chapter 1:

- Emotion efficacy is defined as how effectively a person can experience and respond to a full range of emotions in a contextually adaptive, values-consistent manner.

- Low emotion efficacy is a result of key biopsychosocial vulnerabilities and patterns of maladaptive responses.

- EET operates on the premise that pain is unavoidable but suffering is optional and can be mitigated and tolerated through the use of select skills.

- EET is a transdiagnostic, theoretically driven, contextually based treatment integrating findings from affect science, traditional and third-wave cognitive behavioral therapies, and learning theory.

- The rationale for EET is based on research of three foundational ideas for its treatment structure and content: a transdiagnostic approach is the most effective way to treat clients with emotion problems; transemotional learning, which involves all four components of emotion, is essential to learning; and new learning is enhanced in an activated state.

- Emotion efficacy can be increased through the use of skills that increase the ability to tolerate distressing emotions by responding through emotion awareness, mindful acceptance, values-based action, and mindful coping.

- Orienting clients to EET is an important part of treatment, especially for enhancing motivation for participation and willingness to try new behaviors.

- Each EET session is structured to facilitate skills practice, skills psychoeducation, skills review, feedback, and skills practice assignments.

CHAPTER 2

Emotion Awareness

In this chapter you will learn how to introduce emotion efficacy therapy and how to teach the first EET skills component, *emotion awareness*. Emotion awareness is the foundation for the rest of treatment, so you'll want to take your time to be sure clients understand how to recognize the components of an emotion before you move forward.

Introducing EET is an important part of the treatment, because it may be the first time clients have considered how they experience or respond to emotions, much less a new way of relating to them. By laying out the what, how, and why of the treatment, clients begin to imagine what is possible for them through their participation, and you can increase motivation for treatment compliance.

Keep in mind that many clients who struggle with emotions have a lifelong history of experiencing their emotions as confusing, overwhelming, unpredictable, destructive, and even dangerous. As such, you'll want to regularly validate clients for seeking treatment and recognizing that being willing to face intense emotions and try new ways of responding can feel challenging and takes practice.

EET Skill Objective: **Observe** the emotion

Orienting Clients to Treatment

The first step to beginning EET is to orient your clients to the treatment. As with any therapeutic intervention, building rapport with your clients is essential. You'll want to validate them for seeking treatment and for being willing to take the challenging steps necessary to change. You might also highlight the motivation required to change and how their lives would look different if they had higher emotion efficacy.

Because the goal of the treatment is to increase emotion efficacy, it's especially important to explain the rationale and goals of EET so clients can begin to imagine what is possible for them by participating. Specifically, introducing treatment as a new way of responding to emotional experience can help motivate clients to try the new skills, as well as instill a sense of hope that by learning new behaviors they can create a more meaningful, enriching life.

Following is a handout you can use to summarize how your clients can benefit from EET. (A single-page version of this—and all other handouts in this book—is available in Appendix C and online at http://www.newharbinger.com/34039.)

What You Can Expect from Emotion Efficacy Therapy

EET will help you learn skills so you can be more powerful in how you respond to your emotions:

- You can learn to watch your emotions, seeing them rise and fall like a wave, rather than being overwhelmed or controlled by them.

- You can see the parts of your emotions—thoughts, feelings, physical sensations, and urges—so they are less mysterious and less outside of your awareness.

- You can learn to experience difficult emotions instead of feeling like you have to run away from them. You can learn to accept the emotion without being driven to do something that hurts you, your relationships, or your life.

- You can learn to recognize the "moment of choice"—when you can either do what your emotion is driving you to do, or choose to do something that expresses your values that will enrich your life.

- You can identify your core values—how you want to show up, even when you're emotionally triggered and upset.

- You can learn to act on your values in the moment of choice, rather than act on what your emotions tell you to do.

- You can learn new strategies to dial down your emotions, even when they are very intense.

- You can practice watching, accepting, and dialing down your emotions until you are really good at it.

Emotion Efficacy

The simplest way to EET is to explain to clients that pain is an inevitable part of life, as are the emotions that go with it. And while we cannot avoid pain or difficult emotions, we can reduce suffering by how we understand and respond to our emotional experience. This is what emotion efficacy—and EET—is all about.

In chapter 1, we defined emotion efficacy as how well individuals can—and believe they can—experience a full range of emotions in varying frequency, intensity, and duration in an effective, contextually adaptive, values-consistent manner.

In other words, high emotion efficacy facilitates the ability to experience distressing emotions without avoiding them or reacting to them. Rather, clients will be able to identify a *moment of choice*—an opportunity in time between the emotion trigger and the individual's response—when they can choose to mindfully accept the experience; choose a valued action; and/or, when necessary, choose to cope mindfully. Increased emotion efficacy also means that clients will be able to break out of patterns of emotional responding that are maladaptive and create what is life enriching, in accordance with their values.

Following is a handout you can share with clients to explain emotion efficacy and its components and goals. You'll want to use this to show how EET can help to build emotion efficacy, one skill at a time. Articulating the goals of treatment will help clients begin to imagine a different relationship with their emotions. It will also help them begin to internalize the key skills EET provides.

What Is Emotion Efficacy?

Emotion efficacy is how well you can—and believe you can—respond to emotions, including intense emotions, effectively. This might mean responding by doing nothing, doing something that reflects what you care about in the moment, or practicing skills that decrease the emotion to keep from making the situation more difficult.

This treatment is based on the idea that pain is an inescapable part of being human, as are the emotions that go with it. And while we cannot avoid pain or difficult emotions, the good news is that we can reduce suffering and increase our quality of life by how we understand and respond to our emotional experience. Another way of saying this is that, while we can't escape painful emotions, we can *choose* how we respond to them. That's what emotion efficacy is all about.

The skills you'll learn from emotion efficacy therapy (EET) will help increase your emotion efficacy through the following five components:

- **Emotion awareness**: recognizing and understanding your emotional experience

- **Mindful acceptance**: observing and accepting emotions, instead of reacting to them

- **Values-based action**: responding to painful emotions with actions that reflect your values, instead of your emotions

- **Mindful coping**: when necessary, using skills to decrease the intensity of your emotions

- **Exposure-based skills practice**: using EET skills in an emotionally activated state

We'll be talking about these skills in every session, and by the end of treatment you'll know about and have experience using each of them.

Increasing Emotion Awareness

Once clients have been introduced to the basic goal of EET and understand what emotion efficacy is, the next step is to teach them about emotion awareness. In this section, clients will develop better awareness of their emotional experience through understanding the nature of emotions, the role emotions play in motivation and choices, and how they experience them. By understanding their emotions from a process level, clients will be more able to observe their emotional experience without getting overwhelmed or caught up in it. In addition, clients will learn how to watch emotion by observing its four components: *thoughts, feelings, sensations,* and *urges.*

Clients often believe that their emotions are facts. They think that they have no choice but to react and act on their emotions. Emotion awareness is the first step toward developing the ability to simply observe one's emotional experience. Start by explaining what emotions are and what they are not.

- Emotions are messages sent by the brain to help respond to perceived threats and opportunities.

- Emotions are not the "truth," nor are they static. Rather, they change like the weather.

- Emotions urge us to action. Sometimes those actions help us, but often they are dysfunctional and result in chronic suffering. Bottom line: being easily or constantly triggered doesn't lend itself to quality of life.

Emphasize the good news: while one can't escape distressing emotions, one can choose how to respond to them. That means not assuming that emotions are "true." Rather, one can conceptualize emotions as messages that are based on what the brain thinks is "true."

Many clients with emotion regulation problems show up with low distress tolerance and a heightened vulnerability to stress. Given the natural imperative of distressing emotions—even once skills are learned—your clients will wonder how they can respond differently to distressing emotions. Most clients seeking help for emotion problems have long histories of becoming emotionally dysregulated, reacting through contextually maladaptive behaviors, and/or attempting to alter their reactions (control, suppression, numbing, emotion substitution, etc.) (Brach, 2003).

Reassure your clients that skills practice is key, both in session and during the week outside of session. Like any behavior that is repeated, responding adaptively to emotional distress will get easier the more it is practiced. And knowing there may be other ways of relating to their emotional experience leaves clients with more flexibility and choice in how they respond.

Following is a handout you can use to introduce emotion awareness to your clients.

Emotion Awareness

What Are Emotions?

What are emotions, really? Most simply, emotions are signals that help you respond to what your brain thinks is happening. Here's how they work: the brain responds to internal and external cues (events or observations from our environment). Then the brain produces biochemical messengers, which we experience as emotions. These emotions motivate us to make choices. For example, the emotion we know as anxiety helps us choose to avoid danger. Anger helps us choose to fight when we feel threatened. Sadness helps us choose to withdraw when we need to process a loss or failure.

From birth, our amazing brains are evolutionarily wired to protect us from harm—to help us survive. That means any time your brain is sensing a threat to your well-being, it will do everything it can to send you emotional messages to motivate you to protect yourself. You may have heard about this process referred to as "flight, fight, or freeze," all of which are common responses to intense emotions.

However, while our emotional wiring has been adaptive for the survival of the human race over time, the survival wiring doesn't always serve us when it gets activated in a non-survival situation. Over time, your brain develops a "negativity bias," whereby it constantly scans your environment for anything negative that could be interpreted as a threat so it can protect you. The downside of this protective negativity bias is that you can end up in a state of constant anxiety, or you can be easily triggered—whether or not there is an actual threat.

Author and psychotherapist Tara Brach explains how the negativity bias impacts us: "The emotion of fear often works overtime. Even when there is no immediate threat, our body may remain tight and on guard, our mind narrowed to focus on what might go wrong. When this happens, fear is no longer functioning to secure our survival. We are caught in the trance of fear and our moment-to-moment experience becomes bound in reactivity. We spend our time and energy defending our life rather than living it fully" (2003, p. 168).

EET can help you learn how to respond to non-survival emotions using skills that will help you respond effectively.

Why Do Some People Struggle with Emotions?

You've probably noticed that some people tend to be more emotionally reactive than others. We are all unique human beings, and how we experience emotions also depends on the wiring in our brains. While we are all born wired for survival, some of us are born with a tendency toward heightened emotional sensitivity. Others develop this tendency as a result of difficult experiences that leave them more emotionally reactive to certain cues.

If you are someone who has heightened sensitivity, you may have an increased vulnerability to stress. Even more, the heightened sensitivity to certain cues can become so ingrained and the emotional reactions so automatic that you may forget you have choices when you get triggered. Unfortunately, this emotional reactivity can negatively affect your well-being, quality of life, relationships, personal goals, and long-term health.

For this treatment, we will focus on how you can respond to distressing emotions and increase your emotion efficacy. You will learn how to stop being controlled by your emotions, how to respond in ways that reflect your values, and how to create more of what you want in your life.

Following is a sample therapist-client dialogue of how you could introduce emotion awareness to your clients.

Therapist-Client Dialogue Example: Introducing Emotion Awareness

Therapist: Let's talk a bit about emotions and how we understand them. What do you think of when you think of an emotion?

Client: It's something that tells me how I'm feeling?

Therapist: Right. Your brain sends you messages to help you make choices. So what kind of messages might the brain send if, for example, you see a black bear?

Client: Fear!

Therapist: Exactly. And what might the fear make you want to do?

Client: Run far, far away!

Therapist: Yes. Let's try another example. You know how you've shared that you feel very hurt when you're friends don't call you back?

Client: Yeah, that's really tough for me. I feel really hurt when that happens.

Therapist:	What do you think your brain is trying to tell you through the feeling of hurt?
Client:	Hmm…maybe it's telling me to watch out?
Therapist:	So it could be telling you there's something you need to pay attention to… something that could be negative? What else?
Client:	Well, it also makes me just want to withdraw. I will go to my room and put music on and just try to get some perspective about it—whether I should be mad or let it go.
Therapist:	Right. So your brain is sending you emotional messages to motivate you to take some space?
Client:	Yeah. I guess the message is something like: you're feeling hurt because something bad happened, and you need some time before you can know what to do…
Therapist:	Right. That's what your brain thinks is true—that something bad happened. And it motivates you to withdraw so you can try to figure it out.
Client:	Okay. I'd never thought about it that way.
Therapist:	Uh-huh. Emotions are just messages from your brain based on what it thinks is happening. The more you understand this, the more you'll be able to choose to respond to emotional messages in ways that are helpful.

What Are Emotions Made Of?

In this next section, you will help clients understand the four components of emotion. You might emphasize that, in our culture, emotion is a construct commonly collapsed with just one aspect of emotion that we know as "feeling." However, emotions are much more complex. Distinct from a mere feeling state, emotions are constructs composed of thoughts, feelings, physiological or somatic sensations, and urges. Understanding the four components of emotions will help clients become better observers of their emotions and more clear and articulate about how they experience them. Being able to deconstruct emotional experience will also position clients to create space to find the moment of choice, when they learn to choose to respond adaptively.

Following is a handout you can use to introduce the four components of emotion as well as how emotions are experienced.

Anatomy of an Emotion

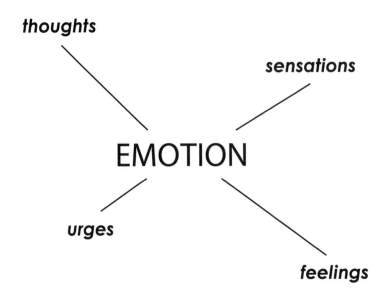

thoughts

sensations

EMOTION

urges

feelings

There are four components that make up your experience of an emotion:

- **Thoughts:** Thoughts are the content of what you're thinking. For example, "I never do anything right," or "I want to get out of here."

- **Feelings:** Feelings are the label or interpretation we give the emotion, for instance, sadness, frustration, joy, and so on.

- **Sensations:** Sensations are anything you feel in the body. This might be a sense of looseness and ease in the body when relaxed or muscle tension when anxious.

- **Urges:** Urges are impulses to do something—or not to do something. Examples include the urge to leave, the urge to yell, the urge to withdraw.

Let's consider one example: If something great happens, you may have the thought, "There is so much to look forward to!" The feeling may be excitement. You may notice sensations of looseness and energy in your body. You may experience the urge to engage with people and/or dance around.

Two more examples: When you feel sad, you may have the thought, "I will always be alone." You may sense tightness in your stomach and a lack of energy in your body. You may have the urge to withdraw from people. If someone threatens you, you may feel angry, you may think, "How dare he say that?!" You may notice the sensation of increased heart rate and energy. You may have the urge to attack the person.

Therapist-Client Dialogue Example: Introducing the Four Components of Emotion

Therapist: I wonder if we could go a little deeper to explore the components of emotion and how they work?

Client: Okay…or how they don't work [laughs mirthlessly].

Therapist: Right [smiles]. So our brain is wired so that when we get cues from our bodies, or our environments, it interprets those cues and sends us messages about how to respond. But it's more complex than that. Do you remember the four components of emotion?

Client: Uh, I think so…feelings, thoughts, sensations, and urges?

Therapist: Great. So let's look at how they work together to make up an emotion. If you were to see a big black bear standing outside your door, what do you imagine you'd feel?

Client: Freaked out! I mean, really scared.

Therapist: Okay. So the feeling would be fear?

Client: Yeah.

Therapist: And what's the thought that goes with seeing that bear?

Client: Probably that I could get hurt!

Therapist: Okay. And what sensations do you think you might experience?

Client: Hmm. I guess my heart rate would go up? And I might get really warm, like I usually do when I get freaked out.

Therapist: Okay, great. And what would you have the urge to do?

Client: Run and hide!

Therapist.   Exactly. We've just walked through the four components of an emotion. Upon seeing a black bear, you had the feeling of fear; you had the thought that you could get hurt; you had the sensation of a racing heart and warmth; and you had the urge to run and hide.

Client: Yeah. So how does that help me?

Therapist:	Good question. You probably don't run into many black bears. But let's look at that situation last week when your boss invited you into her office. What was the feeling then?
Client:	Fear [laughs]. Almost the same as a bear.
Therapist:	And the thought?
Client:	I'm in trouble. She's gonna tell me I've screwed up. She'll give me a box and tell me to pack my desk.
Therapist:	Right. And the physical sensation?
Client:	Hot, sweaty. Heart racing. Throat tight.
Therapist:	Okay, and the action urge?
Client:	Go home and say I'm sick. Get critical of the boss and my job. Say something pissed off; be defensive.
Therapist:	Does seeing these four parts of an emotion help you in any way? If you were observing yourself during that situation?
Client:	I could see I was scared and freaking myself out with those thoughts. And maybe I could see the urges and choose to do something else.
Therapist:	Terrific. That's what observing the four components of an emotion can do; it helps you see how your thoughts can intensify feelings and that you have a choice in how you respond. Learning to observe your emotions, and to notice their components, will help you experience them as less overwhelming, less confusing—and you won't get so caught up in them. Any questions about that? [Answers and/or clarifies any questions.] Now you can practice emotion watching on your own, too, using the Emotion Watching Worksheet.

Following is a worksheet clients can use to practice emotion awareness by observing and recording the four components of emotion when they get triggered, as part of their skills practice outside of session. Also shown is a list of feeling words to assist clients in identifying the specific feeling label that goes with the emotion. Both are available in Appendix C and at the website for this book.

Emotion Watching Worksheet

Observing the Four Components of Emotion

Use this worksheet to record the four components of emotion you experience from specific triggers.

Triggers	Thoughts	Feelings	Sensations	Urges

Feelings Word List

Adored	Disturbed	Infatuated	Satisfied
Afraid	Eager	Inspired	Scared
Amazed	Embarrassed	Interested	Scattered
Angry	Empty	Irritated	Secure
Annoyed	Energetic	Jealous	Shy
Anxious	Enlightened	Joyful	Smart
Ashamed	Enlivened	Lively	Sorry
Blessed	Enraged	Lonely	Stimulated
Blissful	Envious	Loved	Strong
Bored	Exhausted	Loving	Surprised
Bothered	Flirtatious	Mad	Suspicious
Broken	Foolish	Moved	Terrified
Bubbly	Fragile	Nervous	Thankful
Cautious	Frightened	Obsessed	Thrilled
Comfortable	Frustrated	Optimistic	Tired
Concerned	Fulfilled	Overwhelmed	Touched
Confident	Glad	Passionate	Trusting
Confused	Guilty	Pleased	Uncomfortable
Content	Happy	Proud	Unsure
Curious	Helpless	Puzzled	Upset
Delighted	Hopeful	Regretful	Vivacious
Depressed	Horrified	Relieved	Vulnerable
Determined	Hurt	Reluctant	Worried
Disappointed	Hysterical	Respected	Worthless
Discouraged	Impatient	Restless	Worthy
Disgusted	Indifferent	Sad	

Now that your clients understand the goal of emotion efficacy therapy, the nature of emotions, and the components of emotions, they are ready to begin experiencing their emotions with increased awareness. Emotion awareness will set them up to learn the mindful acceptance skills introduced in chapter 3.

Session Structure

You'll want to orient your clients to the structure of each EET session as follows:

- Mindful acceptance skills practice

- Skills practice review and troubleshooting challenges

- Review of previous week's psychoeducation and skill

- Pyschoeducation on new skill

- Practice of new skill

- Imaginal or emotion exposure using new skill

- Homework via skills practice record

Skills Practice Record

A new skill or skills will be taught each week, and clients are asked to practice these skills each day and to keep a record of it using the Skills Practice Record (in reproducible form in Appendix C).

As part of skills practice, clients are also encouraged to do their own emotion or imaginal exposure, using the new skill they've learned. Instructions on how to do this are included in chapter 3.

In addition, clients are encouraged to keep track of any events that are emotionally triggering to them, with the goal of identifying any recurring patterns or themes. Be sure to leave at least ten minutes at the end of your session to answer any questions about the skills they've learned previously or in session, or how to complete the assigned homework. Ask clients to bring their Skills Practice Record each week so you have a sense of how their practice is going outside of session. This will also help you troubleshoot any challenges that come up. After session 2, skills practice will always include at least ten minutes of daily mindful acceptance practice. While some clients will gravitate toward some of the skills more than others, you may encourage them to practice all of them, especially the ones they find more difficult. Often the skills that feel the most difficult will be the most helpful to them. You can let clients know that, by the end of the treatment, they will be asked to create their individualized emotion efficacy plan, but that during treatment they are encouraged to practice all of the skills.

Skills Practice Record

Emotion Efficacy Therapy

Directions: Place a check mark next to the skill you practice each day. Record any triggers at the bottom. Bring this record to your next session.

	Day 1	Day 2	Day 3	Day 4	Day 5	Day 6	Day 7
Observe the four parts of an emotion: sensations, feelings, thoughts, and urges.							
Observe, accept, and surf your emotion wave, with SUDS.							
Observe, accept, and choose a values-based action.							
Observe, accept, and choose a relaxation skill.							
Observe, accept, and choose a self-soothing skill.							
Observe, accept, and choose a coping thought.							
Observe, accept, and choose to practice radical acceptance.							
Observe, accept, and choose a distraction strategy.							
Observe, accept, and choose a time-out.							

Emotional triggers: Record any events or emotions that are distressing during this week.

_____

_____

_____

Summary

Following is a synopsis of content covered in chapter 2:

- EET operates on the belief that pain is an inescapable part of life, but we can reduce suffering and increase quality of life by how we respond to the pain.

- Emotions are messengers that play an important role for our survival. Emotions are not facts. They are just the messages our brain sends to help us survive what it perceives as real. They are messages that urge us to action.

- Emotions are effective messages unless they occur as intense and overwhelming in non-survival situations. Humans have a bias toward negativity that sometimes leads us to interpret neutral or non-survival situations as threatening.

- Watching emotion involves observing the four components: thoughts, feelings, sensations, and urges. Being aware of these components is the first step toward learning to respond to emotions in a new way.

- EET skills are taught in an emotionally activated state to enhance learning and help clients recall the skills when they are triggered.

- Emotion awareness is the first step toward learning to observe emotions instead of reacting to them or acting on them.

CHAPTER 3

Mindful Acceptance

Mindful acceptance is the second component of EET and is derived from the practice of mindfulness meditation and mindfulness-based stress reduction. It builds on the skill of emotion awareness (chapter 2) and prepares clients to practice emotion surfing (chapter 4). Mindful acceptance adds to emotion awareness an intention of nonjudgmental observation and acceptance. It also emphasizes perspective taking on emotional experience that helps clients distinguish themselves from their emotional experience, creating space and flexibility to respond to pain in a contextually adaptive, values-consistent manner.

EET Skill Objective: Observe + Accept the emotion

Psychoeducation on Mindful Acceptance

In EET, we use the skill of mindful acceptance to facilitate a posture of nonjudgmental observation, flexibility, and curiosity about one's experience in the present moment. Mindful acceptance is simply combining that posture with emotion awareness. By making contact with the present moment, and learning to observe and accept all components of emotion, clients can begin the practice of consciously and intentionally choosing their responses.

By practicing mindful acceptance, clients also learn that they are not their emotions. They learn that, as the observer of their experience, they are constant while their emotions come and go. Similar to defusion exercises for thoughts (Hayes et al., 1999), clients learn to defuse from their emotions by observing and accepting all components of the emotion: sensations, feelings, thoughts, and urges. They learn that they can watch and allow emotional experience without collapsing themselves with their emotions. This perspective-taking practice will create the space that allows clients to locate the *moment of choice* (covered later in this chapter) when they are emotionally triggered, and they can choose how to respond.

Mindful acceptance is a radical departure from how people instinctually respond to difficult emotions, especially those who struggle with emotion problems. Humans are wired to survive difficult emotions by avoiding the experience of them, and/or reacting or acting on them to defend or shift the uncomfortable experience. Often, instead of observing and accepting the triggered experience, clients default to maladaptive responses that provide short-term relief, even though they do not ultimately help them effectively respond.

Some clients may also struggle at first with exposing themselves to their pain. To experience pain without avoiding it, acting on it, or attempting to control it may feel like a brave, new, and terrifying world. Clients may have become so skilled in avoiding their emotional experience that they find it difficult just to connect to their experience of the present moment. Discomfort is to be expected, especially since it requires doing the opposite of what our brains are evolutionarily wired to motivate us to do: avoid pain. As with any new behavior, responding to difficult emotions with mindful acceptance will take time and practice, but it is essential to emotion efficacy.

As the treatment progresses, it will be beneficial to help your clients continually reflect on the ways in which avoiding pain, or trying to alter their emotional experience, keeps them trapped in a vicious cycle of emotion dysregulation. This maladaptive responding also prevents clients from showing up in a way that reflects their values and creating what they want. We will explore this in detail in chapters 5 and 6, Values-Based Action Part 1 and Values-Based Action Part 2.

It may also be helpful to emphasize that mindful acceptance does not imply a condoning or approving of the pain or its trigger but rather an allowing of an experience outside of one's control. And, ultimately, practicing mindful acceptance is what will allow clients to respond to pain and difficult emotions in ways that are authentic and life enriching.

Before you begin the session on mindful acceptance, you will want to check in with your clients to see what they may know about mindfulness, so you can gauge how much psychoeducation they may need. Below are a few "primer" videos on mindfulness that may be helpful to clients who are not familiar with mindfulness.

- Short animated clip on mindfulness: https://www.youtube.com/watch?v=5d 46amlJEkI

- Brief introduction with mindfulness expert Jon Kabat-Zinn on mindfulness, taken from psychalive.org, 2013: https://www.youtube.com/watch?v=HmEo6 RI4Wvs

Following is a handout you can use to introduce mindful acceptance, along with a script for conducting mindful acceptance practice with clients.

Mindful Acceptance | Observe + Accept

Mindful acceptance is derived from the practice of mindfulness, which has been shown to reduce psychological stress and improve well-being in numerous studies. The practice of mindful acceptance is essential for emotion efficacy because it will help you better tolerate difficult emotions, recover more quickly, and respond in ways that enrich your life moment to moment.

Mindful acceptance will help you practice observing and accepting emotions instead of reacting to them, avoiding them, or trying to control them. It doesn't mean you have to "like" your emotions; it simply means that you don't resist what you are experiencing.

One helpful metaphor is to think of yourself as the atmosphere and your emotions as the weather. The atmosphere is constant, while the weather is ever-changing. In mindful acceptance, you simply observe and accept changing weather, without reacting, while you as the observer remain constant.

There are many benefits to using mindful acceptance when you are emotionally triggered:

- Practicing mindful acceptance can help you tolerate pain without acting on it.

- Practicing mindful acceptance can help you recover more quickly from the distress of the trigger.

- Practicing mindful acceptance can help you find the space you need to thoughtfully and consciously choose how you will respond to the pain.

Mindful acceptance is practiced by learning to observe and accept the four parts of emotion: sensations, feelings, thoughts, and urges. Following is a simple description for practicing mindful acceptance you can use as you do your skills practice outside of session. Try to practice for at least 10 minutes a day when you are resting or when you get emotionally triggered.

1. Sensation Acceptance

    Scan your body for sensations with the intention of observing and accepting them instead of reacting to them. Just notice all the details of the sensations: size, shape, temperature, tension, and movement. See if you can soften to the sensation and make space for it, without trying to change it…just allowing it to be exactly as it is.

2. Feeling Labeling

    Try to identify the feeling that goes with the emotion. Name it and allow it to be exactly as it is, without judging it.

3. Thought Watching

Clear your mind, and then wait and watch for each thought as it arises; let the thought go without getting involved in it. Come back to the present moment and wait for the next thought to show up. When a thought arises, you might say to yourself, "There's a thought," and then just let it go. If you find yourself struggling to let the thought go, you might just acknowledge it as a "sticky thought" and then let it go.

4. Urge Noticing

Notice if the emotion comes with an urge to do or not do something. Allow yourself to sit with the urge, without acting on it or judging it. Then notice what it's like not to act on it.

The more you practice these mindful acceptance skills, the bigger your emotion efficacy muscle will grow. It will get easier and easier to observe and accept your emotions instead of acting on them. Practicing mindful acceptance will also prepare you to use the other skills you will learn in EET.

Script for Guided Mindful Acceptance

For the next ten minutes I'm going to lead you through a mindful acceptance practice exercise. You will practice observing and accepting your emotional experience in the present moment. Practicing mindful acceptance in a neutral state will build your emotion efficacy muscle and make it easier for you to use this skill when you are triggered.

First, just sit comfortably, and either close your eyes or relax your gaze and pick a spot to focus on in front of you.

Now, take a few minutes to notice any sensations in your body. Scan your body until you find a sensation and rest your attention on it. See if you can let it be just as it is and get curious about it. Notice its size and shape; whether it's moving or staying the same; if there's any temperature or tension to it. See if you can soften to it, or even lean into the sensation…

Now, see if you can identify a feeling label that goes with the sensation…just name it and allow it to be as it is without judgment or reacting to it.

Next, we'll spend a few minutes just noticing and watching our thoughts. Our brains produce different kinds of thoughts all the time, and the key is not to get involved with them. Instead, as each thought arises, you can simply say, "There's a thought," and then let the thought go. Then, just return to the present moment, and wait for the next thought to arise. For the next few minutes, notice your thoughts until I say stop…

Okay, now stop. Next, see if there's an urge that goes with your sensations, feelings, or thoughts. It could be an urge to do something or not do something. Try to just sit with the urge. Notice what it's like not to act on the urge, to just surf it.

[Allow the client to sit with the urge for 30 seconds. Then repeat the sequence one more time.]

Before you come out of this exercise, take a few deep breaths and slowly open your eyes as you bring your attention back to the room.

Using Exposure in EET

Research has shown that rehearsal in an activated state can improve learning, retention, and recall (Szymanski & O'Donahue, 1995). Too often treatment includes knowledge about what to do but not the practice that will help clients encode the new behavior. Many clients who struggle with emotion dysregulation lack both the knowledge and practice of using skills to respond to distress. By using exposure-based skills practice, clients are able to create the new neural pathways they need when they are triggered outside of session.

In EET, we use two types of exposure as a way for clients to access difficult emotions and practice skills in an activated state. The first type, *emotion exposure*, involves exposing to all parts of emotion in an activated state. The second type, *imaginal exposure*, involves imagining a scenario, exposing to the emotion that goes with the scene, and, in an activated state, visualizing behavioral responses to the distressing situation.

You'll want to prepare your clients for exposure exercises by doing psychoeducation on how it works, as well as how to effectively engage in the exercise. Exposure can be especially difficult for clients who have low distress tolerance and who may also be especially sensitive to somatic sensations, as with panic disorder. It will be important to review guidelines for choosing an exposure stimulus that provides enough emotional activation to be effective but not so much that clients become completely dysregulated and can't participate in the exercise.

The following handout will help you provide guidance and psychoeducation to your clients about how to do exposure-based skills practice.

Introduction to Exposure

In this treatment we'll be doing some skills practice we'll call "exposure exercises." The exercises are intended to help you "expose" yourself to the experience of difficult emotions so you can learn how to recover from distress as well as learn new ways of responding that enrich your life. Research shows that when you face distress instead of avoiding it, you can not only increase your tolerance of the distress but also recover more quickly.

Here's how it works. First pick a situation or scene that is distressing to you. For example, try to recall the last time you got upset, and see if you can feel yourself getting activated when you think about it. Then, assess whether it is activating enough to use for your exposure practice using the following SUDS tool.

The SUDS Rating

The SUDS rating stands for *subjective units of distress scale*. In plain terms, this just means how much distress you experience when you think about the situation on a scale of 1 to 10, with 1 being no distress and 10 being the most distress you can imagine. For each situation, you want to predict how upset you might become if you expose yourself fully to the emotion of the situation. Ideally, your distress will be in the 5 to 7 range. If your distress is too low, the exercise is unlikely to be effective, and if it's too high, you may become distracted and unable to stay engaged.

1 = no distress

3 = noticeable distress

5 = moderate distress

7 = distressing and uncomfortable

10 = worst distress imaginable

If at any point in the exposure exercise you begin to feel too distressed to stay with it, you should let the therapist know and/or stop the exercise. You are in the driver's seat.

Therapist-Client Dialogue Example: Introducing Mindful Acceptance with Emotion Exposure

Therapist: Let's try an exercise with mindful acceptance skills. Just take a few minutes to think of a recent situation that was distressing to you. You want to choose something you predict will be around a 5 to 7 on the SUDS scale, with 1 being no distress and 10 being the worst distress you can imagine.

Client: [Pauses] Okay, like maybe when my boyfriend is always late to pick me up and doesn't call.

Therapist: Okay. How distressing do you predict that scene will be for you?

Client: Oh, it gets me going. Probably like a 6.5.

Therapist: Okay, good. Let's take a few minutes to get into that scene. Just close your eyes and I'll talk you through it.

Client: Okay [closes eyes].

Therapist: Imagine the last time you were waiting for him to pick you up. Put yourself in the physical location you were in. Remember what you can see around you, what you can hear. Can you see yourself there, and are you feeling the emotion?

Client: Oh, yeah. I feel it.

Therapist: Okay. Where do you feel the emotion in your body?

Client: Wow. I hadn't really thought about it, but my shoulders get really tight and I start to feel warm, even just sitting here thinking about it.

Therapist: Okay, great. So let's explore what it would be like to open to all these emotional experiences, starting with the tightness and warmth you're feeling. Can you allow those sensations to just be there, without judging them, without reacting to them, and instead opening and softening to them?

Client: Okay [takes a deep breath].

Therapist: And is there a feeling that goes with the sensation?

Client: I'm angry. No...I'm scared. I guess I'm afraid he doesn't really love me. If he did, he would be more excited about seeing me—he would be on time. Or at least have the decency to call and let me know he's running late.

Therapist: So you're scared he doesn't really love you.

Client: Yeah. I know it sounds dramatic, but that's the thought I'm having.

Therapist: Okay, good. Let's practice watching your thoughts and letting them go for a few minutes.

Client:	Okay. Just tell you?
Therapist:	Yes. You can just say, "I'm having the thought that he doesn't really love me," and then let that thought go, and wait for the next one to arise.
Client:	Okay. I'm having the thought that "I'm not pretty enough."
Therapist:	Okay, now let that thought go, and wait for the next.
Client:	Okay… I'm having the thought that "I'm overreacting," and now I'm letting it go.
Therapist:	Good.
Client:	[Pauses] I'm having the thought that "He doesn't need me as much as I need him." That one's hard to let go [sighs].
Therapist:	That's okay. Just acknowledge it by saying, "There's a sticky thought," and let it go.
Client:	Okay.
Therapist:	Can you identify an urge that goes with these thoughts?
Client:	Hmm. Well, definitely the urge to shake him and tell him off!
Therapist:	Okay. Can you try to just sit with that urge by observing and accepting it? See if you can allow it to be just as it is? Maybe you can imagine making space to feel that urge without acting on it.
Client:	I'll try.
Therapist:	[Pauses fifteen seconds] What's happening now in your body?
Client:	It just kind of relaxed…and my mind isn't going so fast.
Therapist:	So the tension you were feeling has relaxed?
Client:	Yeah. It's still there a little, but way less.
Therapist:	Okay. And your thoughts are slowing down?
Client:	Yeah. I'm still having the thought "He doesn't really love me"…but…it stopped feeling so "sticky" once my body relaxed. Kind of like they were connected to each other.
Therapist:	Right. So let's stay with that thought for a moment. See if you can just acknowledge that thought, without reacting to it, without judging it, and instead just letting go of it.

Client:	Okay.
Therapist:	What's happening now?
Client:	I am having the thought that "This is really different."
Therapist:	You mean letting go of your thoughts?
Client:	Yeah. I didn't realize I had a choice. Maybe I can do this when it actually happens.
Therapist:	That's the goal. So where is your SUDS level in this moment?
Client:	Um… I think it's around a 2 or 3.
Therapist:	Okay, great. Let's wrap up the exercise. Take a deep breath in and let it out slowly as you open your eyes and come back to the room.

Moment of Choice

Once clients understand how to practice mindful acceptance, you'll want to explain how to locate the moment of choice. Locating the moment of choice is important for emotion efficacy because this is how clients find the space to choose how to respond to difficult emotions in ways that are effective and hopefully life enriching.

The moment of choice is when clients will choose to use EET skills: emotion surfing (chapter 4), values-based action (chapter 5), relaxation and self-soothing (chapter 7), coping thoughts (chapter 8), and distraction and time-outs (chapter 9). You'll want to emphasize that finding and using this "moment" is essential to increasing emotion efficacy.

Following is a handout you can share with your clients to introduce the moment of choice. (For a single-page version of the handout, visit http://www.newharbinger.com/34039, or see Appendix C.)

Moment of Choice

As humans, we don't have control over whether or not we have emotions. Emotions will arise naturally in response to what's happening inside us and around us. But we can control how we respond to our emotions, and that's where we find true emotion efficacy.

This concept was illuminated by neurologist and psychiatrist Victor Frankl as follows:

Between stimulus and response there is space.

In that space lies our freedom and power to choose our response.

In those choices lie our growth and happiness. (n.d.)

How effectively we respond to difficult emotions depends on being able to locate this "moment of choice." This moment is the time when you realize that you're emotionally triggered, and you realize you have the power to choose how to respond. You might think of it as a "sacred pause" when you can either react, avoid, or try to control it—or you can choose a response that is life enriching.

In EET, you'll learn a variety of skills you can choose to use in your moment of choice to help you respond to your emotions in a way that brings you close to what you want to create in the moment.

EET Model = Observe + Accept Emotions > Locate Moment of Choice > Choose EET Skill

Therapist-Client Dialogue Example: Talking to Clients about Locating the Moment of Choice

Therapist: So now that you know how to observe and accept the components of an emotion, you're ready to practice locating the moment of choice.

Client: What's that?

Therapist: The moment of choice is the moment you recognize your choice in the face of distress. It's when you recognize you could choose a response that is conscious and authentic rather than letting your emotions run the show.

Client: But what if I can't find it? What if I'm still so upset after practicing mindful acceptance that I still act on my emotion?

Therapist: It takes practice to locate the moment of choice, but it gets easier the more you try it. All that's needed to find it is to pause long enough to realize you have a choice in how you respond. Does that make sense?

Client: I think so.

Therapist:	Let's try it. How about we try to locate the moment of choice using a triggering situation right now? Can you think of a triggering situation that's happened recently?
Client:	Sure. Last week when one of my coworkers took credit for an idea I came up with.
Therapist:	What was the trigger, or the moment you realized this had happened?
Client:	She announced it as her own idea in the middle of an office-wide marketing meeting.
Therapist:	Okay, let's go with that. Just close your eyes, and we'll take a few minutes to get into the scene. Just locate yourself at the meeting and remember what she said, and let yourself get emotionally activated.
Client:	[With eyes closed] Oh, I'm activated!
Therapist:	Good. So as you think about the moment when you realized she was taking credit for your idea, what comes up for you?
Client:	I wanna reach across the table and strangle her! She knows how hard I've been working to get promoted.
Therapist:	And what did you do?
Client:	I got up and left the meeting.
Therapist:	Okay, let's work with that emotion. Let's begin using mindful acceptance starting with what you sense in your body?
Client:	Yeah... My heart is racing...um...my stomach is tense, really tense. Almost like I got sucker punched.
Therapist:	Okay, let's stay with that sensation of tension for a moment. Just notice the size and shape of the tension, and see if you can allow it to be exactly as it is.
Client:	Okay. Yeah. It's the size and shape of a grapefruit...
Therapist:	Good, now notice if there's any temperature to it...if it's hot or cold or neutral.
Client:	It's warm.
Therapist:	Now, notice what happens as you accept the sensation and make room for it... Does it change or stay the same?

Client:	It's relaxing a little.
Therapist:	Okay, good. Now see if you can identify a feeling label that goes with the sensation and the urge to strangle your coworker.
Client:	Just…outrage. Pure and simple.
Therapist:	Okay, good. Now see if you can soften to that feeling of outrage… Make space for it and just allow it to be as it is.
Client:	It's intense, but okay. I'll try.
Therapist:	Okay, just allow it to be intense then. Continue trying to soften to it, lean into it even.
Therapist:	[Pauses for 30 seconds] What's happening to the feeling now?
Client:	It's starting to feel a little boring.
Therapist:	Boring?
Client:	Yeah, like I'm tired of focusing on it…and it's not that strong anymore.
Therapist:	Okay, let's move into thought watching.
Client:	I'm having the thought "She betrayed me and I shouldn't have trusted her. I'm so stupid!"
Therapist:	Okay. Can you acknowledge the thought that she betrayed you and let it go?
Client:	I don't want to let it go, but I'll try.
Therapist:	It makes sense… Your brain thinks you need to hold on to that thought so you don't get hurt again. But see if you can just acknowledge that it's a sticky thought, and let it go. You can always come back to it another time.
Client:	Okay. Now I'm having the thought "I am so emotionally messed up."
Therapist:	Okay. Can you see that's a judgment thought, and just acknowledge it and let it go?
Client:	Okay… there's a judgment thought…bye-bye!
Therapist:	[Chuckles] Good for you. Now let's check in to see what urge goes with the emotion.

Client: Hmm. Well, I still want to strangle her, but it's less intense.

Therapist: Okay, so can you just notice what it's like to have the urge to want to strangle her? Can you just sit with it for a moment?

Client: Okay.

Therapist: [Waits 30 seconds] What's showing up now?

Client: Well, I feel less like strangling her… It's a pretty violent urge. I'm a little embarrassed.

Therapist: I understand. Can you just allow that feeling to be there without judging it?

Client: Yeah, okay.

Therapist: Staying with the urge, can you see if you can imagine not acting on it, and just sit with it?

Client: Yeah…you mean like not leaving the meeting?

Therapist: Exactly. Just observe and accept that you had the urge to leave.

Client: Okay.

Therapist: Now, can you locate the moment when you had a choice about that?

Client: Well, I might have had a choice right then if I did these mindful exercises when it happened.

Therapist: Right, can you see that moment?

Client: I think so… If when I got outraged I had paused and noticed the moment of choice, I could have chosen to just stay in the meeting?

Therapist: Right. By using mindful acceptance, you might have seen your power in the situation—in the moment of choice.

Client: Yeah, I can see that.

Therapist.   Okay, take a deep breath and let it out slowly as you open your eyes and come back to the room. In our next session we'll learn a new mindful acceptance skill called emotion surfing that you can use to just ride out the emotion, instead of acting on it.

Summary

Following is a synopsis of content covered in chapter 3:

- Mindful acceptance is the practice of observing and accepting (distinct from avoiding, reacting to, or trying to control or alter) the four components of emotional experience through: sensation acceptance, feeling labeling, thought watching, and urge noticing.

- The moment of choice is the space between an emotional trigger and action, when clients can consciously and intentionally choose their response.

- Mindfully accepting emotional experience is essential to locating the moment of choice during an emotionally triggering situation.

- Exposure to emotional experience allows clients to develop more facility and flexibility with how they respond to triggers.

- Practicing mindful acceptance in an activated state will enhance learning, retention, and recall.

CHAPTER 4

Emotion Surfing

Once clients have learned to observe and accept their emotional experience, they are ready to learn about the life cycle of emotion and the next EET skill: *emotion surfing*. You will teach your clients how to surf their emotions as an alternative to three maladaptive responses that fuel and intensify the emotion wave: *emotion avoidance, rumination,* and *emotion-driven behaviors*.

Using the emotion wave metaphor, clients will learn to ride their emotion waves until they dissipate. The wave metaphor works well for many clients because it's an easy visual. Explain that an emotion, from a single trigger, is relatively short-lived (Ekman, 1994). Like a wave, emotion shows up with a leading edge of sharply escalating intensity. Then it peaks and gradually slopes downward—with a long, descending tail end.

EET Skill Objective: Observe + Accept with emotion surfing

All emotions show up, top out, and gradually diminish in this wave effect. Use the metaphor often, and reassure clients that they can learn to ride, or surf, these emotion waves rather than be churned up in them. Emotion surfing is like body surfing, whereby one can become skilled at rising on the leading edge of the wave, riding there for a while, and finally slipping over the crest to the relative calm of the back slope. Emotion surfing involves a similar skill set, requiring five key abilities:

- Observing and accepting the emotion wave as it comes.

- Locating oneself on the emotion wave. (Is the client on the rising edge, at the crest, or on the diminishing back slope of the emotion? You can use the subjective units of distress scale [SUDS], ranging from 0 to 10, to help calibrate wave intensity while the client surfs.)

- Noticing and watching thoughts without getting fused with them.

- Noticing any desire to escape the emotion, and continuing to observe it instead (not engaging in emotion avoidance).

- Noticing any urges or impulses to act on the emotion, and seeing the moment of choice (not engaging in emotion-driven behavior).

We'll cover how to teach emotion surfing in the following pages. But, first, you need to prepare for the question every client asks: "If my emotions are just a wave that will pass, why do they seem to go on forever?" This is important to address because clients often experience negative emotion as overwhelming and endless. They feel controlled by their emotions, with little choice about how long or how intensely they will last.

How Emotion Avoidance Keeps Emotion at High Intensity

The normal wave pattern of emotions will get interrupted and extended by three maladaptive coping strategies. The first is *emotion avoidance*. It's important for clients to realize how the attempt to control and avoid emotions paradoxically maintains, even intensifies, emotional distress.

The effort to suppress painful emotional experiences can take multiple forms (situational, cognitive, somatic, protective, and substitution-based avoidance), but the outcome is always the same: increased suffering.

The following handout describes the forms of emotional avoidance and some of its possible negative consequences.

Consequences of Emotion Avoidance

There are at least five types of emotion avoidance that researchers believe are at the root of many emotion problems.

Situational: people, places, things, and activities

Cognitive: thoughts, images, and memories

Somatic: internal sensations such as racing heart, palpitations, breathlessness, overheating, fatigue, or unwanted sexual arousal

Protective: avoiding uncertainty through checking, cleaning, perfectionism, procrastination, or reassurance seeking

Substitution: avoiding painful emotions with replacement emotions, numbing out, alcohol, drugs, bingeing, or gambling

Why not just keep on avoiding? Because the consequences of emotion avoidance are usually worse than the experience of what we try to avoid.

- Since distress, discomfort, and anxiety are all a guaranteed part of life, emotion avoidance is often only a temporary and superficial "solution."

- Emotion avoidance reinforces the idea that discomfort/distress/anxiety is "bad" or "dangerous." It reduces your ability to face and tolerate necessary pain.

- Emotion avoidance often requires effort and energy. It's exhausting and time-consuming.

- Emotion avoidance limits your ability to fully experience the present.

- Emotion avoidance can keep you from moving toward important, valued aspects of life.

- Emotion avoidance often doesn't work. When you tell yourself not to think about something, you have to think about not thinking about it. When you try to avoid an emotion, you often end up feeling it anyway.

- Emotion avoidance often leads to suffering: addiction, helplessness, hopelessness, depression, damaged relationships, and lost opportunities.

By allowing yourself to experience fears—and difficult thoughts, feelings, sensations, and urges—you can learn to decrease your suffering.

To help clients explore how emotion avoidance impacts their lives, have them identify one or two strong emotions that show up frequently. Then examine which strategies they typically use to avoid the emotional experience:

- Situational: avoiding people, places, or things

- Cognitive: avoiding thoughts, images, or memories

- Somatic: avoiding unpleasant physical sensations

- Protective: avoiding uncertainty through frequent checking, procrastinating, or assurance seeking

- Substitution: avoiding by numbing, suppressing, addictive behaviors, or replacement emotions (i.e., replacing shame with anger)

When you've identified and listed frequently used avoidance strategies for a particular emotion, help clients examine consequences (see the Emotion Avoidance Consequences Worksheet).

There will be advantages (pros) for avoidance. Be sure to acknowledge and list those. Usually the advantages are immediate (brief suppression of emotion) and short-lived, but they are real. It's important to validate that there is often a short, positive effect from emotion avoidance.

Now examine the disadvantages (cons) of avoidance. What negative outcomes have clients endured from their avoidance strategies? Have there been costs in the form of increased anxiety, depression, or shame? Have there been costs in the form of feeling stuck, damaged or lost relationships, or addictions?

Finally, determine both advantages and disadvantages of experiencing this particular emotion.

Document all the pros and cons on the following Emotion Avoidance Consequences Worksheet.

Emotion Avoidance Consequences Worksheet

Emotion	Pros of Avoiding	Cons of Avoiding	Cons of Experiencing	Pros of Experiencing

Therapist-Client Dialogue Example: Introducing Emotion Avoidance

The process of exploring avoidance in session is demonstrated in the following dialogue. The client has identified shame as an emotion he often runs away from.

Therapist:	Let's look at some of the ways you might be avoiding shame. Are there situations—by that I mean people, places, activities—that shame makes you avoid?
Client:	A couple of my friends who've been super successful lately. And the gym, 'cause I'm ashamed of how I've gained weight.
Therapist:	Any thoughts you try to avoid—thoughts that trigger the shame?
Client:	I won't talk to my girlfriend about my job because it sucks, and I feel like a loser to be doing it.
Therapist:	So thinking or talking about your job is hard. This may seem like a strange question, but I wonder if there are any physical sensations associated with shame that you avoid?
Client:	This hot flush I get when I'm embarrassed. It's weird, it can happen at random times, but particularly if someone asks me a question about myself and the answer would make me feel vulnerable.
Therapist:	Remember, we talked about protective avoidance—checking, reassurance seeking, things like that? Does any of that happen around the shame?
Client:	I'm feeling ashamed right now. I do all of this crap—always asking my girlfriend if something I said or did was okay. I'm worried she's going to be put off.
Therapist:	The shame you feel right now—are you trying to avoid that in some way?
Client:	I'm feeling angry.
Therapist:	Which is...?
Client:	I know. Substitution avoidance.
Therapist:	[Now, having explored some of the client's avoidance strategies, the therapist can begin working with the Emotion Avoidance Consequences Worksheet.] If it's okay with you, I'd like to look at some of the ways avoidance affects you. This worksheet can help us explore some of the

good things—there can really be good things—and not so good things about avoidance. Let's start with the pros of trying to avoid shame.

Client: I guess for a minute I feel better. Less embarrassed.

Therapist: Let's write that down... Anything else?

Client: I can just put off the bad feelings about myself. Sooner or later they come again, but I get a reprieve.

Therapist: Got it. What about any cons of avoiding—avoiding your friends, avoiding the gym, avoiding talking to your girlfriend about your job?

Client: I'm totally blimping out 'cause I don't go to the gym. And sometimes I feel lonely, missing my friends. And I feel kind of alone with my girlfriend 'cause I can't talk to her about the stuff that really bothers me.

Therapist: Okay—I'm writing this down—you feel more alone, and it's affecting your fitness and health. What about not talking about yourself to avoid the hot flush, or the reassurance seeking and substituting anger for shame? Are there consequences for that?

Client: My girlfriend gets very annoyed with all of that. She gets pissed when I ask if things are okay, but I keep asking anyway. And she's threatened to leave over my anger—the substitution thing.

Therapist: So there's a lot of downside for avoidance. Are there cons for experiencing the shame when it comes up?

Client: [Mirthless laugh] Just pain. I'd say that is a con.

Therapist: Absolutely—the pain of embarrassment. What about the pros of experiencing the shame?

Client: Well, I wouldn't have all the stuff you listed. The aloneness, the problems with my girlfriend, getting fat. Truthfully, I think I'd be less depressed, happier, if I stopped all the stuff I do to avoid.

After clients have completed the worksheet, emphasize to them that emotion avoidance keeps the emotion wave going long after it would normally subside. Encourage them to find the evidence for this in their Emotion Avoidance Consequences Worksheet. The key lesson is this: when emotions occur, allow them to run their (usually) short course—without attempts at emotion avoidance or emotion-driven behavior.

How Rumination Keeps Emotion at High Intensity

Rumination is a maladaptive coping strategy to manage difficult emotions. As with emotion avoidance, the message to clients is that rumination intensifies and prolongs emotional suffering. And when we allow and face the emotion—without ruminative processes—affective episodes are brief and relatively less painful.

The three main forms of rumination are:

- **Judging:** Judgments about self are an effort to fix or perfect one's flaws. But the long-term outcome is a deeper sense of defectiveness and chronic depression. Judgments about others relieve feelings of defectiveness but result in chronic anger and damaged relationships.

- **Predicting:** Catastrophic predictions about the future provide a temporary hope that one can plan and avoid bad outcomes. But it is the royal road to chronic anxiety because the terrifying predictions create a constant sense of threat.

- **Explaining:** If one can answer the question "Why did this happen?" it provides the hope that painful experiences can be controlled. If one can find the cause, perhaps problems can be prevented or managed. But the "why" question often has no answer and results in a deep sense of helplessness. Or the answer is a personal flaw—bad things have happened through one's own fault. In each case the result is a deepening depression.

Clients need to learn that rumination—thinking about the bad things that either have happened or could happen—intensifies emotion. Rumination prolongs the wave of emotional pain, keeping people stuck at the crest and preventing natural habituation so the wave can subside.

The role rumination plays in sustaining negative emotions makes it crucial for clients to learn how to label and let go of thoughts. Thought watching (see the handout Mindful Acceptance | Observe + Accept, in chapter 3, Apppendix C, and online) promotes the skill of observing thoughts without getting caught up in an endless cycle of content. Later in this chapter, we'll introduce emotion exposure (called emotion surfing), a strategy whereby this same "labeling and letting go" of thoughts shows up again as a key component.

You can use the following handout on rumination to talk with your clients about the role it plays in perpetuating their suffering.

Rumination

Rumination is thinking about something over and over until it becomes painful. Like emotion avoidance, the goal of rumination is to reduce emotional distress. But, paradoxically, rumination keeps you stuck at the top of the emotion wave. Here's how:

Judging thoughts can focus on yourself or others. When you judge yourself, the hope is to fix or perfect your flaws. But the eventual outcome is a deeper sense of defectiveness and chronic depression. Judging others can give you short-term relief from feelings of being defective or helpless. But they result in chronic anger and damaged relationships.

Predicting thoughts help you peer into the future. Catastrophic predictions may give you temporary hope that you can plan for and avoid bad outcomes. But the constant drumbeat of future negative events creates chronic anxiety—because the terrifying predictions create a constant sense of threat.

Explaining thoughts provide hope that painful experiences can be controlled. These thoughts answer the question "Why did this happen?" If you can find the cause for a painful event, perhaps it can be prevented or managed. But the "why" question often has no answer and results in feeling helpless. Or the answer is a personal flaw—bad things have happened through your own fault—which intensifies your emotions.

Rumination—despite our hopes for fixing, solving, and controlling things—ends up fueling emotional pain. It keeps us stuck at the top of the wave in a chronic state of anxiety, sadness, or anger.

Soon you will learn how to label and let go of thoughts—which will be a tremendous help in reducing rumination and the impact of painful thoughts.

How Emotion-Driven Behavior Intensifies Emotion

The third factor that prolongs an emotion wave is *emotion-driven behavior*. Every emotion has an urge. Anger pushes us toward aggression, anxiety toward avoidance, and sadness toward withdrawal and reevaluation. These hardwired responses are part of our survival programming; they help in crisis situations. But used habitually, emotion-driven behaviors have the paradoxical effect of making emotions worse. The data are in: aggression intensifies anger (McKay, Rogers, & McKay, 2003), avoidance creates anxiety disorders (Allen, McHugh, & Barlow, 2008), and withdrawal is the prime driver of depression (Zettel, 2007).

Clients need to learn this fundamental truth: *acting on urges strengthens emotions.* Emotion-driven behavior, regardless of how right or natural it feels, regardless of the perceived imperative, just keeps clients stuck at the top of the wave. Instead clients can notice the urge and identify a moment of choice, when they can either act on the urge or choose to ride the wave, observing it until the emotion dissipates.

Therapist-Client Dialogue Example: How to Talk About Emotion-Driven Behavior

Therapist: When the shame shows up, what does it make you want to do? I'm wondering here about specific behavior.

Client: Withdraw, hide.

Therapist: Okay, let's see where this goes. Something embarrassing happens. That feeling is pushing you to hide. What happens then, emotionally? You've pulled away from people, you aren't letting anybody see you... What do you feel next?

Client: Alone. Stupid. Like I'm this little, stupid person and everybody can see it.

Therapist: So the emotion-driven behavior—hiding, withdrawing—it doesn't...

Client: It doesn't do anything. I just keep twirling the baton in my shame parade.

The Art of Emotion Surfing

Emotion surfing, to be successful, has to eliminate the three emotion dysregulators (or maladaptive responses) just discussed: emotion avoidance, rumination, and emotion-driven behavior.

This is where the three skills clients are developing in the mindful acceptance exercise (see the handout Mindful Acceptance | Observe + Accept, in chapter 3) become critical. The following points should be understood by clients before moving forward:

- Observing sensations and labeling feelings promotes acceptance rather than emotion avoidance.

- Thought watching and letting go reduces rumination—not just the frequency of thoughts but the degree to which the client believes and is captured by negative cognitions.

- Noticing urges and the moment of choice allows a client *not* to choose emotion-driven behaviors.

The following handout may be useful to remind clients how to practice emotion surfing. The handout emphasizes watching the emotion go through its natural course by noticing thoughts, feelings, and sensations; noticing urges and the moment of choice; and noticing where one is on the wave, watching it evolve and finally diminish.

How to Surf an Emotion Wave

Learning to ride an emotion wave is a fundamental part of Emotion Efficacy Therapy. When an intense emotion is triggered—and your automatic response is emotion avoidance, rumination, or emotion-driven behavior—choosing to surf the emotion wave can actually prevent the emotion from intensifying. Using this skill can be daunting or even scary at first, but, with practice, surfing an emotion wave can be your best option.

Riding the emotion wave involves practicing mindful acceptance skills. Here are the steps to take in the face of an intense emotion:

1. Ride your emotion wave when triggered.

2. Notice how emotionally activated you are (check your SUDS level).

3. Identify the peak of the wave.

4. Don't fuel the emotion.

5. Practice mindful acceptance, just allowing the emotion to be as it is, watching the emotion go through its natural course:

   • Watch and let go of thoughts.

   • Label feelings.

   • Accept sensations.

   • Notice urges.

6. Continue mindful acceptance until the triggered emotion resolves.

Therapist-Client Dialogue Example: How to Lead Emotion Surfing

In the following dialogue, the therapist explains emotion surfing to the client.

Therapist: Emotion surfing is basically practicing all the mindful acceptance skills you've learned: thought watching, noticing feelings and sensations, and watching action urges. Only now we'll use them when you're in the middle of an actual emotion surge.

Client: We'll do it here, in session?

Therapist: Right.

Client: How do we know I'll have an emotion to work on? Most of the time I feel pretty calm in here.

Therapist:	There's no way of knowing when an emotion will show up on its own. That's right. So what we'll do is use imagery—visualizing a recent scene when you were upset—to trigger an emotion in here. Then, once we have a moderate-level emotion—SUDS around 5 or 6—we'll practice emotion surfing.
Client:	What happens after I'm triggered? What if I get overwhelmed, like usual?
Therapist:	I'll help you *not* do any of the things that make emotions overwhelming and prolong the wave. Instead of ruminating, we'll notice, label, and let go of thoughts. You'll just say out loud, "I'm having a sad thought" or "I'm having a judgment thought," or whatever it is. Then you'll go back to observing your sensations and feelings, allowing and making room for them, and describing them out loud. Watching and labeling your feelings and sensations will keep you from emotion avoidance—less avoidance means the emotion will be less overwhelming.
Client:	I'm supposed to say everything that's happening out loud to you?
Therapist:	Exactly. I'll ask questions to prompt you. The last thing is noticing those action urges. Say what they are out loud, and then notice that you don't have to act on them.
Client:	Okay. Then what?
Therapist:	Then we keep watching until the emotion calms down a bit—we'll keep track of the SUDS—or changes into something else.

Choosing the Exposure Image

Imaginal exposure, in these early stages of emotion surfing, should focus on recent, emotionally provocative memories that fall in the midrange (5–6 SUDS). Ask clients to think back over the last week or two to a scene where something moderately upsetting happened. Encourage them to fully enter the scene, noticing the details of where they are, who they're with, what is felt physically, and what is heard (people speaking, ambient sounds from the environment, etc.). Have clients stay in the scene until emotional distress reaches 5 or 6 SUDS—they should signal you at this point.

As soon as clients reach the target distress level, have them shut off the scene. This is a brief exposure, so it's crucial that the provocative scene be terminated before the emotion surfing exercise begins.

Now, with the scene eclipsed, the clients begin focusing on internal states. Ask clients to notice any physical sensations and to describe them out loud. Now ask about feelings (emotions) that seem connected to the sensations. These should be verbalized as well.

Encourage clients to label any thoughts that show up ("There's a thought," or "I'm having a judgment thought," or "I'm having the thought that I need to escape") and immediately return attention to sensations and feelings. You should also direct the clients' attention to any action urges and have them describe the urges out loud.

Return again and again to the clients' sensations and feelings. Keep asking, "What are you noticing in your body?" or "What are you feeling right now?" This is the main focus of the exposure. But you'll also continue to include requests throughout to label thoughts and urges. And periodically you'll also ask clients to note SUDS and describe where they are on the wave.

Script for Guided Emotion Surfing

After the provoking scene is "shut off," a typical emotion surfing exercise might look like this:

What do you notice in your body right now? Can you describe the sensations? [Client responds.]

What are the feelings that go with that? [Client responds.]

If there are thoughts, can you just watch them and let them go? Any time a thought shows up, just say so. Any thoughts now? [Client responds.] See if you can just let go of any thoughts that arise.

Where are you on the wave? [Client responds.] SUDS? [Client responds.]

Any urges? Does the emotion make you want to do something? [Client responds.] Notice how you can just observe the urge. You don't have to act on it.

What's happening in your body right now? [Client responds.]

Can you label your feelings? [Client responds.] See if you can just allow the feelings without reacting to them.

Remember to watch and let go of any thoughts. Are thoughts showing up? [Client responds.]

Urges? Something the emotion wants you to do? [Client responds.] See what it's like to just notice the urge without acting on it.

Where are you on the wave? SUDS? [Client responds.]

What are you experiencing in your body right now? [Client responds.] Can you make room for that and just allow that sensation?

Your feelings? [Client responds.] Can you just allow that feeling? Can you let it be there without trying to control or stop it?

Watch the thoughts and let them go. [Client responds.]

Urges? [Client responds.]

Check the wave. Where are you? [Client responds.] SUDS? [Client responds.]

This process continues until the distress is diminished—down to 2 or 3 SUDS—and/ or the feeling has morphed and become softer. Once an exposure session concludes, begin a discussion of what the clients have learned—so far—about emotion surfing. This is a crucial opportunity for the clients to consolidate and draw conclusions about their ability to tolerate affect and what actually happens when emotions are faced rather than avoided.

Therapist-Client Dialogue Example: How to Consolidate Learning After Emotion Surfing

Therapist:	After we got into that scene where your girlfriend criticized you, we spent maybe ten minutes doing emotion surfing. What did you learn?
Client:	Like what?
Therapist:	Like how your emotions work, or how long they last, or what happens when you don't ruminate, avoid, or act on urges?
Client:	Well, the shame feeling kind of dropped off a lot sooner than I thought.
Therapist:	So the emotion didn't last as long? Anything else you noticed?
Client:	If I label my thoughts, I don't get into them as much.
Therapist:	Meaning they seem less important or powerful?
Client:	Yeah. I guess what surprised me most is that the feeling—shame—didn't ruin me. After a few minutes, it didn't seem that terrible.
Therapist:	So you were able to tolerate it better than you would have thought. Anything else?
Client:	[Shrugs.]
Therapist:	These are some important things you've learned: that the emotional pain, when you surf the wave, doesn't last as long; that thought watching helps with rumination; and that you could stand the shame feeling—you didn't have to avoid it.

Following is a handout clients can use to practice the skill of emotion surfing outside of session. Remember, a single-page version of the handout can be found in Appendix C and online at http://www.newharbinger.com/34039.

Emotion Surfing Practice

Once you're emotionally activated, take note of your SUDS level and then begin to practice emotion surfing following the sequence below:

1. Ask yourself, "What sensations do I notice in my body?"

2. Ask yourself, "What's the feeling that goes with it?"

3. Watch and let go of thoughts.

4. Notice urges. Locate the moment of choice instead of acting on the urges.

5. Ask yourself, "Where am I on the wave?" Determine your SUDS rating.

6. Ask yourself, "What's happening in my body?"

7. Ask yourself, "What's happening to the feeling?" Try to allow and make room for that feeling.

8. Watch thoughts and notice urges. Try not to get involved with them.

9. Ask yourself, "Where am I on the wave?"

10. Ask yourself, "What's the sensation in my body?" Try to accept that sensation.

11. Ask yourself, "What's my feeling?" Try to allow and make room for that feeling.

12. Watch thoughts and notice urges. Try not to get involved with them.

13. Ask yourself, "Where am I on the wave?"

Keep going until the distress improves or the emotion shifts. Record your SUDS level when finished.

By this point in EET treatment, your clients should be working on mindful acceptance and emotion surfing. They should continue to do the mindful acceptance exercises for ten minutes daily and record their practice on their Skills Practice Record. This helps them practice key skills in a non-triggered state. However, state-dependent learning research tells us that skills acquired in a relaxed state are not always retrievable when in an activated, emotionally triggered condition (Szymanski & O'Donohue, 1995). That's why practicing emotion surfing during triggered states is so crucial.

Encourage clients to utilize emotion surfing whenever they experience emotional distress during the week. Instead of describing internal experiences out loud, they will simply notice their emotions and apply a label to them. Give them the Emotion Surfing Practice handout to remind them what to observe. Ask clients to keep track of their homework on their Skills Practice Record (see handout). In addition, they should note any emotional triggers that show up and activate painful affect on the Skills Practice Record.

Emphasize to clients that they will not always remember to or succeed with emotion surfing. This is a new skill that will take time and practice. If clients don't successfully surf during an in vivo upset, encourage them to relive the scene using imaginal exposure and do emotion surfing—just as they did during session.

Summary

Following is a synopsis of content covered in chapter 4:

- Emotion arises from a single trigger, and it is relatively short-lived (Ekman, 1994).

- Emotion surfing can be chosen as an alternative to three maladaptive emotional responses: emotion avoidance, rumination, and emotion-driven behaviors.

- Emotion surfing involves noticing the life cycle of the wave without avoiding, ruminating, or acting on urges through emotion-driven behaviors.

- Riding the emotion wave involves practicing mindful acceptance skills: labeling and letting go of thoughts; noticing and labeling feelings; accepting sensations; and watching urges.

- The five types of emotion avoidance are: situational, cognitive, somatic, protective, and substitution.

- The three types of rumination are: judging, predicting, and explaining thoughts.

- Acting on urges, or emotion-driven behaviors, fuels and intensifies emotion.

- Imaginal exposure is used to allow clients to practice using adaptive emotional response skills in an activated state to improve learning, retention, and recall.

CHAPTER 5

Values-Based Action, Part 1

In the foregoing chapters we've explored how painful emotions trigger both urges to engage in emotion-driven behavior and emotion avoidance (behavior exclusively shaped by the desire to escape pain). Both of these coping responses serve to intensify the emotion and prolong suffering. And both of these reactions lead to chronic emotion disorders and emotion dysregulation. While clients may be getting more skilled at observing and accepting emotions and the urges they trigger by riding the emotion wave, they have yet to identify alternative contextually adaptive behavioral choices to emotion avoidance and emotion-driven behavior.

The next two chapters cover the next EET treatment component and skill, *values-based action*, or VBA. In this chapter, we show you how to help your clients clarify their values across their various life domains and visualize using VBA when they are emotionally triggered. In the next chapter, we show you how to help your clients choose VBA when they are in a triggering situation using a powerful experiential exercise.

EET Skill Objective: **Observe + Accept** with values clarification

Values-based action is the basis for a different choice—acting on what matters, on what clients care about—rather than emotionally driven reactions. Once clients have clarified their values in triggering situations, and have learned how to use values-based action, they'll have new, healthier, adaptive response options. These alternative behavioral choices will provide a counterweight to old, maladaptive patterns.

VBA can be defined as behavior that takes one's life in a direction that matters, that's in alignment with what feels important and right for the situation. As such, values are not goals, for which a plan is accomplished or completed. Values and their expression in values-based action represent directions or paths toward something that matters. Let's take honesty in a relationship as an example. A goal of telling the truth about unspoken sexual desires is something that can be achieved in a single conversation. On the other hand, the value of honesty with a partner, for example, cannot be accomplished; every day the value is enacted in specific values-based actions, such as expressing authenticity and truthfulness.

In other words, values-based action is the result of turning abstract values into behavior. Having the value of being supportive to friends can be enacted or expressed, for example, by helping a friend move or visiting someone who's sick. Emotion-driven behavior, by contrast, often carries clients away from values and values-based intentions. Straying from one's values erodes well-being and creates a host of secondary problems such as depression, damaged relationships, a sense of defectiveness, lack of direction, poor choices, and helplessness.

The first step toward being able to use values-based action is to clarify what values are. You can describe the advantages of values clarification to clients as follows:

- Values direct life where one wants it to go. They help life to be about what matters, as opposed to avoiding pain and seeking pleasure.

- Values provide motivation to make difficult but necessary changes. For example, changing anger-driven behavior can be motivated by a value of kindness or love.

- Values-based action provides a clear alternative to emotion-driven or -avoidant behaviors.

- Values help clients make choices that lead to high well-being.

Assessing Client Values

Provide clients with the Values Clarification Worksheet and ask them to circle their ten most strongly held values.

Values Clarification Worksheet

Review the list below and circle your top 10 values.

Accountability	Contribution	Equality
Accuracy	Control	Excellence
Achievement	Cooperation	Excitement
Adventure	Correctness	Expertise
Altruism	Courtesy	Exploration
Ambition	Creativity	Expressiveness
Assertiveness	Curiosity	Fairness
Authenticity	Decisiveness	Faith
Balance	Dependability	Family
Belonging	Determination	Fitness
Boldness	Devoutness	Fluency
Calmness	Diligence	Focus
Carefulness	Discipline	Freedom
Challenge	Discretion	Friends
Cheerfulness	Diversity	Fun
Clear-mindedness	Dynamism	Generosity
Commitment	Economy	Grace
Community	Effectiveness	Growth
Compassion	Efficiency	Happiness
Competitiveness	Elegance	Hard work
Consistency	Empathy	Health
Contentment	Enjoyment	Helping
Continuous improvement	Enthusiasm	Holiness

Honesty	Patriotism	Speed
Honor	Piety	Spontaneity
Humility	Positivity	Stability
Independence	Practicality	Strength
Ingenuity	Preparedness	Structure
Inner harmony	Professionalism	Success
Inquisitiveness	Prudence	Support
Insightfulness	Quality	Teamwork
Intellectual status	Reliability	Temperance
Intelligence	Resourcefulness	Thankfulness
Intuition	Restraint	Thoroughness
Joy	Results-oriented	Thoughtfulness
Justice	Rigor	Timeliness
Leadership	Security	Tolerance
Legacy	Self-actualization	Tradition
Love	Self-control	Trustworthiness
Loyalty	Self-reliance	Truth-seeking
Making a difference	Selflessness	Understanding
Mastery	Sensitivity	Uniqueness
Merit	Serenity	Unity
Obedience	Service	Usefulness
Openness	Shrewdness	Vision
Order	Simplicity	Vitality
Originality	Soundness	

Assessing Values By Domain

Now, encourage clients to talk about the selected values and why they're important. Are there life experiences—either happy or difficult—whereby clients discovered the significance of this value? When have they acted on the value with positive outcomes? Were there times they forgot or failed to follow this value? What were the outcomes then?

After discussing several high-ranking values, introduce the Values Domain Worksheet. The assessment process here is more complex, requiring clients to identify the value and specific values-based action for each relevant life domain. In addition, values in each domain are measured in two ways:

I—Importance

> 0 = unimportant

> 1 = moderately important

> 2 = very important

A—Action (how often the intention was enacted in the past seven days)

> 0 = no action

> 1 = one or two actions

> 2 = three or four actions

> 3 = five or more actions

A crucial function of this worksheet is helping clients identify values, and their corresponding values-based action, that are rated as "very important" yet are rarely acted upon. Have these values been avoided or abandoned because emotion-driven behavior is getting in the way? Are clients so often responding to action urges that key values no longer guide their choices? To put it simply: are emotions—not values—running the clients' lives? This often leads to a difficult but rewarding conversation that can motivate clients to try new ways of responding to difficult emotions. When it becomes clear that emotion-driven behavior is a barrier to being the person they want to be, many clients will respond by asking, "What can I do about this?"

Values Domains Worksheet

1. Intimate relationships   Value: _____ I = _____ A = _____

       Values-Based Action:

2. Parenting   Value: _____ I = _____ A = _____

       Values-Based Action:

3. Education/learning   Value: _____ I = _____ A = _____

       Values-Based Action:

4. Friends/social life   Value: _____ I = _____ A = _____

       Values-Based Action:

5. Physical self-care/health   Value: _____ I = _____ A = _____

       Values-Based Action:

6. Family of origin   Value: _____ I = _____ A = _____

       Values-Based Action:

I = Importance

Rate:

0 = unimportant

1 = moderately important

2 = very important

A = Action: How much action did you take in the last seven days toward your value?

Rate:

0 = no action

1 = one or two actions

2 = three or four actions

3 = five or more actions

7. Spirituality   Value: _____ I = _____ A = _____

   Values-Based Action:

_____

8. Community life/citizenship   Value: _____ I = _____ A = _____

   Values-Based Action:

_____

9. Recreation   Value: _____ I = _____ A = _____

   Values-Based Action:

_____

10. Work/career   Value: _____ I = _____ A = _____

    Values-Based Action:

_____

11. _____ Value: _____ I = _____ A = _____

    Values-Based Action:

_____

12. _____ Value: _____ I = _____ A = _____

    Values-Based Action:

_____

I = Importance	A = Action: How much action did you take in the last seven days toward your value?
Rate:	Rate:
0 = unimportant	0 = no action
1 = moderately important	1 = one or two actions
2 = very important	2 = three or four actions
	3 = five or more actions

Therapist-Client Dialogue Example: Talking About Values

This client came into treatment concerned that her anger was damaging her relationships and the lives of her children. Explosions were triggered when she felt ignored, disrespected, or had been denied something she wanted. The therapist, in the following dialogue, first examines the client's values and then looks at how her emotion-driven behavior impacted her choices.

Therapist: [Showing the client the Values Domain Worksheet] Let's look at this first domain: intimate relationships. Is there a value that guides who you want to be in this part of your life?

Client: Caring. I want to be caring with Bill.

Therapist: And if you were to turn that value into action—as an intention, or values-based action—what would you do?

Client: I'd express concern and interest about some of his struggles—his health, his difficulties at work. I'd appreciate how difficult it is for him to get organized, rather than criticize him.

Therapist: How important is this value—on that 0 to 2 scale?

Client: Very.

Therapist: Okay, let's write in 2. And how often do you act on your value of being caring with Bill?

Client: [Silence] Not so much.

Therapist: Once or twice a week? Three or four times? No action last week? What would you say?

Client: I don't think I was very caring last week.

Therapist: [Writes in "0"] Sometimes there's a gap between what we want to do and what we actually do. That's true for me, too. What about this next domain, parenting?

Client: Same thing, I want to be supportive and caring.

Therapist: Okay, and if you turn that into specific behavior this week, what would that look like?

Client: It would be talking like I cared about them rather than getting angry.

Therapist: So your intention would be…

Client:	Talking with gentleness. With love in my voice. Even when they don't do what I ask or when they get sassy.
Therapist:	How important is that value?
Client:	At the top.
Therapist:	[Writes in "2"] And how often do you act on your intention?
Client:	When they aren't listening or talk back at me? [Therapist nods] Not too much. I pretty much always get upset and start yelling.
Therapist:	[Writes in "0"] So this is another domain where there's a gap between what matters and what you find yourself doing. Let's keep going and look at other domains.
	[The therapist and the client continue with the worksheet. Some of the domains don't matter to the client at all: family of origin, spirituality, and recreation. Some had moderately important values: physical self-care (exercise, community life), volunteering at her kids' school, learning (community college writing class). Finally the conversation circles back to domains where a gap exists between a value's importance and frequency of action.]
Therapist:	Could we go back for a moment to your relationship with Bill? The value of caring was important, but the intention of expressing interest and concern, or validating his difficulties getting organized, was hard to do. What gets in the way, do you think?
Client:	It drives me nuts when he doesn't get things done. And I'm tired of hearing about work. It's the same problem, he's disorganized. So...I get upset and kind of lay into him.
Therapist:	So your frustration leads to anger, and then what?
Client:	You know what. We've been talking about action urges. I have an urge to yell at him and...blame him.
Therapist:	So the urge to yell—your emotion-driven behavior when you're angry—is a barrier to the value of being caring.
Client:	[Looks angry] I don't like it when you say it that way. But...yes.
Therapist:	This is hard. It's painful to look at. Would you be willing to examine that other domain—parenting—where you felt being caring was important?

Values Domain Worksheet
(Client Sample)

1. Intimate relationships   Value: _Caring_   I = _2_   A = _0_

Values-Based Action:

Express concern, interest re: difficulty getting organized

2. Parenting   Value: _Supportive_   I = _2_   A = _0_

Values-Based Action:

Talk with gentleness/love when they didn't listen or are sassy

3. Education/learning   Value: _Learn how to write_   I = _1_   A = _0_

Values-Based Action:

Enroll in community college class

4. Friends/social life   Value: _Listen_   I = _1_   A = _2_

Values-Based Action:

Ask about what's going on, be interested. Don't interrupt or judge.

5. Physical self-care/health   Value: _Healthy stamina_   I = _1_   A = _1_

Values-Based Action:

Cardio exercise 3x week

6. Family of origin   Value: _____   I = _0_   A = _0_

Values-Based Action:

7. Spirituality   Value: _____   I = _0_   A = _0_

Values-Based Action:

8. Community life/citizenship   Value: _Volunteering_____   I = __1__ A = __0__

                                   Values-Based Action:

_Help at children's school_____

9. Recreation   Value: _____   I = __0__ A = __0__

                                   Values-Based Action:

10. Work/career   Value: _Support co-workers___   I = __2__ A = __2__

                                   Values-Based Action:

_Ask how their projects are going_____

Accessing Values During Distress

Next, you will help clients identify frequent triggering situations where strong, negative emotions get activated. The goal here is to match these emotional triggers with a value/intention that clients wish to be guided by. Start by brainstorming with your clients as many triggering situations—eight to twelve—as you can think of.

As an example, the client listed the following situations that were emotionally activating triggers:

- Bill doesn't get something done that he promises to do.

- Bill can't get organized around some job at work or home.

- Bill looks confused and out of it.

- My kids ignore what I ask.

- My kids get loud.

- My kids make fun of the way I talk.

- My kids whisper together, laughing at something I think they need to do.

- My boss says for the umpteenth time that our department is underperforming.

- My boss looks at his shoes, which means he isn't listening to me.

- My friends talk about their problems—which are nothing close to what I'm facing right now.

- My father's weekly call.

- Dealing with my son's teacher—who doesn't get him and doesn't care what he needs.

Now, with a list of triggers, ask clients what value/intention they want to act on in each situation. Typically, they'll focus on one or two key values—kindness or honesty, for example. If clients are having trouble identifying key values, ask who they want to be in the situation. You can say, "You're extremely upset. X, Y, and Z have happened. You're feeling _____, and the emotion is driving you to _____. Notice the power of that urge. Notice the pain and how it pushes you to do something to feel better, to feel free of the hurt. Now you will have a choice: act on your emotional urges or be who you want to be. Tell me about that choice."

For example, the client identified the following values and intentions/values-based actions that could guide her during emotional triggers:

- Kindness: awareness of others' pain and validating their struggles

- Truthfulness: saying what I feel without blaming people for it

- Caring: supporting people rather than causing pain

These three values became a touchstone for the choices the client made. They were an adaptive alternative to her emotion-driven aggression.

Barriers to Values

Clients know how often they don't act on values. They are acutely, painfully aware of this failure. What they may not know is why. An essential step in this treatment is to validate the pain and the enormous challenge in shifting to making choices based on values. There are three huge barriers to living one's values:

- **A lack of clarity about values-based action in the moment.** The client doesn't clearly recognize the two choices during emotion activation: values-based behavior versus emotion-driven responses. This is often the result of an incomplete values-clarification process. Either the client hasn't fully explored his or her values and intentions, or the values have never been applied to triggering situations. The client may have no idea what to do when faced with strong emotions.

- **A hardwired drive to control painful emotion.** The stronger a negative emotion, the stronger becomes the urge for emotion avoidance and emotion-driven behavior. Clients typically arrive in therapy with a long history of trying to control difficult emotion. But the effort to control emotional pain has the unintended and parallel consequence of carrying clients farther from values-based action. Instead, at the moment of choice, clients struggle with urges to act on and control emotions, and their awareness of values can literally disappear.

- **Emotion avoidance and emotion-driven behavior feel good in the moment.** They are also negatively reinforced. The immediate reward for emotion-driven behavior makes it seem like the better, easier choice.

Emphasize to clients that acting on values will be challenging for all of the above reasons. Appreciate that there will be times when emotional triggers obscure the moment of choice, or make values seem unreachable. But while acting on values won't always be possible, knowing what matters will increase the opportunity for more-conscious decision making.

Values-Based Action

Values-based action—in the face of emotional triggers—is only made possible by recognizing the moment of choice, which can be found using the following sequence:

1. Noticing painful emotion, including the components of feelings, thoughts, and sensations;

2. observing the action urge;

3. remembering situation-relevant values/intentions; and

4. deciding to act (on values/intentions or emotion-driven urges).

An authentic moment of choice requires that clients use steps 1 through 3 rather than merely reacting. All the earlier work with emotion awareness and mindful acceptance will come into play—the clients are more skilled at observing feelings; they have been developing the habit of observing and accepting before acting.

Once the moment of choice has been identified, there's no guarantee that clients will choose values-based action. The reinforcement for emotion-driven behavior will still be strong. But you can increase motivation by using the Benefits of Values-Based Action Worksheet. This simple exercise helps clients identify positive outcomes from acting on values across multiple domains.

Benefits of Values-Based Action Worksheet

Now that you've identified your values—and you understand that the moment of choice presents an opportunity to make a helpful decision about how to respond in an emotion-filled situation—let's explore possible reactions. Answer the following questions about your values, your intentions, and your actions around your values.

How does values-based action affect my relationships with friends and family?

_____

How does values-based action affect my relationship with my spouse or partner, or my living situation?

_____

How does values-based action affect my relationships when I am emotionally triggered?

_____

How does values-based action affect my work or school?

_____

How does values-based action affect my financial situation?

_____

How does values-based action affect my health?

_____

How does values-based action affect my long-term goals?

_____

How does values-based action affect my safety and security?

_____

_____

Therapist-Client Dialogue Example: Benefits of Values-Based Action

The client and her therapist explored the benefits of values-based action in the following dialogue:

Therapist: Let's look at the Benefits of Values-Based Action Worksheet. In terms of your children, the values were gentleness, caring, and love. How would acting on those values affect the relationship to your children?

Client: They would feel protected. They'd see that I care rather than seeing me blow up. They wouldn't be so wary of me, and I think I'd enjoy being with them a lot more.

Therapist: [Knowing the importance of putting this in writing] Could you capture those thoughts on the worksheet? [Pause] And what about with Bill? Would a caring response to his not being organized or not getting things done have benefits in that relationship?

Client: [Long pause] Yes, but I feel embarrassed to say... I think our sexual relationship would improve. He gets hurt and kinda withdraws from me. I think there would be more affection and sweetness between us instead of distance.

Therapist: Let's get that down, too. It feels important.

[When the client finishes the Benefits of Values-Based Action Worksheet, a look of sadness comes over her. She reads it over a second time.]

Client: I need to make some changes.

Your clients now have the tools they need to identify the moment of choice, identify a VBA, and visualize using the VBA during emotion exposure as part of their skills practice outside of session. Clients will continue the practice of choosing VBA in the next session, described in the next chapter.

Summary

Following is a synopsis of content covered in chapter 5:

- Values-based action (VBA) is defined as any behavior that is in alignment with or expresses value for the context of the situation.

- VBA is an alternative to acting on painful emotions.

- Clarifying values across life domains is the first step to being able to identify VBA in the moment of choice.

- Lack of clarity about values; a hard-wiring to avoid pain; the habit of acting on emotion; and short-term reinforcement for acting on emotion-driven behavior, or emotion avoidance, are barriers to choosing values-based action in the moment of choice.

- Understanding the benefits of VBA can increase motivation to choose an action based on values in the moment of choice instead of an emotion-driven behavior.

CHAPTER 6

Values-Based Action, Part 2

In chapter 5, we covered how to help clients clarify their values, identify values-based action, and understand the benefits of enacting values-based actions, or VBAs, in all areas of their lives. In this chapter we examine how to help clients choose VBA when they get triggered, in the moment of choice. Through the Monsters on the Bus exercise and an imaginal exposure exercise, clients will combine the values clarification and motivation developed by completing the Values Domain Worksheet and the Benefits of Values-Based Action Worksheet with rehearsal of the VBA.

EET Skill Objective:
Observe + Accept + Choose values-based action

Monsters on the Bus

The "monsters on the bus" metaphor is used in acceptance and commitment therapy (Hayes et al., 1999). It is a powerful experiential exercise to help clients practice tolerating distressing internal events and choosing to act on their values in triggering situations. In EET, we've modified the exercise to specifically include tolerance of distressing emotional experiences manifested in thoughts, feelings, sensations, and urges. By practicing observing and accepting emotional experience, and choosing VBA in the moment of choice, clients learn how to powerfully create what they want for themselves and their lives.

Your clients have already been practicing mindful acceptance, emotion surfing, and identifying the moment of choice. And they now understand the concept of choosing a values-based action in a triggering situation. The next step is for them to practice in session through imaginal exposure, as well as out of session, in vivo. When clients are willing to do this, they will learn that they can take the pain or distress with them on the path of VBA, instead of choosing to avoid painful emotions (emotion avoidance) or to act on their emotions (emotion-driven behaviors).

Facilitating the willingness to tolerate distress in the service of values is the key to choosing VBA. Clients must be motivated enough to allow for the distressing experience and still be able to choose to use a VBA instead of choosing experiential avoidance. This level of motivation and distress tolerance requires developing a clear understanding of why it's better for them to stay on the path to values-based action than to veer onto the path of experiential avoidance.

Following is a step-by-step guide to setting up the Monsters on the Bus exercise and a therapist-client dialogue example of leading a client through the exercise. It may be helpful to use both the Values Domains Worksheet and the Benefits of Values-Based Action Worksheet as a reference with your clients.

Setting Up the Monsters on the Bus Exercise

Prep your clients for this exercise during session using the following steps:

Step 1: Assist clients in choosing a situation from one of their life domains that is distressing, and then help them identify what value they would like to express in the situation. Make sure that the value is rated as "very important" to ensure the likelihood that your clients will be motivated to try a new behavior.

Step 2: Help clients to identify the values-based action that could be enacted to move in the direction of their value in that particular domain. Help them be very specific about how the VBA would be enacted in the situation.

Step 3: Ask clients what emotional barriers—thoughts, feelings, sensations, and urges—come up when they visualize enacting their VBA. Make a list of all the thoughts, feelings, sensations, and urges, writing each one on its own piece of paper. These pieces of paper will represent the "monsters" for the exercise. If you have time and are so inclined, you can even draw a picture of the monster for each emotional barrier.

Step 4: Have clients stand up at one end of the office. At the other end, place a sheet of paper with the VBA written on it so that it's visible to the clients. Place the pieces of paper with the emotional components, which will serve as the "monsters," in any order in a row between the client and the VBA.

Step 5: Tell clients you will be going on the journey with them, as a guide leading them toward their VBA. Explain that they will be driving a bus in the direction of their VBA. Along the way, they will encounter "monsters"—the barriers to reaching their VBA. Let your clients know that while you are guiding them, they are in complete control of what they choose to do along the way.

The following script provides an example of how to approach the next part of this exercise with your clients.

Therapist-Client Dialogue Example: Monsters on the Bus

Therapist: Okay. We've identified your values-based action, which is to sign up for online dating [points to other end of office]. This VBA is in the service of which of your values?

Client: Connection.

Therapist: And the VBA of signing up for online dating represents one way you can move toward connection?

Client: Yes.

Therapist: Okay. [Stands next to client] So here you are driving your bus along the road, which represents your life and all that goes with it. You're driving toward your VBA, connection. Let's go… [Motions to client to pretend to be driving while moving forward.]

Client: [Puts his hands on an imaginary wheel and steps forward with therapist.]

Therapist: [Steps forward to pick up the first "monster" on the sheet of paper and turns to stand in front of client driving the bus] Let's face this first monster. [Reads] "No one is going to want to go out with me."

Client: Yeah. That's probably true [laughs mirthlessly].

Therapist: So it feels true that no one will want to go out with you. Can we stay with this for a moment?

Client: Sure.

Therapist: Great. Can you say more? What's the feeing that goes with that thought?

Client: Um…probably fear of being rejected.

Therapist: Okay. So you worry if you sign up for online dating you'll end up getting rejected—that no one will want to go out with you.

Client: Yeah.

Therapist: Okay. And when you feel afraid that no one wants to go out with you, where do you feel that in your body?

Client: In my gut. Kind of like a knot.

Therapist: Okay, so you're afraid, and you have a knot in your stomach.

Client:	Yeah. And I get that every time I sit down at my computer and think about signing up.
Therapist:	Okay. And what is the urge that goes with this thought, sensation, and feeling?
Client:	Just don't do it! I want to avoid it.
Therapist:	Okay. So when you are having this thought that no one is going to want to go out with you, and the knot in your stomach, and fear, you just want to avoid?
Client:	Absolutely.
Therapist:	So now that we're here, can you locate your moment of choice?
Client:	I see it…but I still want to avoid.
Therapist:	Okay… Shall we try veering off the VBA path?
Client:	Sure.
Therapist:	[Comes back next to client and guides him off to the side of the office, away from the VBA path] So now we're moving toward the path to experiential avoidance.
Client:	Uh, okay. Hmm.
Therapist:	So what's it like hanging out over here?
Client:	Well… I'm not so afraid anymore.
Therapist:	Okay, so you're not feeling the fear so much. What else?
Client:	And the knot is better…
Therapist:	Okay… So there's less tension in your stomach?
Client:	Yeah.
Therapist:	Any thoughts coming up?
Client:	Well, actually the thought that I'll never find a partner is back…
Therapist:	I see. And what's the feeling that goes with that?
Client:	Fear, actually.

Therapist:	So now the fear is from *not* taking steps to try to find a partner?
Client:	Exactly. And now the knot in my stomach is coming back.
Therapist:	Sounds like a different monster over here? The fear that you'll never find a partner, and the sensation is back?
Client:	Seems that way.
Therapist:	So, how's the path to experiential avoidance working for you?
Client:	It's not. I'm still miserable.
Therapist:	Shall we head back to the VBA path?
Client:	Yeah, sure. At least over there I'm trying to do something good for myself.
Therapist:	[Guides client back to start of VBA path] So where were we...? We were hanging out with this monster called "No one is going to want to go out with me." [Steps back in front of the client.]
Client:	Yeah. That's still probably true.
Therapist:	Okay. So how do we move toward your VBA with that thought in your way?
Client:	Run it over?
Therapist:	[Chuckles] Good idea. But, unfortunately, in this game, like real life, we can't kill the monsters.
Client:	[Chuckles] Okay... So how *do* I move forward?
Therapist:	Well, remember you're driving a bus. So if you can't run them over, and you can't go around them or avoid them, what does that leave you with?
Client:	Hmm... Take them with me?
Therapist:	Exactly! You can let them on your bus.
Client:	All right then. [Pretends to open the lever to the bus door.]
Therapist:	[Picks up the sheet of paper with "No one will want to go out with me" on it and rejoins the client, standing next to him] Shall we move forward?
Client:	Sure...

Therapist: What's the next monster? [Picks up the next piece of paper, stands in front of the client, and reads] "I need to make more money before anyone will want to be with me."

Client: Well that's probably true.

Therapist: That feels really true, huh?

Client: [Nods.]

Therapist: Okay, let's stay with that. What's the sensation that goes with that thought?

Client: My chest feels a little tight. And I'm getting warm all over my neck and chest.

Therapist: And what's the feeling that goes with the thought that you need to make more money for someone to want to be with you, and the tightness in your chest, and the warmth in you neck and chest?

Client: Hmm… I feel embarrassed about what I earn at my job. I guess the feeling is shame.

Therapist: You think it's shame?

Client: Yeah, it's shame.

Therapist: Okay. And what's the urge that goes with this emotion?

Client: Well, just don't put myself out there. You know…avoid.

Therapist: Okay, so here we are at your moment of choice again. Shall we veer off the VBA path and onto the path of experiential avoidance?

Client: No way! I've been over there and it's not any better [looks dejected].

Therapist: Are you sure? It might relieve the distress, even for just a little while… You wouldn't be fighting against this particular emotion…

Client: Yeah, I might feel less shame, but then the fear of being alone will kick back in.

Therapist: Okay. So what are you going to choose?

Client: Let the shame monster on the bus!

Therapist:	Are you sure? You'll have to keep driving with these emotions, and with all their thoughts, sensations, feelings, and urges…
Client:	Yeah, I'm sure. They're with me anyway, so I might as well try online dating.
Therapist:	Okay, let's keep going. [Comes back next to the client and moves forward to the next "monster," and turns to face the client] What do we have here? [Reads] It's the thought "If anyone really gets to know me, they won't like me."
Client:	Ooh—that's a good one. [Pauses] Yeah, I gotta be honest, I really do believe that one.
Therapist:	You feel it's true that if anyone gets to know you, they won't like you?
Client:	Yeah. My heart has started racing and my palms just got sweaty.
Therapist:	Okay… And what's the feeling that goes with those sensations?
Client:	Panic.
Therapist:	Okay. So you feel panic and your heart is racing and your palms are sweating when you have the thought "No one who really gets to know me will like me"?
Client:	Yes. It's pretty strong.
Therapist:	This is a big one for you?
Client:	Yeah. It's a big risk, letting someone know me.
Therapist:	Right. There's always the possibility you won't be a match?
Client:	Yeah.
Therapist:	So what is the urge that goes with this emotion?
Client:	Well, to avoid, of course.
Therapist:	Okay. So would you be willing to take that emotion with you toward your VBA?
Client:	In this game or in real life [chuckles]?
Therapist:	Both.

Client:	Well, I know going off on the path to experiential avoidance isn't going to feel good. But it might feel better than risking letting someone get to know me. But... I really want a relationship.
Therapist:	It sounds like you do. And so far you've been willing to take these other monsters with you for the chance of finding connection.
Client:	Yeah. I think I have to let this one on the bus too.
Therapist:	You're sure?
Client:	Yes. I'm ready to try something new. I'm tired of being alone.
Therapist:	Okay. Let's bring this big monster on the bus. [Stands next to client and directs him to the VBA, picks it up, and hands it to him] Congratulations!
Client	Thanks. Now I just have to do it for real.
Therapist:	Yes. Can you commit to signing up for online dating before our next session?
Client:	I will.
Therapist:	Great. And if it gets hard, you'll remember what it was like on the path to experiential avoidance.
Client:	Yeah. It's even more depressing over there.

After the Monsters on the Bus exercise is complete, you'll want to consolidate what clients learned by asking about their experience, specifically: what they predicted would be hard, and what it was like allowing (observing and accepting) the distressing emotion; their experience of moving toward experiential avoidance; and their experience of moving toward the VBA. Be sure to ask them if they can commit to using their VBA in an in vivo situation. You'll also want to emphasize that VBA doesn't involve changing their emotional experience. They just become willing to tolerate it and can then "take it with them."

If clients weren't able to commit to moving forward during the Monsters on the Bus exercise, and instead chose to stay on the path to experiential avoidance, you still have several options. First, you could highlight that the costs of taking the path of VBA seem to outweigh the costs of taking the path to experiential avoidance; then reassess the clients' rating of importance for this value. Second, you can choose a different VBA for which the clients are more motivated and willing to tolerate distress. Third, you can use imaginal exposure (discussed in the following section) as a way to increase their distress tolerance and willingness to allow the suffering while moving toward their VBA.

Imaginal Exposure Using Values-Based Action

Now it's time to practice choosing VBA using imaginal exposure to increase willingness to tolerate distress and to enhance learning, retention, and recall. Just as in previous sessions, imaginal exposure begins by using the O+A+C (observe + accept + choose) model. Once clients have practiced O+A+C and located their moment of choice, they will visualize choosing their values-based action, rating their SUDS level just before and after.

Imaginal exposure with rehearsal of the VBA helps clients more easily access the willingness to do a new behavior in future in vivo situations. From a neuroscience perspective, the rehearsal visualization makes new neural connections, allowing them to more easily fire together again in similar future situations.

Following is a step-by-step practice guide and a therapist-client dialogue example of conducting imaginal exposure with VBA.

Conducting Imaginal Exposure with VBA

Prep your clients to work with imaginal exposure during session using the following steps:

Step 1: Selecting a distressing situation. Ask clients to describe a recent distressing event in which they became emotionally triggered and responded with experiential avoidance or other emotion-driven behavior.

Step 2: Identifying the value and the VBA. Prompt your clients to identify which of their values relates to this situation. Then identify a specific VBA that the clients would have preferred to enact. You'll want to ask clients to articulate exactly what this alternative behavior would look like—everything the clients say and do, including their tone of voice and body language.

Step 3: Visualizing enacting the VBA. Have clients briefly visualize enacting the VBA, mentally rehearsing the scene several times until they are clear about what they will do.

Step 4: O+A+C. Begin the exposure by having clients form a clear image of the triggering scene. Encourage them to notice the environment where the trigger occurred: watch the action in the scene, hear what's said, feel whatever physical sensations are part of the scene, notice if there's an urge to do something or not to do something. As clients become emotionally activated, ask them to continue to describe the sensations, thoughts, feelings, and urges that come up. Encourage an accepting attitude whereby the clients "make room" for the emotion, allowing it to be what it is with no effort at controlling or avoiding it.

While clients are still visualizing the triggering event, have them observe any action urges that arise. Is there a desire to be verbally aggressive, to withdraw, to stonewall, to be defensive? Ask the clients to describe such urges, and get them to notice that the urges don't have to become action. This is the moment of choice, and it's important for the clients to stay with it for several minutes: observing the emotional pain, accepting and allowing the pain to be there without avoidance, and choosing not to act on emotion-driven urges.

Step 5: Imaginal exposure with VBA. Now that your clients have identified the moment of choice, check for SUDS. Then introduce the VBA as a guided visualization. Ask your clients to continue the distressing scene, but instead of having them imagining the emotion-driven behavior that accompanied the actual scene, have them visualize the alternative VBA they rehearsed earlier. As noted before, encourage clients to watch themselves saying and/or doing the new behavior, with a tone of voice and posture matching the VBA. For the next three to five minutes, ask clients to repeat this visualization, moving from the triggering scene—and the moment of choice—through the new, values-based response several times. Ask clients to rate their SUDS at the end. The entire exposure sequence—O+A+C + VBA—should last eight to ten minutes.

Step 6: Consolidating what was learned. Help clients consolidate what they have learned through a brief conversation. Did the exposure increase acceptance for the target emotion? What did they observe about the moment of choice? How did visualizing an alternate response (VBA) impact them? Did it reduce their distress? Increase their distress tolerance? Did it increase confidence that the client could choose VBAs in distressing situations?

Therapist-Client Dialogue Example: Imaginal Exposure + VBA

Step 1: Selecting a distressing situation.

Therapist: It sounds like you had a difficult incident with one of your children. Tell me what happened.

Client: My youngest child refused to clean up his room. When I asked, he threw himself on the bed screaming. I shouted that he should get up and do what I asked, and then I dragged him off the bed. He fought me, and I pinned him to the ground and screamed at him to respect me and do what I ask when I ask it.

Step 2: Identifying the value and the VBA.

Therapist: Can you identify a key value you hold for your relationship with your son?

Client: I think it would be caring.

Therapist: Great. And what would be a values-based action to move you in the direction of caring in this situation?

Client: I want to let him know that I get that he's unhappy. I'd like to interrupt his playtime in a calm way.

Therapist: Okay, great. How would you do that? Can you imagine a way to slow the situation down so it doesn't escalate?

Client: I could give him a few minutes to think about the consequences of not stopping and cleaning his room.

Therapist: Great idea. So how long will you give him?

Client: I guess I could give him five minutes.

Step 3: Visualizing enacting the VBA.

Therapist: Okay, great. Let's take a few moments and visualize the situation... Imagine you go into his room and see him playing, and you ask him in a calm voice to clean up his room. When he protests, you tell him he has five minutes to think about it, or else there will be a consequence.

Client: Got it.

Therapist: So now take a moment and close your eyes, and talk me through it in your own words.

Client: Okay. I'm going into the room. I see him playing and I say—calmly— "Honey, I need you to stop what you're doing and clean up your room." And then he starts to pout and says, "I don't want to." So I calmly say, "I know it's hard for you to stop playing." I see he is not stopping, so I say, "I'll give you five minutes to make up your mind, and when I come back I would like you to stop and clean your room, or there will be a consequence." And then I walk away.

Therapist: Great. Now let's do that one more time. Talk me through it.

Client: Okay. I come into his room and see him playing there. I calmly ask him to stop playing and clean up his room. He starts pouting and says he doesn't want to. I don't react, but I calmly say that I understand he doesn't want to stop playing, and that I'll give him five minutes to make up his mind, and that when I come back I need him to be cleaning or there will be a consequence.

Therapist: Okay. Good work.

Step 4: O+A+C + VBA.

Therapist: Now let's move into the exposure. I'll talk you through it. Start by imagining the scene, noticing anything you see, hear, or sense. You've asked him to clean his room and he protests. What are you noticing right now about your urge to yell?

Client: It's strong. I want to take control.

Therapist: Stay with that. Notice the urge, but be aware you have a choice. You could yell or not yell.

Client: Okay, I'm really pissed, though. I really can't stand it when he acts that way.

Therapist: Right. Notice the pain, how helpless and disrespected you feel. Can you describe that?

Client: Yeah. Being ignored—I feel like I'm nothing, like I don't matter.

Therapist: Okay, keep watching that feeling and try to just allow it. Make room for it without controlling or pushing it away. Can you do that?

Client: I'm just watching it.

Therapist: And what about that urge to yell? Can you see your moment of choice right now? That you could actually have this pain without yelling?

Client: Yes. I'm watching myself feeling the urge. I see the choice.

Step 5: Imaginal exposure with VBA.

Therapist: Okay, good. What is your SUDS rating in this moment?

Client: A 6, maybe.

Therapist:	Okay. Now, can you see yourself calmly and gently telling your son that you understand how hard it is to stop playing? [Pauses] And now can you explain there will be a consequence if you have to pick up his toys? Imagine saying that with a calm, caring voice.
Client:	Yes, I can see that.
Therapist:	Now, notice that he isn't stopping, and hear yourself giving him five minutes to decide.
Client:	I'm still pissed off, but I can imagine doing that.
Therapist:	Good, let's go through the scene again, starting when he refuses to clean up and throws himself on the bed. Notice the pain and the urge to yell. Now see yourself going through each step of your intention. [The client repeats the sequence several times.] What is your SUDS rating now?
Client:	A 3, maybe. I feel calmer.

Step 6: Consolidating what was learned.

Therapist:	Let's talk about the exposure. What was it like just being with your feelings and accepting them while observing your moment of choice?
Client:	Well, I'm getting better at watching my feelings and not being so overwhelmed by them.
Therapist:	Great. And what about adding the visualization of doing your VBA—imagining carrying out your intention to be caring with your boy?
Client:	It's weird, just making it up—something that didn't really happen. But somehow I feel like I could do it. After rehearsing in my mind, I think it makes it easier to actually pull off.

During the balance of treatment, you can return to using imaginal exposure with O+A+C + VBA each time your clients get emotionally triggered during the week and don't use a VBA. You can also encourage clients to relive problematic events using this exposure outside of session. Remind your clients that every time they enact a new values-based action they are building their emotion efficacy muscle.

Summary

Following is a synopsis of content covered in chapter 6:

- The key to overcoming barriers to enacting VBA is accessing the willingness to tolerate distress while moving in the direction of values in the moment of choice.

- Motivating clients to choose values-based action in the moment of choice can be accelerated by comparing the costs of emotion avoidance with the benefits of moving in their valued direction.

- Visualizing choosing VBA in the moment of choice can increase willingness to enact values-based action during in vivo exposure.

- Imaginal exposure practice using values-based action can enhance learning, retention, and recall. It can also increase willingness to enact VBAs in distressing situations.

CHAPTER 7

Relaxation and Self-Soothing

As clients develop the skill to observe, accept, and choose (O+A+C) when responding to emotion, they are learning distress tolerance and beginning to change the belief that they can't stand pain. The emotional distress that they have habitually run from or acted on may seem less overwhelming now. They have seen the pain, they have observed emotions that once felt "too hot to handle." And they're able to locate the moment of choice—when they can choose to act or not act on emotion-driven urges.

But emotion efficacy is more than believing one has the ability to face and endure pain, or act on values instead of emotion. It also means knowing that one has the skills to cope with pain. For example, when emotional distress shows up as a sudden urge, and the pain hits, there's an instantaneous appraisal: "Do I have the ability to withstand this? Do I know what it takes to live with this emotion?" The answers to these questions come at a point of decision when the client chooses acceptance versus avoidance.

EET Skill Objective: Observe + Accept + Choose
mindful coping (relaxation/self-soothing)

Mindful Coping

Mindful coping, as with all key EET components, begins with the practice of mindful acceptance. Clients observe and "surf" a strong emotion. The exposure practice is brief—usually five minutes or less—and gives clients the opportunity to strengthen beliefs that they can experience difficult emotions without running.

As with previous O+A+C exercises, the object is to watch and *not* act on emotional pain and urges. However, mindful coping requires a second phase to the O+A+C process. Once the exposure is terminated, the focus shifts to a specific coping strategy. Now the client copes down distress until some downregulation is achieved.

Just as with values-based action, clients will use *mindful coping skills* in the face of emotional triggers in the moment of choice. The sequence is similar to choosing a VBA:

1. Noticing painful emotion, including the components of feelings, thoughts, and sensations;

2. observing and accepting the action urge;

3. recognizing that the emotion is so powerful that they first need to practice mindful acceptance; and

4. choosing a mindful coping skill to downregulate emotion before they choose a values-based action.

Mindful coping will help build the emotion efficacy muscle and, in particular, develop the skills necessary to hold—and not avoid—pain as well as to downregulate it.

Advantages of Mindful Coping

Emotion coping strategies are usually taught in the relatively comfortable environment of a therapist's office or DBT group meeting. The clients rehearse the coping process and may promptly forget it when facing the exigencies of an emotional storm. The difficulty of retrieving skills learned in a relaxed state—while aroused—is explained by state-dependent learning research (Szymanski & O'Donohue, 1995). These studies suggest that knowledge or skills learned in a specific state are harder to remember in a different one. Mindful coping solves this problem by inducing emotional arousal through imaginal exposure before practicing coping. The clients are thus placed in the same emotionally triggered state in which they will need to use the coping skills in vivo.

The second advantage of mindful coping is that it affords repeated practice opportunities across multiple contexts. Craske and colleagues have shown that exposure works best when the avoided stimulus is encountered in many environments and contexts (Craske, Treanor, Conway, Zbozinek & Vervliet, 2014). The same can be said for exposure plus coping. Imaginal exposure creates opportunities to practice coping skills in the face of varied emotions and triggering situations.

Introducing Mindful Coping to Clients

The steps to introduce mindful coping include the rationale for using this coping strategy, along with a brief description of the five EET mindful coping skills: *relaxation* and *self-soothing* (this chapter), *coping thoughts* and *radical acceptance* (chapter 8), and *distraction* and *time-out* (chapter 9).

What follows are the steps for guiding a mindful coping skills practice, along with a sample dialogue.

Step 1: Lead clients into a brief imaginal exposure.

Step 2: Achieve the target range for emotional arousal (5–6 SUDS), then terminate exposure.

Step 3: Initiate mindful acceptance and identify the moment of choice.

Step 4: Initiate mindful coping (using one of the five EET skills) until there is some reduction in distress (SUDS).

Therapist-Client Dialogue Example: Introducing Mindful Coping

Therapist: Today we're going to start something new—mindful coping. It will be added onto the emotion exposure you've already been doing—so after each exposure you will use these new coping skills to reduce distress.

Here's why this will help. Mindful coping skills will give you more confidence and security that you can deal with emotions—no matter how big. They'll strengthen your feeling of efficacy—the sense that you have what it takes to face any emotional storm. You'll get lots of practice coping in an emotionally aroused state, which will help you remember these skills when you get emotionally triggered out in the world.

Client: What are the coping skills? What am I supposed to learn?

Therapist: There are five of them. First, you'll learn basic relaxation skills—deep breathing, relaxing muscles, and so forth. Then self-soothing, which are calming experiences—like listening to peaceful sounds or music, looking at something beautiful, smelling a lovely fragrance. Things like that.

We'll work on relaxation and self-soothing today. Later, we'll develop some coping thoughts to calm you as well as distraction strategies to give you more distance from upsetting emotions. So far, so good?

Client: Sure, okay.

Therapist: Mindful coping is pretty simple. We'll do an exposure, as usual, to something that was recently upsetting. You'll keep watching the scene till the emotion is moderately strong—5 or 6 SUDS. Then we'll stop the exposure and begin mindful coping till the emotion quiets a little bit. We'll practice with both relaxation and self-soothing to see how each of them works for you.

O+A+C + Mindful Coping

The protocol for using mindful coping is the same using all five skills that are covered in chapters 7 through 9. The steps for O+A+C + mindful coping are as follows:

Step 1: Give clients a week to practice new mindful coping exercises at home.

Step 2: In session, choose a recent situation when the clients were emotionally triggered. Encourage them to visualize the scene, paying attention to visual, auditory, and kinesthetic elements.

Step 3: While the clients "watch" the scene, periodically check SUDS. When SUDS reach 5 or 6, or five minutes has elapsed, end the exposure and take a final SUDS rating.

Step 4: Ask clients to observe and accept any sensations, thoughts, feelings, and urges that arise. Encourage them to "make room" for all parts of the emotion.

Step 5: Begin mindful coping. Coach the clients through the process. Continue mindful coping until there is some (even a small) reduction in SUDS.

Step 6: Review outcomes with the clients—go over what worked and what didn't.

Now let's look at the two mindful coping skills covered in this chapter: relaxation and self-soothing.

Mindful Coping with Relaxation

Key relaxation skills taught in EET are diaphragmatic breathing, relaxation without tension, cue-controlled breathing, and the five-senses exercise.

Diaphragmatic breathing. This is the classic first step in a relaxation program. Diaphragmatic breathing starts by having clients place one hand on their chest and the other just above the belt line. The clients are then instructed to breathe slowly and deeply, so the hand on the abdomen moves while the hand on the chest does not (see the Mindful Coping Through Relaxation handout).

Relaxation without tension. This skill requires clients to focus on five muscle groups: face (forehead and jaw); neck and shoulders; arms and hands; chest, back, and abdomen; and legs (buttocks, thighs, calves, and feet). Clients are instructed to observe a specific muscle group, noting any area of tension. Then they take a deep breath, subvocally recite a cue word at the top of the breath, and then release the breath while relaxing away tension in the target muscle group. This process should be done twice with each muscle group.

Cue words can include relaxing colors (golden light, sea blue), places associated with peace (Tuolumne Meadows, Shenandoah National Park), commands ("relax now"), or spiritual mantras (*om*). Whatever cue word is chosen, by noting it at the moment of relaxation the cue becomes associated with and begins to trigger muscle release (see the Mindful Coping Through Relaxation handout). Once relaxation without tension is mastered, the procedure can be shortened to focus on a single muscle group, or even a specific tense muscle, as needed during mindful coping practice.

Cue-controlled breathing. Developed by Ost (1987), this skill is a quick, effective relaxation procedure. It distills relaxation without tension to a single sequence: a deep breath, the subvocalized cue word at the top of the breath, and the release of breath while relaxing away tension throughout the body. The goal is to relax all muscle groups simultaneously. Clients use the same cue word established during relaxation without tension. They do five to ten cue-controlled breaths during each practice session (see the Mindful Coping Through Relaxation handout).

The five senses. This technique is designed to induct clients into the present moment. It relaxes by moving attention from negative thoughts into a focus on current sensory experience. Clients are taught to spend thirty seconds on each sense, observing the following sequence:

- Auditory experience: trying to notice each sound in earshot

- Olfactory experience: observing fragrances, odors, and scents from clients' own bodies or the environment

- Kinesthetic experience: noticing touch, including the sense of temperature, texture, or pressure where one's body touches the floor or chair

- Visual experience: observing colors, shapes, and objects

- Gustatory experience: identifying and observing any kind of taste (see the Mindful Coping Through Relaxation handout)

The following sample script can be a model when your clients are ready to be introduced to using the mindful coping skill of relaxation.

Therapist-Client Dialogue Example: Relaxation as a Mindful Coping Skill

In the following example of mindful coping, the client has chosen a recent fight with her sister for the exposure.

Therapist: As you close your eyes, bring up the scene where you had a fight with your sister. You're in the restaurant—Salute. See the configuration of tables, the room; hear the murmurs of conversation and click of silverware. Feel the texture of the tablecloth under your hands. Now see your sister across from you, notice how she's dressed. Hear her voice—she's telling you that you've neglected her. Just watch the scene and listen to what she says… What are your SUDS?

Client: A 3 or 4.

Therapist: Stay with it. Watch her across from you. Listen to her words… See if you can accept the feelings. Try to make room for them… Just allow whatever you feel as you listen to her talk. What are your SUDS?

Client: Around 5.

Therapist: Okay. Notice the action urge. Your emotion is pushing you to say something harsh. Just watch the urge, the moment you must choose.

Client: I feel like telling her she's worthless and walking out.

Therapist: Yes, notice the urge. And that you can choose to do that or not. Keep listening to what she says… What are your SUDS?

Client: A 6.

Therapist: Good. Let go of this image now. It's time for mindful coping. What relaxation exercise would feel best at this moment?

Client: A deep breath [takes several diaphragmatic breaths].

Therapist: Any tense places in your body?

Client: My shoulders.

Therapist: Can you use your breath and the cue word to relax away tension in your shoulders…? Where are your SUDS?

Client: A 4 or 5.

Therapist: What would help now?

Client: I'd like to try the five senses.

Therapist:	Good. Notice what you hear. If thoughts interrupt, just go back to listening. Notice anything you can smell…notice your sense of touch… Now focus on what you see…notice anything you can taste… Where are your SUDS?
Client:	A 3.
Therapist:	The emotion is softening, less intense. What was that experience like?
Client:	It's very different to observe my anger and the urge to blow up. To just allow it, rather than have to do something. Breathing away the stress in my shoulders worked the best. Using the five senses is okay, but I don't think it would work that well in real life. We'll see, I guess.

The following handout (also in Appendix C and online at http://www.newharbinger .com/34039) can be given to your clients to assist them in practicing the mindful coping skill of relaxation outside of session.

Mindful Coping Through Relaxation

When a powerful emotion has been triggered and you are suddenly facing your moment of choice, a mindful coping skill can help downregulate your emotions before you decide on a values-based action. Practice these relaxation techniques daily so that you can rely on them in your moment of choice.

Diaphragmatic Breathing

Place one hand on your abdomen, just above the belt line, and the other on your chest.

Take a slow, deep breath into the abdomen. The hand on the abdomen should move but not the hand on the chest.

If you are having difficulty pushing the breath into your abdomen (and the hand on your chest is moving), you can do one of two things:

- Press your hand into your abdomen, and then inhale so that the breath pushes your hand out.

- Lie down and put a phone book over your abdomen. Breathe so that your inhale pushes the phone book up.

Practice 15 diaphragmatic breaths three times a day.

Relaxation Without Tension

Choose a cue word. Identify a word or phrase that you associate with relaxation. This could be a color (golden light, sea blue), a place that calms you (Tuolumne, Shenandoah), a command (relax now), or a spiritual mantra (om, peace on earth, I let go). This cue word will become associated with, and soon trigger, deep relaxation.

Observe a muscle group (see next paragraph) and notice any tension. Take a deep, diaphragmatic breath. At the top of the breath, say to yourself the cue word. Now, as you exhale, relax away any tension in the target muscle group. Do this process twice with each muscle group, in any order.

The five muscle groups you will relax are:

- Face (forehead and jaw)

- Neck and shoulders

- Arms and hands

- Chest, back, abdomen

- Legs (buttocks, thighs, calves, feet)

Practice this skill three times a day.

Cue-Controlled Breathing

Use the same cue word you established with Relaxation Without Tension.

Take a deep, diaphragmatic breath. At the top of the breath, say to yourself the cue word. Now, as you exhale, relax away any tension throughout your body at once. Let your body slump forward slightly as you exhale and release all tension.

Take 15 cue-controlled breaths three times a day to practice this new skill.

Five-Senses Exercise

For 30 seconds, focus on every sound you can hear: voices, traffic noise, machinery noise such as the hum of an air conditioner, sounds of movement, sounds your body makes. Try to keep your attention fully on these sounds. If your mind wanders, gently bring it back to focusing on what you hear.

For 30 seconds focus on what you can smell: fragrances, odors, scents from your own body or the environment. Try to keep attention on what you smell; return to this focus when your mind wanders.

For 30 seconds focus on your sense of touch, including temperature and texture, noticing the pressure where your body touches the floor or chair. Return to your sense of touch when your mind wanders.

For 30 seconds focus on visual sensations, observing color and shapes, and noticing the objects in your environment. When you get distracted, bring your attention back to what you see.

For 30 seconds focus on your sense of taste. What residual tastes do you notice in your mouth—bitter, sweet, sour, salty? Are there more subtle tastes? If you get distracted, bring your attention back to taste.

Practice this exercise twice daily as a way to focus attention away from negative thoughts and onto present-moment experience.

Mindful Coping with Self-Soothing

Used extensively in dialectical behavior therapy, self-soothing exercises facilitate calming physical experiences for each of the five senses. Clients are encouraged to find and test self-soothing practices focused on sight, sound, taste, smell, and touch, including ones they can do at home and ones appropriate for public places.

The worksheet that follows can be given to clients to help them discover new methods of self-soothing as a way to mindfully cope in the moment of choice.

Mindful Coping Through Self-Soothing

This worksheet will help you identify some ways to soothe yourself using each of your five senses.

Sense of Smell

Using your sense of smell can activate specific thoughts, memories, or sensations that can be calming. If you identify smells that make you feel good in advance, you will be prepared to use them when triggered. Following are some examples, and feel free to add your own ideas:

_____ Burn scented candles or incense that you like.

_____ Wear scented oils, perfume, or cologne that makes you feel happy, confident, or sexy.

_____ Carry perfumed cards from magazines, or ones that you make, in your purse, wallet, or car.

_____ Go someplace where you know the scent is pleasing to you, such as a bakery or coffee shop.

_____ Lie down in a park where you can smell grass, flowers, or other outdoor smells.

_____ Buy flowers or find flowers in your neighborhood.

_____ Hug someone whose smell makes you feel calm.

_____ Other ideas: _____

Sense of Sight

Sight is an important sense for humans in that a large portion of our brain is devoted to what we see. What we look at can have powerful effects on our emotions, for better or for worse. If you identify images that make you feel good in advance, you will be prepared to use them when upset. Following are some examples, and a place for you to add your own ideas:

_____ Look online, through magazines, and in books to select pictures you like. Make a collage of them to hang on your wall, add as a screensaver on your computer, or keep with you in your purse or wallet to look at throughout the day.

_____ Find a physical place that's soothing for you to look at, like a park, a lake, a museum, or other landmark. Or take a picture of that place.

_____ Go online or to the bookstore and find a collection of photographs or paintings that you find relaxing, such as the nature photographs by Ansel Adams.

_____ Draw or paint a picture that's pleasing to you.

_____ Carry a picture of someone you love, someone you find attractive, or someone you admire.

_____ Other ideas: _____

Sense of Hearing

Certain sounds can be very soothing. For example, everyone has his or her own tastes or preferences in music. By identifying in advance songs or sounds you know are soothing for you, you will be prepared to use them to help calm down. Following are some examples, and a place for you to add your own ideas:

_____ Listen to soothing music: classical, opera, oldies, new age, Motown, jazz, emo, whatever works for you. It might be instrumental or music with singing. Go online to iTunes and listen to a variety of music to determine what helps you relax. Look for preselected compilations for relaxation and meditation.

_____ Listen to audiobooks or CDs. Many public libraries will let you check out audiobooks. Try some to see if they help you relax. You don't even have to pay attention to the story line; sometimes just listening to the sound of someone's voice can be relaxing.

_____ Watch TV or stream shows on your computer. Find a show that's boring or sedate, not anything activating, like reality TV, or that would make you angry, like the news. Keep the volume at a low level.

_____ Listen to a gentle talk-show podcast, like a gardening or music show.

_____ Listen to white noise, a fan, or sound machine. White noise is a blend of sounds that blocks out other distracting sounds. A sound machine has recorded sounds such as birds, waterfalls, wind, rain, and waves. Many people find these machines very relaxing.

_____ Listen to the sounds of rushing or trickling water. Find a personal electronic water fountain or a nearby fountain in a park or a mall.

_____ Listen to a relaxation or meditation exercise. Exercises like these help you imagine yourself relaxing in different ways.

_____ Other ideas: _____

Sense of Taste

Our tongues have distinct regions on them that use taste buds to differentiate flavors and tastes of food. These sensations can also trigger memories and feelings. By identifying tastes you know are soothing for you in advance, you will be prepared to use them to deal with upsets. Following are some examples, and a place for you to add your own ideas:

_____ Enjoy your favorite meal. Eat it slowly and mindfully so you can savor all of its various flavors.

_____ Carry gum, mints, mouth spray, or other tasty treats with you to taste when you're feeling upset.

_____ Eat a "comfort" food that's soothing to you.

_____ Drink something you find soothing, such as tea, coffee, or hot chocolate.

_____ Suck on a popsicle or ice cube, especially if you're feeling warm.

_____ Find a piece of ripe, juicy fruit and eat it slowly.

_____ Other ideas: _____

Sense of Touch

Our skin is the largest organ in the body, and it's completely covered with nerves that carry sensations to our brain. This makes skin a powerful emotional messenger. By identifying tactile sensations you know are soothing for you in advance, you will be prepared to use them to quiet your emotions. Following are some examples, and a place for you to add your own ideas:

_____ Work in the garden, touching the cool earth.

_____ Carry something soft or velvety in your pocket to touch when you're upset.

_____ Take a hot or cold shower and observe the sensations of water on your skin.

_____ Take a warm bath with bubbles or scented oil.

_____ Get a massage. If you're not comfortable taking your clothes off, look for massage types such as Shiatsu, which simply requires you to wear loose-fitting clothes. Or find a seated chair massage for a shoulder and neck rub.

_____ Massage yourself.

_____ Play with a pet—yours or someone else's. Stroking an animal's fur or skin can provide a soothing tactile experience. In fact, having a pet can have many health benefits, such as lower blood pressure, lower cholesterol levels, and reduced risk for heart disease. If you can't find a pet, visit your local animal shelter, where you can play with the rescued animals.

_____ Wear your most comfortable clothes, for instance a worn-in T-shirt, baggy sweats, and so on.

_____ Other ideas: _____

This worksheet, and all the worksheets in this book, is available in appendix C and for download at http://www.newharbinger.com/34039.

Therapist-Client Dialogue Example: Self-Soothing as a Mindful Coping Skill

The client has downloaded and been practicing a "relaxing sounds" app. She has brought with her a photo of a meadow where she camped in the high Sierras, along with a small bar of soap with a fragrance of violets. In session, the client has just completed an imaginal exposure to a scene in which her son had refused help with his homework and told her to leave him alone. The exposure lasted five minutes, and the client has reached 5 on the SUDS scale.

Therapist:	Let's shift now. Let go of the scene. What self-soothing technique would you like to start with?
Client:	Smelling violets. [Smells the soap bar for a minute] Reminds me of my father's nursery—the hothouse in back. I loved being in there.
Therapist:	Where are your SUDS?
Client:	I don't know...4 maybe.
Therapist:	Want to add anything else?
Client:	I'll look at the meadow. And I have the sound of a brook. [Plays it on her phone and takes a deep breath] That's nice...
Therapist:	I can see you're feeling a little more peaceful. Where are your SUDS now?
Client:	A 3, or a little less.
Therapist:	Good. What was that like for you?
Client:	The fragrance and the sound helped most. I can get lost in it, kind of drift away.
Therapist:	Could you experiment with some of these self-soothing strategies during the week?
Client:	Yeah. I have earphones. And I can keep the soap and the picture with me.

Using Mindful Coping Outside Session

After practicing exposure with relaxation and self-soothing, prepare clients to use mindful coping outside of session. Start by identifying some of the likely situations when clients could get triggered. Emphasize the importance of responding initially with O+A+C.

Observing and accepting remains the first, and most important, response to any painful emotion. Then clients must choose: values-based action versus emotion-driven urges.

Only after a period of O+A+C should the clients consider coping responses. Coping, at this point, is limited to relaxation and self-soothing, and clients are encouraged to choose among those available responses mindfully. This means making a best choice—mindfully and intuitively—based on what's happening in the triggering situation. First, clients practice mindful acceptance, and then they choose additional coping strategies, as needed—until the emotional storm begins to subside.

Ultimately, the choice of whether to use coping strategies at all is a mindful one. Many clients will use them sparingly, and only in situations when they are feeling overwhelmed. They make the choice by staying aware of the moment and the risk of emotion-driven behavior. If the risk is high, mindful coping will give clients a sense of efficacy—that they can successfully ride the wave.

Summary

Following is a synopsis of content covered in chapter 7:

- Distinct from coping skills that are used in other interventions, mindful coping skills are practiced only *after* the practice of mindful acceptance. This sets up coping skills to be used intentionally, consciously, and in a contextually adaptive manner.

- Mindful coping skills are for crisis situations when clients have become so emotionally flooded that they are unable to access values-based action and need to intentionally and mindfully downshift their emotion.

- The six mindful coping skills in EET include: relaxation, self-soothing, coping thoughts, radical acceptance, distraction, and time-out.

- Relaxation is a skill that can be used to downregulate emotion including all four components of emotion: thoughts, feelings, sensations, and urges.

- Self-soothing is a mindful coping skill that applies pleasurable experiences to each of the five senses in order to downregulate emotion using all four components of emotion.

- Mindful coping also helps clients recover enough to choose values-based action.

- The knowledge that clients can use mindful coping increases their emotion efficacy by contributing to their belief that they have the skills to recover when necessary.

CHAPTER 8

Coping Thoughts and Radical Acceptance

The next mindful coping skills in EET are *coping thoughts* and *radical acceptance*. Both skills have to do with the way we think about the triggering event and the emotions that go with it. As one of the four contributing components of an emotion, thoughts are powerful forces in creating and maintaining emotion.

As we have discussed in previous chapters, emotions follow whatever the brain is registering as "true." If thought content is a result of threatening stimuli, emotions may manifest as tense sensations; feelings of fear, anxiety, and dread; and the urge to fight, freeze, or flee in some way. Or if thought content is a result of pleasurable stimuli, emotions may manifest as relaxed sensations; feelings of joy, contentment, and confidence; and the urge to engage. If clients struggle with automatic negative thoughts, replacing those thoughts with coping thoughts or practicing radical acceptance can help them increase distress tolerance and regulate their emotions by downshifting emotion.

EET Skill Objective: Observe + Accept + Choose
mindful coping (coping thoughts/radical acceptance)

Coping Thoughts

Automatic negative thoughts are often made up of judgment or danger thoughts about the self and/or the self in relationship to the world. Frequently, these thoughts reflect a person's maladaptive core beliefs organized around schemas, which contribute to and maintain distressing emotions (Rafaeli, Bernstein & Young, 2011). Coping thoughts are simply personalized, strength-based declarations about resiliency, history, or perspective that shifts the client's attention to help effectively navigate the difficult emotion.

Distinct from some other interventions that use coping strategies to increase emotion regulation and distress tolerance, all coping skills in EET are taught to be used mindfully. Similarly, coping thoughts are used differently than in other treatment interventions. Coping thoughts are taught as a mindful skill because they are used only after clients observe and accept their emotional experience. For example, after clients have practiced mindful acceptance and have located the moment of choice, they may choose to use coping thoughts to support them in decreasing distress.

In order to use coping thoughts, it's important to "cope ahead" by having some preselected cognitions in response to different triggers. To select effective coping thoughts, you'll work with your clients to identify common automatic negative thoughts they have in response to triggers and then come up with coping thoughts that can be used to replace them.

Following is a step-by-step guide to help clients recognize automatic negative thoughts and replace them with coping thoughts.

Mindful Coping with Coping Thoughts

Use the following steps to introduce your clients to coping thoughts:

Step 1: Identifying triggering situations. Start by pulling out the blank Replacing Automatic Thoughts with Coping Thoughts worksheet (which you'll find at the end of this section, in Appendix C, and in downloadable format at http://www .newharbinger.com/34039). Then ask your clients to recall a recent triggering situation and have them write it down in the "Trigger" column.

Step 2: Identifying automatic negative thoughts. Next, ask your clients to try to remember the automatic thought(s) that came up for them in the situation. You can prompt them with questions such as, "When you experienced that trigger, do you remember what you were thinking?" or "What did you believe about yourself in that moment?" Ask them to write their thought(s) in the "Automatic Negative Thoughts" column.

Step 3: Creating coping thoughts. Now it's time to get creative. You want to guide your clients in creating a coping thought to replace the negative automatic thought. The key with effective coping thoughts is to choose statements that the clients can get on board with. If they choose a thought that reflects an unrealistic possibility, it's unlikely they will believe it, and therefore unlikely they will get any relief from it.

For example, if a client's automatic negative thought is "I'll never be good enough," an effective coping thought might be "I always try my best." However, an example of an ineffective coping thought might be "I am the best," which may not be true, depending on the context, and may actually reinforce the negative automatic thought if the client doesn't believe it.

You'll want to do a reality check with your clients for each coping thought, asking your clients questions to ensure that they are creating coping thoughts that will be effective. Ask them, "Is that statement true for you?" or "Is that realistic?" Once your clients have created a coping thought for this situation, guide them through completing the worksheet by recording a few more triggering situations, automatic thoughts, and coping thoughts. Give clients the Client Coping Thoughts handout so they can record the coping sequence.

Step 4: O+A+C + coping thoughts. The next step is to show your clients how to practice using coping thoughts during imaginal exposure. Just as with values-based action, using imaginal exposure will accelerate new learning, retention, and recall when clients encounter a triggering situation in vivo. First, you'll help clients practice observing and accepting the situation. Then, in the moment of choice, guide them to use one or more previously developed coping thoughts. The dialogue example provided later in this chapter can be a model for this step.

Following is a handout on coping thoughts you can give to clients to help them understand this skill, and a blank worksheet for clients on which to log their triggers, automatic thoughts, and coping thoughts. (Both are available in reproducible format in Appendix C, and for download at the website for this book.) To help them understand this exercise, a filled-out sample of the second worksheet is also provided for clients.

Client Coping Thoughts

Coping thoughts can be used when you are facing a difficult emotion. They may be especially helpful after you've practiced observing and accepting the difficult emotion, and you're still struggling with specific ruminations, or a repetitive automatic thought is fueling your emotion wave.

You now know that your emotions will follow whatever you pay attention to. If you're triggered, you're likely to have negative automatic thoughts. One way to tolerate the distress and shift your emotion is to replace the negative automatic thought with a coping thought. The key with a coping thought is that you believe it to be true and realistic. If you don't believe the thought, it's unlikely to be effective.

Following are some examples of coping thoughts:

"This situation won't last forever."

"I can feel anxious/sad/angry without reacting."

"I can tolerate this emotion until the wave goes down."

"This emotion won't kill me, it just doesn't feel good right now."

"I've dealt with this situation before, and I can do it again."

"I can take all the time I need to just let go and relax."

"I can let this emotion run the show, or I can use values-based action."

"Just because I feel this emotion, doesn't mean I have to act on it."

"I am not my emotions… I can choose my next action."

Replacing Automatic Thoughts with Coping Thoughts

Use this worksheet to record specific triggers, the automatic thoughts that go with them, and alternative coping thoughts with which you can replace them.

Trigger	Automatic Thought	Coping Thought
1.	1.	1.
2.	2.	2.
3.	3.	3.
4.	4.	4.
5.	5.	5.

Replacing Automatic Thoughts with Coping Thoughts

(Client Sample)

Trigger	Automatic Thought	Coping Thought
1. Turning in a project to my boss.	1. My work isn't as good as it should be.	1. I'm doing my best, which is all I can do.
2. Being at a party with people I don't know.	2. If I don't say the right thing at this party, people are going to think I'm a loser.	2. I can have this thought without acting on it.
3. My wife comes home and goes straight to the bedroom.	3. My wife doesn't love me anymore.	3. My defectiveness schema is talking, but I'm not listening.
4. Anytime...	4. Something's wrong with me.	4. I have strengths and weaknesses, just like everybody else.
5. My boss doesn't talk to me at the office-wide lunch.	5. My boss doesn't like me.	5. It's not my job to be liked. It's my job to do my job.

Therapist-Client Dialogue Example: Using Coping Thoughts in Exposure

Therapist: Now that you've completed the Coping Thoughts worksheet, let's do an exposure exercise to practice using the coping thoughts we've developed for one of the triggering situations and an automatic negative thought.

Client: Okay. Which one should I choose?

Therapist: Just take a look at what you have there, and choose a situation that you predict will be somewhere around a 5 or 6 on the SUDS scale, with 1 being no distress and 10 being the worst distress you can imagine.

Client: [Pauses] Well, I think when my wife comes home and goes straight to the bedroom.

Therapist: Okay. And how distressing do you predict that scene will be for you?

Client: I would say a 6.

Therapist: Okay, good. Let's take a few minutes to get into that scene. Just close your eyes and I'll talk you through it.

Client: Okay [closes eyes].

Therapist: Imagine the last time your wife came home and went to the bedroom. Put yourself in the physical location you were in. Try to remember what you were doing. Remember what you can see around you, what you can hear, anything you can sense. Can you see yourself there, and are you feeling the emotion?

Client: Yes.

Therapist: Okay. Where do you feel the emotion in your body?

Client: I have a tight feeling in my stomach.

Therapist: Okay, let's start with that. See if you can allow that sensation to just be there, without judging it, without reacting to it, and instead opening and softening to it.

Client: [Pauses] Yeah, I'm trying.

Therapist: You might imagine that instead of avoiding the sensation, you are leaning into it…

Client:	Okay.
Therapist:	Just notice if the sensation is changing or staying the same; notice what size and shape it is...whether there's a temperature to it.
Client:	Yeah. It's hard and tight, about the size of a baseball. It's not moving. I don't feel any temperature.
Therapist:	Has it changed since you've been observing it?
Client:	It's a little less intense now.
Therapist:	Okay, good. Can you identify a feeling that goes with the sensation?
Client:	Uh, maybe fear? I feel afraid.
Therapist:	So there's a tight sensation in your stomach, and the feeling that goes with it is fear?
Client:	Yeah.
Therapist:	Okay. And is there an urge to do something or not do something?
Client:	Well, I don't want to talk to her... I think I'm scared I'll see that she really doesn't want to talk to me. The urge is also to shut my office door...to hide out.
Therapist:	Okay. Just see if you can sit with that urge to not talk to her, and also the urge to shut the door and hide. Notice what it's like to allow that urge to be there.
Client:	It feels terrible.
Therapist:	Okay, can you allow it to feel terrible...? Just make space for it to be exactly as it is?
Client:	Yeah. I just wish it would change.
Therapist:	Sure—it feels terrible and it makes sense you'd rather not feel that. See if you can stay with this and instead allow the feeling, and be curious about it for a few moments longer.
Client:	Okay. Hmm.
Therapist:	What came up for you?
Client:	Well, it got a little less terrible as soon as I just accepted that it felt terrible.

Therapist:	When you stopped avoiding or resisting, the emotion wave went down?
Client:	Yeah.
Therapist:	Okay. Let's now think about the negative automatic thought that comes up for you in this situation.
Client:	That "My wife doesn't love me anymore."
Therapist:	Your SUDS?
Client:	A 6 or a little more.
Therapist:	Okay, let's shut off the scene with your wife now and work on coping thoughts. What's the coping thought that might help you most?
Client:	I guess that I don't have to listen to my defectiveness schema?
Therapist:	Okay. So you can just say, "I'm having the thought that she doesn't really love me anymore," and then say your coping thought.
Client:	Okay. "My defectiveness schema is talking, but I don't have to listen."
Therapist:	How is that working for you?
Client:	Well, it takes my attention off of the fear. And…it makes me question whether it's true that she doesn't love me anymore.
Therapist:	Okay. Stay with it for a moment, just saying it to yourself a few times. [Waits 45 seconds] What's showing up for you now?
Client:	Well, I feel better…
Therapist:	Your SUDS dropped?
Client:	Yeah. I was up to almost 7, and then once I said the coping thought I dropped to about a 4.
Therapist:	So the thought that it's your defectiveness belief talking and not the absolute truth was helpful?
Client:	Yes. I'm actually surprised how much the feeling of fear changed… It's like my whole perspective changed…
Therapist:	Great. Let's try a second coping thought now. What do you think might most help now?
Client:	Hmm. Maybe that "My emotions aren't the truth"?

Therapist:	Okay, your emotions aren't the truth. So try saying that to yourself a few times silently.
Client:	Okay…
Therapist:	[Waits twenty seconds or so] So are you thinking differently about the trigger?
Client:	Yeah… I'm thinking that maybe she went to her room because she wants to change clothes and have a few moments to herself. Since she works as a nurse when she's at her job, she's with people nonstop, so maybe she just needs a little time-out. Maybe it has nothing to do with me.
Therapist:	Great. So that thought helped you look at this differently?
Client:	Yes, it helped to just allow the emotion, and then using the coping thought definitely helped too.
Therapist:	Good. So let's just check in again. Where is your SUDS level in this moment?
Client:	It's around a 2.
Therapist:	Okay, great. Let's wrap up the exercise, take a deep breath, and let it out slowly as you open your eyes and come back to the room.

Radical Acceptance

Radical acceptance is a key component of dialectical behavior therapy, which was developed by Marsha Linehan (1993). It is the practice of accepting the reality of things exactly as they are without resisting or trying to change them. To grasp the concept of radical acceptance, it can be helpful to understand what it is and what it isn't: Radical acceptance *is* a complete and total embracing of an unchangeable reality. Radical acceptance is *not* approval, passivity, forgiveness, compassion, or love.

By practicing radical acceptance of a triggering situation, event, or memory, clients learn to be mindful while downregulating emotion. Clients will find that they have more freedom to choose how they respond. Radical acceptance can be a difficult skill to choose when life is painful, disappointing, or scary; it's the opposite of what most of us want to do when things are different than what we would hope.

It's important to note that radical acceptance is distinct from mindful acceptance. Radical acceptance means accepting the unchangeable reality of "what is"; mindful acceptance means accepting one's emotional experience.

Following is a handout you can use to help your clients understand radical acceptance.

The Art of Radical Acceptance

What It Is

Part of successfully navigating intense emotions is knowing when it's time to try to improve your situation and when it's time to accept it. *Radical acceptance* is another mindful coping skill that allows you to accept "what is" and stop suffering from rejecting the reality in front of you. We have a choice in every moment: to reject the reality of what is or to accept it. The choice we make will determine whether we continue to suffer or create space for something else to exist.

Our natural response to distressing emotions is to fight against the reality that we think caused them. In doing this, we can make ourselves and others miserable. Choosing radical acceptance—to accept "what is"—is a huge shift for most people. It feels like the opposite of what your emotions urge you to do when you encounter pain.

What It's Not

Radical acceptance does not mean you like or condone what happened. It just means that you accept the reality that it happened. In other words, some situations in life are simply unjust or unfair. In other situations, you may share responsibility for what happened. Either way, just because you accept that it happened doesn't mean you're condoning it.

The more you practice radical acceptance, the easier it will become to stop resisting what you cannot change.

Following are a few examples of radical acceptance:

"My girlfriend broke up with me, but it doesn't mean I have to retaliate or try to win her love back."

"I have suicidal thoughts all the time, but that doesn't mean I like having them or that I will act on them."

"I didn't set a reminder to pay that phone bill, so I will have to take responsibility for the consequences."

Radical acceptance requires a willingness to look at things differently. Sometimes our disappointments and moments of frustration were preventable. We can also practice radical acceptance by accepting what we might have done differently, and taking responsibility for how we didn't. For example, could you have prevented being late to an appointment, forgetting to do work assignments, or behaving in a way that was less than stellar? Moreover, could you have prevented lying to hurt someone or allowing yourself to be motivated by hate? Many times we have culpability in "what is." Accepting that is key to practicing radical acceptance.

While the outcomes of these situations may have serious consequences, they can also be opportunities for growth if you can view them as moments of learning. Often people who struggle with intense emotions believe that life is something that "happens" to them, instead of recognizing their own power in creating their experience.

The good news is that if we have responsibility in the things happening, we also have the power to make different choices—choices that can alleviate suffering and bring us closer to living the life we want in accordance with our values.

It's not unusual for clients to struggle with understanding radical acceptance, especially if the situation they are struggling to accept was traumatic. Following is a sample therapist-client dialogue of how you can talk to you clients about radical acceptance. The Radical Acceptance worksheet at the end of this chapter is another tool to help your clients understand and practice this skill.

Therapist-Client Dialogue Example: Radical Acceptance

Therapist: Have you heard of radical acceptance?

Client: Um, I think so. Is it a Buddhist thing?

Therapist: I believe it is something that Buddhists practice, but we are using it here as a mindful coping skill.

Client: I see. So what's radical about it?

Therapist: Good question. The radical part of radical acceptance refers to how complete and total the acceptance is. In other words, you don't just partly accept the reality of what is—you fully accept that what exists is unchangeable.

Client: Okay…

Therapist: So let's use an example of something you've been struggling with, or wish would change, but that you can't change. You can use the worksheet, starting with the section "Assessing the situation."

Client:	I guess the fact that I have chronic pain, and no matter what I do, I can't seem to get rid of it.
Therapist:	Okay, great example. Because you have done everything in your power, right? You exercise, eat healthy, and get plenty of sleep just like your doctor has told you to?
Client:	Yep. And I still hurt every day [eyes well up].
Therapist:	Yeah. This is an ongoing challenge for you.
Client:	Uh-huh.
Therapist:	So let's continue with the worksheet. What's next?
Client:	[Looks at the worksheet] So the situation is my pain… I'm not really sure that any past events led to the situation because the doctor doesn't really know why I hurt.
Therapist:	Okay. What's next?
Client:	[Continuing with the worksheet] I don't think I or anyone else played a role in my pain. I really don't have much control over it, and what control I do have I'm already taking.
Therapist:	That's right. You're already doing all the things your doctor says can help the pain.
Client:	And I can't control the fact that it still hurts every day.
Therapist:	Right.
Client:	[Continuing with the worksheet] So my response to the pain at first was to be really depressed. I just thought about all the things I can't do anymore because it makes the pain worse. And I was really mad.
Therapist:	Who were you mad at?
Client:	I don't know… God? My parents for giving me these genes?
Therapist:	Okay. And how did that affect your thoughts and feelings?
Client:	Gosh, I ended up miserable and depressed! I just went round and round with it. I mean, now it's better because I at least accept I have the pain, but I still haven't accepted what I can't do…like running for example.
Therapist:	Good point. You've accepted it halfway, but not all the way?

Client:	Yeah.
Therapist:	And how is that affecting you?
Client:	I'm still pretty down about it. I mean, I just never really liked any other exercise. Nothing else gives me that feeling of being so…free.
Therapist:	I get it. And how does being down affect you and your life?
Client:	Well, I haven't been exercising at all because I'm down, so I've gained weight…and can't really fit into my favorite clothes now. And it makes me not want to go out with my friends because I'm self-conscious about how I look. And now my friends are frustrated with me that I don't want to hang out like I used to.
Therapist:	So it's really affecting you to not be able to radically accept the limitations that come with your pain?
Client:	Yeah. It really is.
Therapist:	What would it look like if you applied radical acceptance to the reality that you have chronic pain.
Client:	Yeah…it's got to be better than this.
Therapist:	Okay. So using the worksheet, let's walk through what they might look like.
Client:	Okay.
Therapist:	When you think about your pain, can you connect to the resistance you have about how it limits your activity?
Client:	Oh, yeah!
Therapist:	Okay. So move on to step 2.
Client:	Okay. So I know how to do mindful acceptance…should I just talk through it right now?
Therapist:	Exactly. Go ahead and close your eyes, if it's helpful, and just notice each component of the emotion that goes with that resistance. Tell me what you're experiencing as you practice observing and accepting.
Client:	All right… So the first thing I notice is a tightness in my chest and throat. So I'm just noticing that sensation…trying to allow it.

Therapist:	Great. Just make room for it and observe whether it changes or shifts, whether it has any temperature to it.
Client:	Yeah, there's no temperature, but it got less strong as soon as I started making room for it.
Therapist:	Great. What else are you aware of?
Client:	I'm having the thought that this isn't fair!
Therapist:	Okay. Can you just acknowledge that thought, and try to let it go?
Client:	Yeah…but now I'm angry.
Therapist:	Okay, let's stay with that for a moment.
Client:	Yeah… [Starts to cry a little] I'm just so, so…disappointed.
Therapist:	Yeah. Not being able to run has been a huge adjustment for you.
Client:	Yeah. It feels so unfair…there's the thought again.
Therapist:	So see if you can allow the anger and the disappointment, and also acknowledge the thought and let it go…
Client:	Okay [still sniffling].
Therapist:	Just stay with that for a moment…allowing and letting the thought go.
Client:	[After thirty seconds] Okay… I'm feeling less angry, but I have the urge to keep thinking about how unfair this is.
Therapist:	The thought just keeps coming up over and over again?
Client:	Yeah.
Therapist:	Okay. Let's move into choosing radical acceptance. First, just practice letting go of the resistance. Continue to allow the emotion while also trying to let go of any rejection of the reality that you can't run. Let me know what's coming up.
Client:	All right…so I am not going to resist that I have pain that keeps me from running, and I'm going to tell myself that I can't change that?
Therapist:	Exactly. No resisting. If you start to notice your mind, body, feelings, or urges are resisting, try to radically accept it by telling yourself that the reality of not being able to run is unchangeable, and just watch your emotion.

Client:	Okay. I'm feeling the anger still, so I'm going to tell myself that the facts are that I have chronic pain that keeps me from running, and it can't be any other way, because it just is this way.
Therapist:	Good work… What's it like when you tell yourself that?
Client:	Well [exasperated sigh], it actually makes it seem senseless for me to be angry.
Therapist:	Why's that?
Client:	Well, it makes it so clear that it's not going to do anything but ruin my life. And as long as I'm angry, I'm disappointed and depressed, and then I don't do anything I want.
Therapist:	Okay. So it seems like it makes more sense not to continue feeling angry and disappointed about not being able to run, because you can't change that?
Client:	It's just keeping me stuck.
Therapist:	And what's happening to the emotion?
Client:	It's shifted…and now I have the urge to figure out what I *can* do so I don't stay heavy and so I feel like going out again.
Therapist:	Okay, great. So it seems like you're focusing on what you *can* control and are letting go of what you can't?
Client:	Yeah. Can we talk about that?
Therapist:	Sure!

Radical Acceptance

Assessing the Situation

Think of a situation you have no control over, but about which you struggle to accept. Then answer the following questions:

Describe briefly the distressing situation:

What past events led to the situation?

What role, if any, did you play in creating the situation?

What roles, if any, did others play in the situation?

What do you have control of in this situation?

What do you *not* have control of in this situation?

What was your response to this situation?

How did your response affect your own thoughts and feelings?

How did your response affect the thoughts and feelings of others?

How could you have changed your response to this situation so that it led to less suffering for yourself and others?

How could the situation have occurred differently if you had chosen to radically accept the situation?

How to Practice Radical Acceptance

Once you've identified the situation and have a clear understanding of it, you can use these steps to practice radical acceptance during imaginal exposure or when you get upset.

1. Recognize your resistance to the reality of "what is."

2. Practice mindful acceptance of the emotion that goes with the situation or reality. Using the four components of emotion, make room for all your thoughts, feelings, sensations, and urges, allowing them to be there without reacting or acting on them.

3. Stop resisting by reminding yourself of the facts, such as: "This is just the way it is, I can't change it" or "I have to accept the consequences of my actions."

As with all skills, it takes time and practice to master them. Remind your clients that the more they practice using coping thoughts and radical acceptance when they get triggered, the easier these skills will be—and the more relief they will bring.

Summary

Following is a synopsis of content covered in chapter 8:

- The use of coping thoughts is a mindful coping skill used to replace negative automatic thoughts with alternative thoughts that reinforce adaptive ways of responding.

- Radical acceptance is a mindful coping skill used to decrease resistance and increase acceptance of unchangeable realities.

- Because emotions follow what we pay attention to, using coping thoughts and radical acceptance can help increase distress tolerance and decrease negative emotion.

- Like all mindful coping skills, coping thoughts and radical acceptance are used mindfully, after observing and accepting the four parts of emotion *and* when clients are too emotionally triggered to continue mindful acceptance or to choose a values-based action.

- Practicing coping thoughts and radical acceptance in an activated state will enhance learning and help clients recall the skills when they are triggered.

CHAPTER 9

Distraction and Time-Out

The previous two chapters covered four mindful coping skills—relaxation, self-soothing, coping thoughts, and radical acceptance. The last two mindful coping skills clients will learn are *distraction* and *time-out*. As with all the mindful coping skills, distraction and time-out are not substitutes for mindful acceptance or values-based action. Rather, mindful coping is a choice that is only used when clients are still significantly emotionally dysregulated, even after practicing mindful acceptance and/or values-based action. You'll want to keep emphasizing to clients that sometimes *just* practicing mindful acceptance or values-based action is all it takes to tolerate distress, regulate emotions, and move in the direction of one's values. Mindful coping, on the other hand, is used when clients get emotionally overwhelmed, and are still in too much pain, even after choosing to mindfully accept the pain and/or choose a values-based action.

EET Skill Objective: Observe + Accept + Choose
mindful coping (distraction/time-out)

Distraction

Distraction follows the exposure of observing and accepting. In the moment of choice, distraction allows clients to shift attention away from stimuli that trigger emotion: provoking thoughts, sensations, and situations.

Some theorists in the mindfulness and acceptance community view distraction as a form of avoidance and therefore discourage it. In EET, however, distraction is used mindfully—to intentionally shift attention to alternative present-moment experiences after observing and accepting emotions. Because clients always begin with mindful acceptance, distraction is not used to avoid their experience but rather to mindfully regulate their emotions in an effective, contextually adaptive, and values-consistent manner. Moreover, distraction is taught as a skill to use only in crisis situations, as a last resort. For example, when clients are in danger of harming themselves or others, sometimes the best and only choice is to distract themselves from the urge to act on their emotions.

The mindful coping protocol for distraction is the same as described in previous chapters. After reaching the target SUDS level (typically 5 to 7), clients practice one or more previously chosen distraction strategies. Ideally, they will have preselected techniques from each of the five distraction categories:

- **Shifting attention to someone else.** Here clients shift attention to those they care for, often making a specific plan to provide help or support. Thinking about values-based behavior can provide an effective alternative to triggering situations and cognitions.

- **Shifting attention to something else.** The goal of this technique is to use memory and imagination to create an alternative focus. Prayer, mantras, and passive forms of entertainment are also part of this mix.

- **Focusing on productivity.** While clients probably won't practice this in your office, having a list of house- and self-care tasks can offer an effective response to emotional storms at home.

- **Using alternatives to self-destructive behaviors.** When clients struggle with emotion-driven urges that are dangerous or destructive, creating an alternative physical sensation is often the best distraction strategy (Linehan, 1993). Such approaches include holding an ice cube, screaming into a pillow, snapping a rubber band on the wrist, or even using a red marker or pen to draw on the body instead of cutting.

- **Doing pleasurable activities.** Pleasure sensations can rapidly shift mood and help clients downregulate. The list of pleasurable activities included in the Distraction Strategies handout is merely a conversation starter. You'll need to make a more complete and customized list with your clients, and then choose some portable pleasures that you can use in the office.

The following handout (also available at http://www.newharbinger.com/34049 and in Appendix C) will help clients identify mindful coping strategies to distract themselves when they have already tried to use mindful acceptance and/or values-based action and are still feeling triggered.

Distraction Strategies

The following handout will help you identify mindful coping ideas to distract yourself when you have already tried to use mindful acceptance and/or values-based action and are still feeling triggered.

Pay Attention to Someone Else

One effective way to shift your attention when you are emotionally triggered is to place your attention on someone else. Following are some examples of how you might do this, as well as a space for your own ideas:

_____ Call your friends and ask if they need help doing something, such as a chore, grocery shopping, or housecleaning.

_____ Ask any family members who live nearby if you can assist them with something: running errands, yard work, babysitting, walking the dog, etc.

_____ Call your local soup kitchen, homeless shelter, volunteer organization, or advocacy group and sign up to help.

_____ Bake cookies for a neighbor or coworker.

_____ Send a "just because" card to someone you haven't talked to in a while.

_____ Write a thank-you email to someone who did something kind for you.

_____ Write a handwritten letter to someone who has changed your life for the better and tell him or her why.

_____ Make a list of people you admire and want to be like and write down why.

_____ People-watch. Go to a local store, shopping center, bookstore, or park and notice what other people do, how they dress. Listen to their conversations. Observe as many details about other people as you can.

_____ Play counting games while people-watching, for example, count the number of blue-eyed people versus brown-eyed people you see.

_____ Think about someone you care about. What do you imagine he or she is doing right now?

_____ Keep a picture of those you love in your wallet or purse. These people can range from family members to friends to public figures you admire. Look at the photo whenever you need comfort.

_____ Imagine having a healing, peaceful conversation with someone you deeply care about or admire. What would he or she say to you that would help you feel better? Imagine him or her saying this to you.

_____ Other ideas: _____

Pay Attention to Something Else

Our brains are amazing thinking machines. They produce millions of thoughts every day. Our emotions follow what we think about, and you can intentionally shift your thoughts when you're triggered to decrease your emotional activation. Following are some examples of how you might do this, as well as a space for your own ideas:

_____ Pay attention to the natural world around you. Observe the flowers, trees, sky, and landscape as closely as possible. Observe any animals that are around. Listen to all the sounds around you. Or, if you live in a city without much nature, observe what you can see and hear.

_____ Keep a copy of your favorite prayer or saying with you. When you feel distressed, read it to yourself. Imagine the words calming and soothing you. Use imagery (such as white light coming down from the sky) to soothe you as you read the words.

_____ Walk around your neighborhood or a park and notice the scenery, the colors, the textures of your surroundings.

_____ Listen to music that's pleasing to you. Also try listening to new music: from a different genre or from another country.

_____ Listen to an engaging audiobook. Close your eyes and really try to pay attention.

_____ Watch a TV show or movie you know will hold your attention and take your focus off yourself. Think about whether you would have written a different plot or ending.

_____ Learn a new language.

_____ Learn how to play a musical instrument.

_____ Write a letter to God or your higher power.

_____ Write in your journal.

_____ Other ideas: _____

Be Productive

Many people don't schedule time to take care of themselves or their living environments. Doing tasks and chores can be an effective way to shift your attention away from your distress. Following are some examples, and a place for you to add your own ideas:

_____ Make a to-do list.

_____ Wash the dishes.

_____ Make phone calls to people with whom you are not angry and want to catch up with.

_____ Clear your room or house.

_____ Clean out your closet and donate old clothes.

_____ Redecorate a room in your house.

_____ Organize your books, files, drawers, etc.

_____ Make a plan of action for finding a job, or for finding a better job if you already have one.

_____ Make appointments with various people—doctor, dentist, optometrist, accountant, etc.—and arrive on time.

_____ Get a new hairstyle or haircut.

_____ Get a manicure or pedicure.

_____ Get a massage.

_____ Wash your car.

_____ Plan something: a party, event, your next vacation.

_____ Mow the lawn.

_____ Plant a garden, or do gardening work in your own space or in a community garden.

_____ Clean out your garage.

_____ Do homework or other work.

_____ Clean your bathtub and take a bath.

_____ Go grocery shopping and cook a nice dinner for yourself.

_____ Pay bills.

_____ Other ideas: _____

Do a Pleasurable Activity

_____ Call or text a friend.

_____ Visit a friend or invite a friend to come over.

_____ Exercise: lift weights; do yoga, tai chi, or Pilates, or take classes to learn how; stretch your muscles; ride your bike; go swimming or hiking; play something you can do by yourself, such as basketball, bowling, handball, miniature golf, billiards.

_____ Get out of your house and go for a drive in your car, or ride public transportation.

_____ Plan a daytrip to somewhere you've always wanted to go.

_____ Sleep or take a nap.

_____ Eat something you really like.

_____ Cook your favorite meal.

_____ Watch TV or stream shows on the Internet.

_____ Go to a sporting event.

_____ Play video games.

_____ Join an Internet dating service.

_____ Create your own blog or website.

_____ Go shopping.

_____ Go to a bookstore and read.

_____ Go to your place of worship.

_____ Sing or learn how to sing.

_____ Take pictures.

_____ Join a club or attend a meet-up group.

_____ Make a movie or video with your phone.

_____ Go to a flower shop and smell your favorite flowers.

_____ Knit, crochet, or sew, or learn how.

_____ Make a scrapbook.

_____ Write a loving letter to yourself when you're feeling good, and read it when you're feeling upset.

_____ Draw or paint a picture, or learn how.

_____ Make a bucket list of things you want to do before you die.

_____ Make a list of 10 things you're good at or that you like about yourself.

_____ Masturbate or have sex with someone you care about.

_____ Join a public-speaking group and write a speech.

_____ Pray or meditate.

_____ Other ideas: _____

Alternatives to Self-Destructive Behaviors

Some people who struggle with overwhelming emotions use self-destructive behaviors to temporarily relieve their distress. Instead of continuing to hurt yourself, consider using some tools to help shift your emotions rather than acting on them. Following are some examples, and a place for you to add your own ideas:

_____ Instead of hurting yourself, hold an ice cube in one hand and squeeze it. The sensation from the cold ice will be numbing and distracting.

_____ Write on yourself with a red felt-tip marker instead of cutting. Draw exactly where you would cut. Use red paint or nail polish to make it look like you're bleeding. Then draw stitches with a black marker. If you need more distraction, squeeze an ice cube in the other hand at the same time.

_____ Snap a rubber band on your wrist each time you feel like hurting yourself. This is very painful, but it causes less permanent damage than cutting, burning, or otherwise mutilating yourself.

_____ Dig your fingernails into your arm without breaking the skin.

_____ Throw foam balls, rolled up socks, or pillows against the wall as hard as you can.

_____ Scream as loud as you can into a pillow or scream someplace where you won't draw attention, like your car or at a loud concert.

_____ Cry. Sometimes people don't cry because they're afraid that if they start they'll never stop. This never happens. In fact, the truth is that crying can make you feel better because it releases stress hormones.

_____ Other ideas: _____

Mindful Coping with Distraction

When you feel that your clients are ready to be introduced to skillful distraction, you can take the following steps:

Step 1: Psychoeducation on distraction. Review the Before You Act, Distract handout with your clients. Emphasize that distraction isn't about avoiding experience—your clients have already faced their feelings during exposure. Distraction is merely a tool to increase behavioral choices—values-based behavior instead of emotion-driven urges.

Highlight the way distraction works: Emotions mirror what we pay attention to. If we pay attention to people, things, or sensations that anger or upset us, our feelings will reflect that. And the intensity of those emotions can make it hard to act on our values. If we switch attention to something else, our feelings will reflect the new experience we've chosen.

By shifting our attention to alternative present-moment experience, there are several potential benefits:

- Clients will be less likely to be swept into destructive emotion-driven behaviors.

- Clients will be more likely to be willing and able to act on values.

- Clients will build their ability to tolerate distress.

- Clients will learn that emotions subside if you observe and accept them.

This is good news because it means we have some power over shifting our emotions by changing our attention.

If possible, you'll want to give both handouts—Distraction Strategies and Before You Act, Distract—to your clients as homework in the previous session so they can select one or more strategies they think will work for them.

Step 2: Choosing distraction strategies. Talk with your clients to determine what distraction strategies they want to use in both their lives and the exposure practice. You'll want to discuss them with your clients, being very specific about how they will be used. It's also important to do a reality check about whether the strategies they've chosen will work for them in situations in which they imagine they might be needed.

Step 3: Observe + Accept + Choose distraction. Select a recent emotionally triggering experience to use in imaginal exposure. Keep clients focused on the scene until arousal reaches 5 to 6 SUDS, or five minutes have elapsed.

During exposure, coach clients to observe and accept all parts of the emotion, and make room for whatever shows up.

Next, erase the scene and commence mindful coping with a distraction technique chosen by the clients. Support the clients to stay with the distraction, if effective, or choose another one. Check for SUDS both during the five or so minutes of mindful coping and at the end. A small reduction in SUDS is desirable but not necessary. Practicing mindful coping, even without a drop in distress, will still increase distress tolerance.

Finally, talk to your clients about their experience to consolidate learning.

The following dialogue sample can be used to guide you and your clients through the art of distraction as a mindful coping skill after clients have completed the Distraction Strategies worksheet.

Therapist-Client Dialogue Example: Mindful Coping with Distraction

Therapist: Let's see what distraction strategies appeal to you [looks over the list to see which strategies the client checked]. You checked, "Do something for someone else." Can you say more about that?

Client: I'd like to pay attention to something else by planning my daughter's birthday party. And I'd like to pay attention to someone else by helping my brother with his disability claim.

Therapist: Could you do either of those things here?

Client: Sure. I have paper to make a list of things I'll need for the party. And I brought the disability application papers.

Therapist: Great. Did you choose any other distractions?

Client: Yes. I brought a little peace meditation from Pema Chödrön. I also made a list of small chores I want to get done in the house—I think it would help if I tried to do something productive. 'Course, I can't do that stuff here.

Therapist: Very good. Anything else?

Client:	When I'm upset, I don't really do anything to hurt myself, so I skipped over those ideas. In terms of being productive, I brought my needlepoint project.
Therapist:	What do you plan to make?
Client:	A pillow for the couch.
Therapist:	Any pleasurable activities?
Client:	Well, peaches are in season so I brought one to eat (pulls a peach out of her bag).
Therapist:	Perfect. You've got the idea. Could you choose two or three distraction strategies that we can practice right now?
	[The client chooses planning her daughter's birthday party, the Pema Chödrön peace meditation, and eating a peach. Imaginal exposure focuses on feelings of hurt and anger at her father. After five minutes of exposure to the scene, and trying to make room for the feelings, the client is at a 4 on the SUDS scale. It's a little low, but mindful coping proceeds anyway.]
Therapist:	Good. Let go of the scene now, and we'll use distraction to shift your attention to something else. Which of the distraction strategies would feel best now? Just use your intuition.
Client:	I'll try the peach [takes a few bites, piercing the juicy sweet flesh, letting the nectar caress her tongue and slide down the back of her throat, letting out a soft moan].
Therapist:	Where are your SUDS?
Client:	Around 3.
Therapist:	Want to stick with eating the peach, or do something else?
Client:	I'll read the Pema Chödrön meditation [looks for it, then settles in to read silently]… I like this, I'm gonna read it again [closes her eyes]… I can feel it.
Therapist:	Your SUDS?
Client:	A 2 or 2½.
Therapist:	Good. We'll practice again in a minute. What was that like for you?

Client: It was calming. I was already pretty over that thing with my father; I couldn't get too worked up about it. The peach was good, but particularly the Pema Chödrön meditation helped me refocus and go somewhere else. [Folds her hands and looks at them] I can see how this helps.

Use the following handout to help your clients understand when to use distraction as a mindful coping skill in the moment of choice.

Before You Act, Distract

Emotions mirror what we pay attention to. If we pay attention to people, things, or situations that anger or upset us, our feelings will reflect that. And the intensity of those emotions can make it hard to act on our values. If we switch attention to something else, our feelings will reflect the new experience we've chosen. We have the power to shift how we feel by shifting our attention. There are several benefits from using distraction:

- You're less likely to be swept into destructive, emotion-driven behaviors.

- Your upset is likely to subside more quickly than if you act on your emotion.

- You're more likely to feel able to act on your values.

Avoiding Avoidance

Sometimes it's hard to tell if you're using mindful coping to avoid your emotions or to move in the direction of your values. If you're not sure, you can ask yourself this basic question: "Am I using this skill to move toward my values or to avoid my emotion?" Using distraction after you observe and accept your emotional experience can be a life-improving, values-consistent choice in situations when you're getting overwhelmed and need to "downshift" an emotion wave.

Mindful Coping with Distraction

Follow these steps for mindful distraction:

Step 1: Select a triggering event. Visualize an upsetting event until you are at the target level of arousal (usually 5 to 6 SUDS).

Step 2: Observe and accept. Observe and accept the sensations, emotions, and urges that come up for at least 5 minutes. Make room for all the experience.

Step 3: Choose distraction. Begin using a distraction technique of your choice for at least 5 minutes. You may also choose additional distraction strategies, if you want.

Remember, if you experience a strong, painful emotion in the course of daily life, you can do one of two things: You can stay with the feeling, noticing the moment of choice, and responding with a values-based action. Or, if the pain is pushing you hard toward emotion-driven behavior and you can't muster a values-based response, you can mindfully choose distraction (or any of the other mindful coping skills).

Time-Out

The last mindful coping skill is called time-out. When clients are in triggering environments or situations, sometimes the best choice is to leave, or to take a "time-out." This is particularly true if they are at risk of acting on emotion-driven urges that might damage a relationship or result in losing a job. Guide clients in coping ahead by helping them determine which situations they can safely walk away from and how to do it (i.e., a short script for exactly what to say, and how to handle resistance from the other person).

The following handout will help clients identify when to take a time-out.

Take a Time-Out

Sometimes when you get emotionally triggered, the best thing you can do is leave, or take a "time-out." If you find yourself in an extremely distressing situation with someone or something, and, after trying to practice mindful acceptance or enact a values-based action, you're still very upset, it's often best to distance yourself and shift your attention away from the trigger to a more positive present-moment experience.

Try to remember that if you're already overwhelmed by your emotions, it will be more difficult to resolve your problem in a healthy way. If you stay in the situation, you may make it worse than it is already. If you can put some distance between you and the situation, and give yourself time to calm your emotions, you can better think about what to do next.

It may be helpful to rehearse doing this, or to write a short script ahead of time, so that you'll know exactly how you want to excuse yourself from the situation. If you don't feel you have time to excuse yourself, sometimes just walking away is the best you can do to keep from making a difficult situation worse.

Mindful Coping with Time-Out

Use the following steps to introduce your clients to the skill of time-out:

Step 1: Psychoeducation on time-out. Review the Take a Time-Out handout with your clients. Emphasize that, in extreme cases, the best choice can be to put distance between the triggering person or situation. As a tool, time-out gives clients a chance to increase behavioral choices—to enact values-based behavior instead of emotion-driven urges—by walking away from a situation before making it worse.

Remind clients that they have some power over shifting their emotions by changing where they focus their attention. By shifting attention to a different present-moment experience, there are several potential benefits:

- Clients will be less likely to be swept into destructive emotion-driven behaviors.

- Clients will be more likely to be willing and able to act on values.

- Clients will build their ability to tolerate distress.

- Clients will learn that emotions subside if you observe and accept them.

If possible, you'll want to give the handout to your clients as homework in the previous session so they can select one or more strategies they think will work for them.

Step 2: Choosing a time-out strategy. Talk with your clients to determine how they might excuse themselves from an overwhelming experience. Discuss how to walk away from a situation—what they would do and/or say—if necessary.

Step 3: Observe + Accept + Choose time-out. Select a recent emotionally triggering experience to use in imaginal exposure. Keep clients focused on the scene until arousal reaches 5 to 6 SUDS, or five minutes have elapsed.

During exposure, coach clients to observe and accept all parts of the emotion, and to make room for whatever shows up.

Next, erase the scene and commence visualization of the time-out in the way the clients have planned it. Check for SUDS both during the five or so minutes of mindful coping and at the end. A small reduction in SUDS is desirable but not necessary. Practicing mindful coping, even without a drop in distress, will still increase distress tolerance.

Finally, talk to your clients about their experience to consolidate learning.

The following dialogue sample can be used to guide you and your clients through the art of time-out as a mindful coping skill.

Therapist-Client Dialogue Example: Mindful Coping with Time-Out

Therapist: You've come up with great ideas for how you might use distraction as a mindful coping skill, but what about a situation, like the one with your father, when you seem to get consistently hooked into a fight?

Client: Yeah, I really have trouble with that.

Therapist: Sometimes even after you practice mindful acceptance or try to do a values-based action, the emotions are still just too powerful not to get sucked in?

Client: Yes. And sometimes I end up making the situation worse.

Therapist: So that's when you could take a time-out…

Client: So how does that work?

Therapist: To choose a time-out in the moment of choice, you would simply leave the situation. And you can improve your chances of successfully doing that with some planning. You can figure out how to leave a situation when you're so triggered that you might act on emotion-driven urges.

Client: Like the night he came home drunk and wanted to get into the whole situation around the divorce between him and my mom…?

Therapist: Right. So let's look at that. How could you have taken a time-out in that situation?

Client: I could have told him I was too upset to have a conversation, and that I'd call him the next day.

Therapist: Perfect. You've got the idea. You walk away from the situation and come back to it later when you feel that you're not so emotionally triggered that you can't practice mindful acceptance and values-based action.

Client: Yeah, but what if he just keeps yelling at me?

Therapist: What do you think you could do?

Client: At that point, the best choice is probably just to leave. 'Cause I know nothing good can happen when he is drunk and angry like that. No matter how hard I try to be reasonable, or use mindful acceptance, he will just piss me off until I explode.

Therapist: Right. That's exactly the time to use a time-out.

Now that your clients have practiced distraction and time-out using exposure, you will want to help them be clear about when to use distraction or time-out out of session. As a review, the criteria for using mindful coping are:

- When clients are in danger of losing behavioral control and engaging in destructive, emotion-driven responses.

- When clients are overwhelmed with pain and seem stuck in a deepening emotional crisis, even after practicing mindful acceptance.

- When clients are in too much pain to act on their values.

Clients should be encouraged not to use distraction—or any other form of mindful coping—if: they haven't first done exposure (O+A+C) and located their moment of choice, or the primary motivation is avoidance as opposed to having exhausted available choices (sitting with the feeling or acting on values).

The following sample dialogue is one way you might approach this conversation.

Therapist-Client Dialogue Example: Mindful Coping in Vivo

The therapist explains to the client how to use mindful coping in daily life.

Therapist: This week, when strong emotions come up, you have some new choices. The first thing is always to make room for the feeling—observe it and accept it. Then try to figure out what valued action you can choose, rather than actions driven by your emotions. Sometimes—often—that will be enough. But sometimes your feelings could be so strong that they seem overwhelming…maybe values-based action seems impossible and you're about to do something harmful. That's when mindful coping comes in.

Client: Why only then? We've practiced it a lot, shouldn't I use it whenever I'm upset?

Therapist: Mindful coping is for situations when you're so overwhelmed that you're at risk of losing control. Otherwise, stay with observing, accepting, and choosing—O+A+C. Just allow the emotion, and then choose a values-based action.

Client: So I only do mindful coping if I'm in total meltdown?

Therapist: [Nodding] If you're overwhelmed and in danger of doing something hurtful.

Client: How am I supposed to figure that out?

Therapist: Remember the work we did on being mindful of the moment of choice—the moment when you could do old, destructive behaviors or act on your values? That same mindful awareness can help you decide whether to use coping skills. Just watch what's happening—can you think about what you value in this situation, or is that the last thing on your mind? Now make a mindful choice—if you're overwhelmed and can't act on your values, select a mindful coping strategy.

Client: How?

Therapist: See if you can make the choice intuitively—the strategy that would feel best right then. That's another form of mindfulness. We could also make a list of the mindful coping strategies you've already practiced, and you could keep it with you. When you're overwhelmed, you could look at it and see what would feel best for that moment.

Summary

Following is a synopsis of content covered in chapter 9:

- Distraction and time-out are mindful coping skills that can be used to shift attention and downregulate emotion. Shifting attention away from the triggering stimuli will downregulate emotion, giving clients more choices in how to respond.

- Neither distraction nor time-out is used as an avoidance strategy. Like all mindful coping skills—relaxation, self-soothing, coping thoughts, and radical acceptance—distraction or time-out is chosen mindfully, after observing and accepting the four parts of emotion.

- Distraction and time-out is only for use in "crisis" situations, when clients become flooded and are too emotionally triggered to continue mindful acceptance or to choose a values-based action.

- Distraction skills include: paying attention to someone or something else, shifting thought content, using productivity tasks or chores, and alternatives to self-destructive behaviors.

- Time-out is used in situations when leaving is the best way to prevent a difficult situation from becoming worse.

- Mindful coping using distraction and time-out is rehearsed through imaginal exposure and in vivo practice to enhance learning, recall, and retention.

Chapter 10

Pulling It All Together

At this point we've covered all the EET components and their related skills: emotion awareness, mindful acceptance, values-based action, and mindful coping. Additionally, we've covered how to help your clients practice the skills in an emotionally triggered state to enhance learning, retention, and recall. You also know how to help clients consolidate what they've learned to create an ongoing emotion efficacy practice. In this chapter we: provide a client handout to facilitate consolidated learning; provide a brief outline and eight-session schedule for delivering EET; address potential treatment challenges and opportunities you may encounter; offer tips for using EET in a group format; and give suggestions for assessing your clients' levels of emotion efficacy to inform treatment planning.

Consolidating Learning

The work from here on is to help clients to consolidate their learning and identify what skills work best for them. Knowing they have a toolbox of skills they can use in triggering situations, and having many written down, will give them something to refer to when they need to review their choices in triggering situations.

You can use the Emotion Efficacy Therapy Skills handout and Personalized Emotion Efficacy Plan worksheet (available, as with all session materials in this book, in Appendix C and at http://www.newharbinger.com/34039) to facilitate this process. Clients can complete this worksheet after session and then bring it to the last session for review.

Emotion Efficacy Therapy Skills

You now have a whole new set of skills to use to help you make choices that are effective and consistent with your values when you get triggered. Use the following list to review the EET skills you've learned and to complete the Personalized Emotion Efficacy Plan worksheet.

Mindful Acceptance

_____ Sensation Acceptance

_____ Feeling Labeling

_____ Thought Watching

_____ Urge Noticing

_____ Emotion Surfing

Mindful Coping

_____ Relaxation

_____ Self-Soothing

_____ Pleasurable Activities

_____ Coping Thoughts

_____ Distraction

_____ Time-Out

Values-Based Action

_____ Identify your value and the corresponding action in the moment of choice

---

Personalized Emotion Efficacy Plan

Use this list of EET skills to remember what works for you when you get emotionally triggered. In addition, there is space for you to write down what else you have learned or want to remember about your relationship with your emotions.

Mindful Acceptance Skills (**O** + **A**)

When I am triggered, I can practice the following mindful acceptance skills:

_____ **Sensation acceptance:** Identify any sensations, describe them to myself, make room for them to be exactly as they are, without reacting or judging.

_____ **Feeling labeling:** Identify any feeling labels, sit with the feeling, allow it to be exactly as it is without reacting or judging.

_____ **Thought watching:** Watch my thoughts as they arise, and then let them go. Notice any "sticky" thoughts and let them be exactly as they are, without reacting or judging.

_____ **Urge noticing:** Notice any urges to do something or not to do something. Notice what it's like not to act on the urge.

Values-Based Action (O + A + Choose Values-Based Action)

When I've practiced mindful acceptance (observe + accept) and want to choose to move toward my values, I can choose the following values-based actions:

Situation   VBA

_____   _____

Situation   VBA

_____   _____

Situation   VBA

_____   _____

Situation   VBA

_____   _____

Situation   VBA

_____   _____

Mindful Coping (O + A + Choose Mindful Coping)

When I have practiced mindful acceptance and/or have tried to use values-based action and still feel at risk of acting on destructive urges, I can choose the following skills:

_____ **Relaxation:** Use diaphragmatic breathing, relaxation without tension, cue-controlled breathing, or the five-senses exercise to downshift emotion.

_____ **Self-soothing:** Stimulate each of my five senses to downshift emotion.

_____ **Coping thoughts:** Use a coping thought to reframe the situation and downshift emotion.

_____ **Radical acceptance:** Practice radical acceptance to allow difficult situations instead of resisting them, to downshift emotion.

_____ **Distraction:** Shift my attention to alternative present-moment experiences to downshift emotion.

_____ **Time-out:** Remove yourself from situations that are triggering where you risk making a difficult situation worse.

_____ **Other:** I want to remember the following about my relationship with my emotions:

_____

_____

_____

_____

_____

_____

_____

EET 8-Week Protocol Schedule

The following schedule covers all the EET skills in eight sessions. Modifications can be made depending on whether treatment is being delivered in a group or individual format. For a step-by-step protocol, see Appendix C.

Session 1: Emotion Awareness (chapter 2)

Session 2: Mindful Acceptance with Emotion Surfing (chapters 3 and 4)

Session 3: Values-Based Action, Part 1 (chapter 5)

Session 4: Values-Based Action, Part 2 (chapter 6)

Session 5: Mindful Coping Through Relaxation and Self-Soothing (chapter 7)

Session 6:   Mindful Coping Through Coping Thoughts and Radical Acceptance (chapter 8)

Session 7:   Mindful Coping with Distraction and Time-Out (chapter 9)

Session 8:   Consolidating, Troubleshooting, and Wrap-Up (chapter 10)

Potential Treatment Challenges and Opportunities

Following are guidelines and suggestions for working with common issues that may come up when doing EET with clients.

Difficulty with Specific Skills

When clients encounter difficulty with a skill, there may be valuable lessons for them. In other words, the skills that are more difficult may be the skills that can offer them the most emotion efficacy when mastered.

For example, clients with a diagnosis of panic disorder may struggle with sensation acceptance. Given their propensity to interpret sensations as messages of danger, clients can experience alarm in the absence of an actual threat. Given this vulnerability, they may tend to avoid observing and accepting physical sensations even though this skill could be the most effective strategy when they get triggered. Helping your clients become attuned to this paradox can serve to increase their willingness to engage in the skills they find more difficult.

Sensation acceptance can also be challenging for clients who struggle with chronic pain. The key, as with all clients, is to assess whether the skill can be effective for them when they are emotionally triggered. For clients with high levels of chronic pain, it may be more effective to choose an EET skill that doesn't focus attention on their bodies, which can be triggering and further fuel the emotion wave.

Similarly, clients who tend to ruminate may struggle with watching their thoughts. You should work with clients to help them see that their difficulty with thought watching is a sign that they may benefit even more over time from learning to observe and let go of their thoughts. In the short term, you'll want to help clients learn to evaluate what works best for them in the moment of choice.

Increased Awareness and Demoralization

Now that your clients have increased their emotion awareness, they are more likely to notice the times they choose to act on maladaptive emotion-driven behaviors. While they may actually be making fewer maladaptive choices when they get triggered, it's possible for clients to feel frustrated and demoralized about how often they let their emotions drive their behavior.

You may need to reassure clients that increasing emotion efficacy is a process. Remind them that not acting on their emotions will feel unnatural—especially in the beginning— but every time they choose mindful acceptance, values-based action, or mindful coping, it will get easier. In the same way it takes time to break old habits, it takes time to form new ones. They are building their emotion efficacy muscle.

Tailoring Treatment for Clients, aka "The Stretch"

The intention in each session should be to empower clients to engage with the skills to the fullest extent possible. The level of emotion efficacy clients come in with, and achieve during treatment, will vary greatly depending on their vulnerabilities, schemas, and coping patterns. In addition, clients come to treatment at varying levels of intellectual and cognitive ability, and social support, which can impact their ability to learn and, ultimately, the outcome of treatment.

As with any intervention, EET will be most effective if clients set realistic goals that are challenging enough to yield new learning without overwhelming them. Finding this sweet spot requires regular inquiry around their emotional process and what's possible. We refer to this possibility zone as a "stretch" in EET. For some clients, just learning to be present with their emotions will feel like a big stretch; for others, engaging in values-based action with their partners when they are triggered will be a stretch.

Some clients will easily learn and assimilate EET skills; they will experience incredible breakthroughs in emotion efficacy during treatment. For others, the process of increasing emotion efficacy may be slower, more challenging, and more painful. The key is to work with clients where they are while facilitating new learning opportunities through exposure and daily homework practice. You'll want to check in weekly with clients to help them assess how they can "stretch" in their daily practice using one or more EET skills.

Inducing Emotion Activation

While most clients who seek treatment for emotion problems are able to access the difficult emotions that go with triggering thoughts or situations, some clients aren't easily activated during exposure. They may struggle to reach emotion activation unless they experience an in vivo trigger. There are several possible reasons for this. They may not allow themselves to become emotionally activated because they fear getting overwhelmed and not being able to recover. Or they may be less vulnerable to internal triggers but are very sensitive to external triggers, which makes it difficult to induce distress during emotion or imaginal exposure. In the former case, the fear of overwhelm would likely improve during the course of treatment, especially as clients learn new ways of relating to their emotions. In the latter case, the exposure benefit may be more likely to come outside of session, when clients can seek out in vivo triggers to practice using the skills. Either way, you'll become aware of their experience by assessing their SUDS level and working with them to achieve an optimal level of arousal.

Assessment

If you plan to track your clients' progress during treatment (and we recommend that you do), you will want to administer outcome measures at the beginning of treatment and then regularly throughout. In addition to your own observations and experience with clients, you can also use a variety of self-report scales to track clients' emotion efficacy by measuring distress tolerance, experiential avoidance, emotion dysregulation, values-based living, and related tracking measures.

Gathering data will help you tailor ongoing treatment to meet the needs of your clients. For example, if you notice that clients are struggling with emotion avoidance, you can take extra time to review this with them. Or you may have clients who are improving but still suffer from a lack of confidence in their ability to use EET skills. You might take time to review and validate the ways clients are making better choices for themselves when they get triggered.

If you have completed treatment, then you probably also have a good sense of what skills your clients have mastered and which are more difficult. This may be a good time to stop and do a more formal assessment if you haven't been tracking outcomes throughout treatment.

The following outcome measures are included in Appendix A for your use:

Distress Tolerance Scale (DTS) (Simons & Gaher, 2005)

Difficulties in Emotion Regulation Scale (DERS) (Gratz & Roemer, 2004)

Valued Living Questionnaire (VLQ) (Wilson, Sandoz, Kitchens, & Roberts, 2010)

Emotion Efficacy Scale (EES)

Depression, Anxiety, and Stress Scale–21 (DASS–21) (S. H. Lovibond & P. F. Lovibond, 1995)

Acceptance & Action Questionnaire (AAQ-2) (Bond et al., 2011)

Keep in mind when using a symptom inventory, such as the DASS—or any symptom inventory for assessment of emotion efficacy—that sometimes symptoms may not significantly decrease. This isn't necessarily an indication that clients are not benefiting from treatment. For example, clients with chronic pain may experience significant stress symptoms on a daily basis, and this may or may not change during treatment. However, emotion efficacy can still increase those clients' ability to tolerate distress, make values-consistent choices, and regulate their emotions even when they're triggered. Or clients may experience a reduction in symptoms during treatment but still choose emotion avoidance in very distressing situations. On a case-by-case basis, you'll want to assess and think carefully about how to tailor treatment to best target growth edges for each of your clients.

EET and Beyond

If treatment with clients goes past the eight-week EET protocol timeline, you'll want to continue to support them in increasing their mastery with EET skills. Practicing regular mindful acceptance in session will allow you to continue to track how your clients are working with their emotional experiences. You'll also want to keep track of how effectively your clients are responding to emotional triggers outside of session, using a check-in to review how the week went, what triggers occurred, and how they were handled. In addition, validate and highlight what worked, and troubleshoot what didn't. Keep coming back to the psychoeducation and skills practice, using exposure to practice a recent trigger or a future feared situation.

Be sure to emphasize the benefits of daily practice. Remind clients that they are more vulnerable to emotional triggers when they are in a state of constant activation. One way clients can bring down their level of anxiety is to practice mindful acceptance, moment to moment, even when they aren't emotionally triggered. Maintaining a lower baseline will have mental, physical, and social health benefits, in addition to lowering their vulnerability to become emotionally triggered.

You can create a structure for your sessions to ensure that clients are using the skills both in and outside the session:

- Mindfulness practice

- Week in review: validate and highlight what worked; troubleshoot what was difficult or ineffective

- Review psychoeducation and an EET skill to practice in exposure

- Exposure practice with an identified past trigger or anticipated situation

- Homework planning with specific intentions and assignments

It may also be helpful to remind your clients that emotion efficacy is a lifelong practice. The more they practice, the less their emotions will feel overwhelming—and the more fulfilling and meaningful their lives will be.

Summary

Following is a synopsis of content covered in chapter 10:

- Increases in emotion awareness can initially result in demoralization in clients who realize how often they are driven by their emotions. They may need reassurance that it takes time to build their emotion efficacy muscle.

- Sometimes the skills that are most difficult for clients are those that will be most beneficial for them.

- Each client will need to learn to identify what constitutes a "stretch," or how far to push into the pain.

- Some clients struggle to become emotionally activated during imaginal and emotion exposure; they may need to focus on in vivo exposure practice outside of session.

- When conducting exposure with clients who are highly reactive, you'll want to clearly outline how they can identify optimal scenes to work with in exposure as well as how they can ground when they come out of exposure.

- Using assessment during and after EET can help tailor treatment to meet a client's specific needs.

- Conducting exposure in a group format requires having clear guidelines around confidentiality, disclosure, and participation.

- EET was designed to be delivered in an eight-session protocol, which can be modified for group or individual formats.

APPENDIX A

Outcome Measures for Assessment

This appendix includes six outcome measures you may want to use to assess your clients' treatment progress.

Distress Tolerance Scale

Directions: Think of times that you feel distressed or upset. Select the item from the menu that best describes your beliefs about feeling distressed or upset.

1. Strongly agree

2. Mildly agree

3. Agree and disagree equally

4. Mildly disagree

5. Strongly disagree

1.	Feeling distressed or upset is unbearable to me.	1 2 3 4 5
2.	When I feel distressed or upset, all I can think about is how bad I feel.	1 2 3 4 5
3.	I can't handle feeling distressed or upset.	1 2 3 4 5
4.	My feelings of distress are so intense that they completely take over.	1 2 3 4 5
5.	There's nothing worse than feeling distressed or upset.	1 2 3 4 5
6.	I can tolerate being distressed or upset as well as most people.	1 2 3 4 5
7.	My feelings of distress or being upset are not acceptable.	1 2 3 4 5
8.	I'll do anything to avoid feeling distressed or upset.	1 2 3 4 5
9.	Other people seem to be able to tolerate feeling distressed or upset better that I can.	1 2 3 4 5
10.	Being distressed or upset is always a major ordeal for me.	1 2 3 4 5
11.	I am ashamed of myself when I feel distressed or upset.	1 2 3 4 5
12.	My feelings of distress or being upset scare me.	1 2 3 4 5
13.	I'll do anything to stop feeling distressed or upset.	1 2 3 4 5
14.	When I feel distressed or upset, I must do something about it immediately.	1 2 3 4 5
15.	When I feel distressed or upset, I cannot help but concentrate on how bad the distress actually feels.	1 2 3 4 5

Difficulties in Emotion Regulation Scale (DERS)

Please indicate how often the following statements apply to you by writing the appropriate number from the scale below on the line beside each item.

1	Almost never	(0–10%)
2	Sometimes	(11–35%)
3	About half the time	(36–65%)
4	Most of the time	(66–90%)
5	Almost always	(91–100%)

1. I am clear about my feelings.   1 2 3 4 5

2. I pay attention to how I feel.   1 2 3 4 5

3. I experience my emotions as overwhelming and out of control.   1 2 3 4 5

4. I have no idea how I'm feeling.   1 2 3 4 5

5. I have difficulty making sense out of my feelings.   1 2 3 4 5

6. I am attentive to my feelings.   1 2 3 4 5

7. I know exactly how I am feeling.   1 2 3 4 5

8. I care about what I am feeling.   1 2 3 4 5

9. I am confused about how I feel.   1 2 3 4 5

10. When I'm upset, I acknowledge my emotions.   1 2 3 4 5

11. When I'm upset, I become angry at myself for feeling that way.   1 2 3 4 5

12. When I'm upset, I become embarrassed for feeling that way.   1 2 3 4 5

13. When I'm upset, I have difficulty getting work done.   1 2 3 4 5

14. When I'm upset, I become out of control.   1 2 3 4 5

15. When I'm upset, I believe I will remain that way for a long time.   1 2 3 4 5

16. When I'm upset, I believe that I will end up feeling very depressed.   1 2 3 4 5

17. When I'm upset, I believe that my feelings are valid and important. 1 2 3 4 5

18. When I'm upset, I have difficulty focusing on other things. 1 2 3 4 5

19. When I'm upset, I feel out of control. 1 2 3 4 5

20. When I'm upset, I can still get things done. 1 2 3 4 5

21. When I'm upset, I feel ashamed at myself for feeling that way. 1 2 3 4 5

22. When I'm upset, I know that I can find a way to eventually feel better. 1 2 3 4 5

23. When I'm upset, I feel like I am weak. 1 2 3 4 5

24. When I'm upset, I feel like I can remain in control of my behaviors. 1 2 3 4 5

25. When I'm upset, I feel guilty for feeling that way. 1 2 3 4 5

26. When I'm upset, I have difficulty concentrating. 1 2 3 4 5

27. When I'm upset, I have difficulty controlling my behaviors. 1 2 3 4 5

28. When I'm upset, I believe there is nothing I can do to make myself feel better. 1 2 3 4 5

29. When I'm upset, I become irritated at myself for feeling that way. 1 2 3 4 5

30. When I'm upset, I start to feel very bad about myself. 1 2 3 4 5

31. When I'm upset, I believe that wallowing in it is all I can do. 1 2 3 4 5

32. When I'm upset, I lose control over my behavior. 1 2 3 4 5

33. When I'm upset, I have difficulty thinking about anything else. 1 2 3 4 5

34. When I'm upset, I take time to figure out what I'm really feeling. 1 2 3 4 5

35. When I'm upset, it takes me a long time to feel better. 1 2 3 4 5

36. When I'm upset, my emotions feel overwhelming. 1 2 3 4 5

Valued Living Questionnaire (VLQ)

Below are areas of life that are valued by some people. We are concerned with your quality of life in each of these areas. One aspect of quality of life involves the importance one puts on different areas of living. Rate the importance of each area (by circling a number) on a scale of 1 to 10. 1 means that area is not at all important. 10 means that area is very important. Not everyone will value all of these areas, or value all areas the same. Rate each area according to your own personal sense of importance.

Area	not at all important	extremely important
1. Family (other than marriage or parenting)	1 2 3 4 5 6 7 8 9 10	
2. Marriage/couples/intimate relations	1 2 3 4 5 6 7 8 9 10	
3. Parenting	1 2 3 4 5 6 7 8 9 10	
4. Friends/social life	1 2 3 4 5 6 7 8 9 10	
5. Work	1 2 3 4 5 6 7 8 9 10	
6. Education/training	1 2 3 4 5 6 7 8 9 10	
7. Recreation/fun	1 2 3 4 5 6 7 8 9 10	
8. Spirituality	1 2 3 4 5 6 7 8 9 10	
9. Citizenship/community life	1 2 3 4 5 6 7 8 9 10	
10. Physical self-care (diet, exercise, sleep)	1 2 3 4 5 6 7 8 9 10	

In this section, we would like you to give a rating of how consistent your actions have been with each of your values. We are not asking about your ideal in each area. We are also not asking what others think of you. Everyone does better in some areas than others. People also do better at some times than at others. We want to know how you think you have been doing during the past week. Rate each area (by circling a number) on a scale of 1 to 10. 1 means that your actions have been completely inconsistent with your value. 10 means that your actions have been completely consistent with your value.

During the past week

Area	not at all consistent with my value				completely consistent with my value
1. Family (other than marriage or parenting)	1 2 3 4 5 6 7 8 9 10				
2. Marriage/couples/intimate relations	1 2 3 4 5 6 7 8 9 10				
3. Parenting	1 2 3 4 5 6 7 8 9 10				
4. Friends/social life	1 2 3 4 5 6 7 8 9 10				
5. Work	1 2 3 4 5 6 7 8 9 10				
6. Education/training	1 2 3 4 5 6 7 8 9 10				
7. Recreation/fun	1 2 3 4 5 6 7 8 9 10				
8. Spirituality	1 2 3 4 5 6 7 8 9 10				
9. Citizenship/community life	1 2 3 4 5 6 7 8 9 10				
10. Physical self-care (diet, exercise, sleep)	1 2 3 4 5 6 7 8 9 10				

From Wilson, Sandoz, Kitchens, & Roberts (2010). Used with permission.

Emotion Efficacy Scale (EES)

Using the scale below, rate each statement as it applies to you to indicate how much you agree or disagree.

1. strongly agree

2. moderately agree

3. agree/disagree equally

4. moderately disagree

5. strongly disagree

1.	I usually know what I am feeling.	1 2 3 4 5
2.	I have skills to recover when I get upset.	1 2 3 4 5
3.	When I get upset, I believe I can manage my emotions.	1 2 3 4 5
4.	When I get upset, I believe I will lose control.	1 2 3 4 5
5.	When I'm upset, I always act on my emotions.	1 2 3 4 5
6.	I cannot function when I'm distressed	1 2 3 4 5
7.	When I become upset, I do everything I can to avoid feeling uncomfortable.	1 2 3 4 5
8.	When I'm upset, I can express what's important to me.	1 2 3 4 5
9.	I usually fulfill my values and responsibilities, even when I get upset.	1 2 3 4 5
10.	I can identify what's most important to me, even when I'm upset.	1 2 3 4 5

Depression, Anxiety, and Stress Scale–21 (DASS–21)

Name: **Date:**

Please read each statement and circle a number—0, 1, 2, or 3—which indicates how much the statement applied to you *over the past week*. There are no right or wrong answers. Do not spend too much time on any statement.

The rating scale is as follows:

0 Did not apply to me at all

1 Applied to me to some degree, or some of the time

2 Applied to me to a considerable degree, or a good part of the time

3 Applied to me very much, or most of the time

1.	I found it hard to wind down.	0 1 2 3
2.	I was aware of dryness of my mouth.	0 1 2 3
3.	I couldn't seem to experience any positive feeling at all.	0 1 2 3
4.	I experienced breathing difficulty (e.g., excessively rapid breathing, breathlessness in the absence of physical exertion).	0 1 2 3
5.	I found it difficult to work up the initiative to do things.	0 1 2 3
6.	I tended to overreact to situations.	0 1 2 3
7.	I experienced trembling (e.g., in the hands).	0 1 2 3
8.	I felt that I was using a lot of nervous energy.	0 1 2 3
9.	I was worried about situations in which I might panic and make a fool of myself.	0 1 2 3

10. I felt that I had nothing to look forward to.   0 1 2 3

11. I found myself getting agitated.   0 1 2 3

12. I found it difficult to relax.   0 1 2 3

13. I felt downhearted and blue.   0 1 2 3

14. I was intolerant of anything that kept me from getting on with   0 1 2 3
    what I was doing.

15. I felt I was close to panic.   0 1 2 3

16. I was unable to become enthusiastic about anything.   0 1 2 3

17. I felt I wasn't worth much as a person.   0 1 2 3

18. I felt that I was rather touchy.   0 1 2 3

19. I was aware of the action of my heart in the absence of physical   0 1 2 3
    exertion (e.g., sense of heart rate increase, heart missing a beat).

20. I felt scared without any good reason.   0 1 2 3

21. I felt that life was meaningless.   0 1 2 3

From S. H. Lovibond & P. F. Lovibond (2005).

Acceptance and Action Questionnaire (AAQ-2)

Below you will find a list of statements. Please rate how true each statement is for you by circling a number next to it. Use the scale below to make your choice.

1. Never true

2. Very seldom true

3. Seldom true

4. Sometimes true

5. Frequently true

6. Almost always true

7. Always true

1.	It's okay if I remember something unpleasant.	1 2 3 4 5 6 7
2.	My painful experiences and memories make it difficult for me to live a life that I would value.	1 2 3 4 5 6 7
3.	I'm afraid of my feelings.	1 2 3 4 5 6 7
4.	I worry about not being able to control my worries and feelings.	1 2 3 4 5 6 7
5.	My painful memories prevent me from having a fulfilling life.	1 2 3 4 5 6 7
6.	I am in control of my life.	1 2 3 4 5 6 7
7.	Emotions cause problems in my life.	1 2 3 4 5 6 7
8.	It seems like most people are handling their lives better than I am.	1 2 3 4 5 6 7
9.	Worries get in the way of my success.	1 2 3 4 5 6 7
10.	My thoughts and feelings do not get in the way of how I want to live my life.	1 2 3 4 5 6 7

From Bond et al. (2011).

APPENDIX B

Research and Results

Here we provide research results from a quantitative outcome trial for emotion efficacy therapy.

Hypotheses and Results

H_1: An eight-week emotion regulation treatment will be effective in reducing emotion dysregulation, as measured by the DERS; increasing self-efficacy beliefs about regulating negative emotions, as measured by the MNESRES; and reducing depression, anxiety, and stress symptoms, as measured by the DASS–21.

Results and Significance of Pre- vs. Posttreatment Scores for Hypothesis 1		
Variable	Univariate MANOVAs	Planned Comparison Pre vs. Post
	F (1,21)	d
Hypothesis 1: Emotion Regulation		
DERS	32.36***	-1.21***
MNESRES	42.17***	1.38***
DASS-Depression	5.23*	-0.49*
DASS-Anxiety	5.01*	-0.48*
DASS-Stress	19.37***	-0.94***

Note. N = 22. ^p < 0.10; * p < 0.05; ** p <0.01; *** p < 0.001
Cohen's d: 0.2 = small; 0.5 = medium; 0.8 = large.
DERS = Difficulties with Emotion Regulation Scale.
DASS = Depression, Anxiety, and Stress Scale.

MNESRES = Multidimensional Negative Emotions Self-regulatory Scale.
DTS = Distress Tolerance Scale.
MEAQ = Multidimensional Experiential Avoidance Questionnaire.

H$_2$: An eight-week emotion regulation treatment will be effective in reducing experiential avoidance, as measured by the MEAQ; and increasing distress tolerance, as measured by the DTS.

Results and Significance of Pre- vs. Posttreatment Scores for Hypothesis 2		
Variable	Univariate MANOVAs	Planned Comparison Pre vs. Post
	F (1,21)	d
Hypothesis 2: Distress Tolerance and Experiential Avoidance		
DTS	15.45***	1.34***
MEAQ-Total	14.47***	-0.81***
MEAQ-Behavioral Avoidance	8.53**	-0.62**
MEAQ-Distress Aversion	12.26**	-0.75**
MEAQ-Procrastination	6.90*	-0.56*
MEAQ-Distraction & Suppression	0.04	-0.04
MEAQ-Repression & Denial	8.22**	-0.61**
MEAQ-Distress Endurance	2.31	0.32

Note. N = 22. ^p < 0.10; * p < 0.05; ** p <0.01; *** p < 0.001
Cohen's d: 0.2 = small; 0.5 = medium; 0.8 = large.
DERS = Difficulties with Emotion Regulation Scale.
DASS = Depression, Anxiety, and Stress Scale.
MNESRES = Multidimensional Negative Emotions Self-regulatory Scale.
DTS = Distress Tolerance Scale.
MEAQ = Multidimensional Experiential Avoidance Questionnaire.

Emotion Regulation Measures

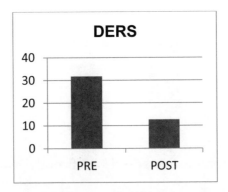

Emotion dysregulation decreased significantly (d = -1.21)

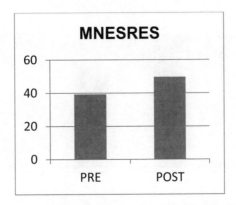

Efficacy regulating negative emotions increased significantly (d = -1.38)

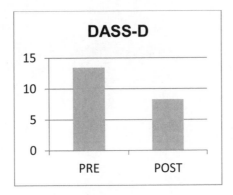

Depressive symptoms decreased significantly (d = -0.49)

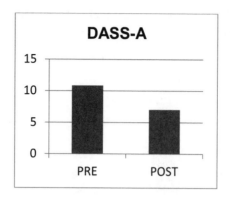

Anxiety symptoms decreased significantly (d = -0.48)

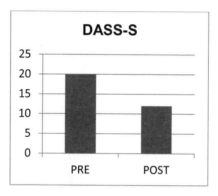

Stress symptoms decreased significantly (d = -0.94)

Transdiagnostic Drivers

Experiential Avoidance

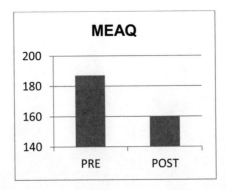

Experiential avoidance decreased significantly (d = -0.81)

Distress Tolerance

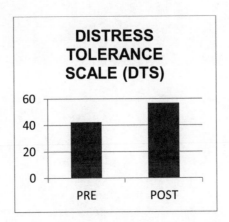

Distress tolerance increased significantly (d = 1.34)

Appendix C

EET Eight-Session Protocol

Included here are session-by-session outlines for delivering the eight-session EET protocol, and all scripts, handouts, and worksheets in single-page format, for copying. Note that all handouts and worksheets are also available for download at http://www.newharbinger.com/34039.

The session overview for group therapy is as follows:

Session 1:   Emotion Awareness

Session 2:   Mindful Acceptance: Emotion Surfing

Session 3:   Values-Based Action: Part 1

Session 4:   Values-Based Action: Part 2

Session 5:   Mindful Coping: Relaxation and Self-Soothing

Session 6:   Mindful Coping: Coping Thoughts and Radical Acceptance

Session 7:   Mindful Coping: Distraction and Time-Out

Session 8:   Consolidating, Troubleshooting, and Wrap-Up

EET Session 1: O+A

Components Covered: Emotion Awareness (chapter 2)

Session 1 is dedicated to introducing group members to EET. It's also designed to help clients develop a sense of what's possible by learning how to have a new relationship with emotions. Clients also learn what emotions are, how they work, and how they are experienced. In addition, Session 1 sets the tone for treatment, establishing guidelines about the structure for the session, participation expectations, and between-session skills practice.

Materials

- What You Can Expect from Emotion Efficacy Therapy handout
- What Is Emotion Efficacy? handout
- Emotion Awareness handout
- Anatomy of an Emotion handout
- Emotion Watching Worksheet
- Feelings Word List handout
- Session 1 Skills Practice handout
- Skills Practice Record

Overview

1. Welcome and administration of pretreatment measures
2. Introduction of leader and group members
3. Overview of EET treatment and structure
4. Psychoeducation on emotions and emotion awareness
5. Emotion watching exercise
6. Introduction to skills practice and the Skills Practice Record
7. Session 1 skills assignment

Procedures

1. Welcome and administration of pretreatment measures

If you are using pretreatment measures, administer them at the very beginning of group. (A list of recommended measures is provided in chapter 10, and full versions are available in Appendix A.)

2. Introduction of leader and group members

When working within a group format, there are several dynamics you'll want to be prepared to address. First, take some time in the beginning of treatment to create comfort and rapport with the group. You can do this by articulating the intention to create a safe space.

Take a few minutes to introduce yourself to the group, and allow enough time for each person to introduce him- or herself. Depending on the context and the group, you may ask clients to share something about their relationship with their emotions, ranging from what their most difficult emotion is to what brings them to treatment. As an icebreaker, you might ask group members to share their least favorite emotion. This will help establish some connection among group members and to normalize the common struggle with emotions that has brought each client to treatment.

Review guidelines for disclosure as well as confidentiality. While you cannot legally enforce confidentiality among participants, you'll want to ask them to keep what is shared private so that the group will be a safe space to engage in the treatment. In addition, you can remind your clients that while at times they will be asked to share or to give feedback, it is up to them whether to disclose anything personal. Participation in the group is intended to focus on learning EET skills, which does not depend on disclosing personal or specific details.

3. Overview of EET treatment and structure

Using the What You Can Expect from Emotion Efficacy Therapy handout, review EET treatment and outline the session structure for the group:

- Mindful acceptance practice

- Skills practice review and troubleshooting problems with homework

- Review of previous session's skill(s)

- Psychoeducation on new skill for the coming week

- Practice new skills using imaginal exposure

- Homework via Skills Practice Record

You'll want to emphasize that EET treatment involves regular skills practice between and outside of group sessions, and that the effectiveness of treatment will depend, in part, on how willing clients are to practice the skills on their own.

Using the handouts What You Can Expect from Emotion Efficacy Therapy and What is Emotion Efficacy?, introduce clients to the concept of emotion efficacy and to the skills they will be learning.

4. Psychoeducation on emotions and emotion awareness

Using the handouts Emotion Awareness and Anatomy of an Emotion, introduce clients to what emotions are, how they work, and what they're made of. (See chapter 2 for further detail on how to introduce this.)

5. Emotion watching exercise

Using the Emotion Watching Worksheet, have group members identify a situation that evokes strong emotion, and have them name the four parts of the emotion that go with it. Refer them to the Feelings Word List handout for help identifying the feeling label that goes with the emotion.

6. Introduction to skills practice and the Skills Practice Record

Explain the importance of skills practice outside of session. Then introduce them to the Skills Practice Record. Emphasize that emotion efficacy is like a muscle that needs to be exercised to build up. Skills practice between sessions will allow clients to become more efficient and effective at using the skills. It will also give them a chance to figure out where they need help troubleshooting.

7. Session 1 skills assignment

Use the Session 1 Skills Practice handout to review the skills practice for the week and to give clients a reminder of what they should practice.

What You Can Expect from Emotion Efficacy Therapy

EET will help you learn skills so you can be more powerful in how you respond to your emotions:

- You can learn to watch your emotions, seeing them rise and fall like a wave, rather than being overwhelmed or controlled by them.

- You can see the parts of your emotions—thoughts, feelings, physical sensations, and urges—so they are less mysterious and less outside of your awareness.

- You can learn to experience difficult emotions instead of feeling like you have to run away from them. You can learn to accept the emotion without being driven to do something that hurts you, your relationships, or your life.

- You can learn to recognize the "moment of choice"—when you can either do what your emotion is driving you to do, or choose to do something that expresses your values that will enrich your life.

- You can identify your core values—how you want to show up, even when you're emotionally triggered and upset.

- You can learn to act on your values in the moment of choice, rather than act on what your emotions tell you to do.

- You can learn new strategies to dial down your emotions, even when they are very intense.

- You can practice watching, accepting, and dialing down your emotions until you are really good at it.

Emotion Efficacy Therapy (EET) © 2016

What Is Emotion Efficacy?

Emotion efficacy is how well you can—and believe you can—respond to emotions, including intense emotions, effectively. This might mean responding by doing nothing, doing something that reflects what you care about in the moment, or practicing skills that decrease the emotion to keep from making the situation more difficult.

This treatment is based on the idea that pain is an inescapable part of being human, as are the emotions that go with it. And while we cannot avoid pain or difficult emotions, the good news is that we can reduce suffering and increase our quality of life by how we understand and respond to our emotional experience. Another way of saying this is that, while we can't escape painful emotions, we can *choose* how we respond to them. That's what emotion efficacy is all about.

The skills you'll learn from emotion efficacy therapy (EET) will help increase your emotion efficacy through the following five components:

- **Emotion awareness**: recognizing and understanding your emotional experience

- **Mindful acceptance**: observing and accepting emotions, instead of reacting to them

- **Values-based action**: responding to painful emotions with actions that reflect your values, instead of your emotions

- **Mindful coping**: when necessary, using skills to decrease the intensity of your emotions

- **Exposure-based skills practice:** using EET skills in an emotionally activated state

We'll be talking about these skills in every session, and by the end of treatment you'll know about and have experience using each of them.

Emotion Efficacy Therapy (EET) © 2016

Emotion Awareness

What Are Emotions?

What are emotions, really? Most simply, emotions are signals that help you respond to what your brain thinks is happening. Here's how they work: the brain responds to internal and external cues (events or observations from our environment). Then the brain produces biochemical messengers, which we experience as emotions. These emotions motivate us to make choices. For example, the emotion we know as anxiety helps us choose to avoid danger. Anger helps us choose to fight when we feel threatened. Sadness helps us choose to withdraw when we need to process a loss or failure.

From birth, our amazing brains are evolutionarily wired to protect us from harm—to help us survive. That means any time your brain is sensing a threat to your well-being, it will do everything it can to send you emotional messages to motivate you to protect yourself. You may have heard about this process referred to as "flight, fight, or freeze," all of which are common responses to intense emotions.

However, while our emotional wiring has been adaptive for the survival of the human race over time, the survival wiring doesn't always serve us when it gets activated in a non-survival situation. Over time, your brain develops a "negativity bias," whereby it constantly scans your environment for anything negative that could be interpreted as a threat so it can protect you. The downside of this protective negativity bias is that you can end up in a state of constant anxiety, or you can be easily triggered—whether or not there is an actual threat.

Author and psychotherapist Tara Brach explains how the negativity bias impacts us: "The emotion of fear often works overtime. Even when there is no immediate threat, our body may remain tight and on guard, our mind narrowed to focus on what might go wrong. When this happens, fear is no longer functioning to secure our survival. We are caught in the trance of fear and our moment-to-moment experience becomes bound in reactivity. We spend our time and energy defending our life rather than living it fully" (2003, p. 168).

EET can help you learn how to respond to non-survival emotions using skills that will help you respond effectively.

Why Do Some People Struggle with Emotions?

You've probably noticed that some people tend to be more emotionally reactive than others. We are all unique human beings, and how we experience emotions also depends on the wiring in our brains. While we are all born wired for survival, some of us are born with a tendency toward heightened emotional sensitivity. Others develop this tendency as a result of difficult experiences that leave them more emotionally reactive to certain cues.

If you are someone who has heightened sensitivity, you may have an increased vulnerability to stress. Even more, the heightened sensitivity to certain cues can become so ingrained and the emotional reactions so automatic that you may forget you have choices when you get triggered. Unfortunately, this emotional reactivity can negatively affect your well-being, quality of life, relationships, personal goals, and long-term health.

For this treatment, we will focus on how you can respond to distressing emotions and increase your emotion efficacy. You will learn how to stop being controlled by your emotions, how to respond in ways that reflect your values, and how to create more of what you want in your life.

Anatomy of an Emotion

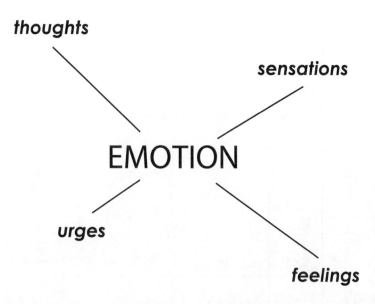

There are four components that make up your experience of an emotion:

- **Thoughts:** Thoughts are the content of what you're thinking. For example, "I never do anything right," or "I want to get out of here."

- **Feelings:** Feelings are the label or interpretation we give the emotion, for instance, sadness, frustration, joy, and so on.

- **Sensations:** Sensations are anything you feel in the body. This might be a sense of looseness and ease in the body when relaxed or muscle tension when anxious.

- **Urges:** Urges are impulses to do something—or not to do something. Examples include the urge to leave, the urge to yell, the urge to withdraw.

Let's consider one example: If something great happens, you may have the thought, "There is so much to look forward to!" The feeling may be excitement. You may notice sensations of looseness and energy in your body. You may experience the urge to engage with people and/or dance around.

Two more examples: When you feel sad, you may have the thought, "I will always be alone." You may sense tightness in your stomach and a lack of energy in your body. You may have the urge to withdraw from people. If someone threatens you, you may feel angry, you may think, "How dare he say that?!" You may notice the sensation of increased heart rate and energy. You may have the urge to attack the person.

Emotion Watching Worksheet

Observing the Four Components of Emotion

Use this worksheet to record the four components of emotion you experience from specific triggers.

Triggers	Thoughts	Feelings	Sensations	Urges

Feelings Word List

Adored	Disturbed	Infatuated	Satisfied
Afraid	Eager	Inspired	Scared
Amazed	Embarrassed	Interested	Scattered
Angry	Empty	Irritated	Secure
Annoyed	Energetic	Jealous	Shy
Anxious	Enlightened	Joyful	Smart
Ashamed	Enlivened	Lively	Sorry
Blessed	Enraged	Lonely	Stimulated
Blissful	Envious	Loved	Strong
Bored	Exhausted	Loving	Surprised
Bothered	Flirtatious	Mad	Suspicious
Broken	Foolish	Moved	Terrified
Bubbly	Fragile	Nervous	Thankful
Cautious	Frightened	Obsessed	Thrilled
Comfortable	Frustrated	Optimistic	Tired
Concerned	Fulfilled	Overwhelmed	Touched
Confident	Glad	Passionate	Trusting
Confused	Guilty	Pleased	Uncomfortable
Content	Happy	Proud	Unsure
Curious	Helpless	Puzzled	Upset
Delighted	Hopeful	Regretful	Vivacious
Depressed	Horrified	Relieved	Vulnerable
Determined	Hurt	Reluctant	Worried
Disappointed	Hysterical	Respected	Worthless
Discouraged	Impatient	Restless	Worthy
Disgusted	Indifferent	Sad	

Emotion Efficacy Therapy (EET) © 2016

Session 1 Skills Practice

_____ Using the Emotion Watching Worksheet, practice emotion awareness by observing and recording the four components of emotion when you get emotionally triggered. If you don't find yourself able to practice when you get triggered, you can find something to intentionally activate your emotions. For example, recall a recent difficult situation or a distressing memory. If it's helpful, you can use the list of feeling words to identify the specific feeling label that goes with the emotion.

_____ Practice observing the parts of emotion for at least 10 minutes a day.

_____ Record the four parts of the emotion on the worksheet.

_____ Record your skills practice in the first row on your Skills Practice Record.

_____ Bring all of these materials to review in your next session.

Skills Practice Record

Emotion Efficacy Therapy

Directions: Place a check mark next to the skill you practice each day. Record any triggers at the bottom. Bring this record to your next session.

	Day 1	Day 2	Day 3	Day 4	Day 5	Day 6	Day 7
Observe the four parts of an emotion: sensations, feelings, thoughts, and urges.							
Observe, accept, and surf your emotion wave, with SUDS.							
Observe, accept, and choose a values-based action.							
Observe, accept, and choose a relaxation skill.							
Observe, accept, and choose a self-soothing skill.							
Observe, accept, and choose a coping thought.							
Observe, accept, and choose to practice radical acceptance.							
Observe, accept, and choose a distraction strategy.							
Observe, accept, and choose a time-out.							

Emotional triggers: Record any events or emotions that are distressing during this week.

_____

_____

_____

EET Session 2: O + A

Components Covered: Mindful Acceptance, Emotion Surfing, and Exposure-Based Skills Training (chapters 3 and 4)

Session 2 is the most content-heavy of all the sessions. Group members add the key component of mindful acceptance to emotion awareness, which is used in every exposure-based skills training both within and outside of session for the duration of treatment. The types and consequences of emotion avoidance are also highlighted to increase motivation for trying new behaviors. Finally, clients begin working with emotion exposure and learning how to do their own exposure-based skills practice both in session and between sessions.

Materials

- Mindful Acceptance | Observe + Accept handout

- Script for Guided Mindful Acceptance

- Consequences of Emotion Avoidance handout

- Emotion Avoidance Consequences Worksheet

- Rumination handout

- Script for Guided Emotion Surfing

- Introduction to Exposure handout

- Session 2 Skills Practice handout

- Skills Practice Record

- Emotion Surfing Practice handout

- Values Clarification Worksheet (for homework)

Overview

1. Skills practice review

2. Psychoeducation on mindful acceptance

3. Mindful acceptance practice

4. Introduction to emotion avoidance

5. Psychoeducation on emotion surfing

6. Psychoeducation on exposure and practice

7. Skills practice assignment

Procedures

1. Skills practice review

Using the Skills Practice Record, ask group members to share how their skills practice went since the last session, providing validation and an opportunity for troubleshooting. If necessary, briefly review the concept of emotion efficacy and the four parts of emotion.

2. Psychoeducation on mindful acceptance

Using the Mindful Acceptance | Observe + Accept handout, introduce clients to the idea of observing and accepting their emotions.

3. Mindful acceptance practice

Using the Script for Guided Mindful Acceptance, lead your clients through mindful acceptance practice. Be sure to leave time for feedback both as an opportunity for troubleshooting and to consolidate learning.

Remind group members that each session will begin with mindful acceptance practice. Tell them that, as part of their homework for the remainder of treatment, they should practice this for at least ten minutes a day and record it on their Skills Practice Record.

4. Introduction to emotion avoidance

Use the Consequences of Emotion Avoidance handout to introduce your clients to the different kinds of avoidance, as well as how emotion avoidance negatively impacts their lives. Then have them assess the pros and cons using the Emotion Avoidance Consequences Worksheet.

5. Psychoeducation on emotion surfing

Introduce clients to emotion surfing, emphasizing what happens to emotion when we try to avoid the emotion versus accepting it and "riding the wave." Set up the exposure and lead clients through an emotion surfing exercise practicing mindful acceptance using the following script.

Be sure to leave time for feedback both as an opportunity for troubleshooting, and to consolidate learning.

Mindful Acceptance | Observe + Accept

Mindful acceptance is derived from the practice of mindfulness, which has been shown to reduce psychological stress and improve well-being in numerous studies. The practice of mindful acceptance is essential for emotion efficacy because it will help you better tolerate difficult emotions, recover more quickly, and respond in ways that enrich your life moment to moment.

Mindful acceptance will help you practice observing and accepting emotions instead of reacting to them, avoiding them, or trying to control them. It doesn't mean you have to "like" your emotions; it simply means that you don't resist what you are experiencing.

One helpful metaphor is to think of yourself as the atmosphere and your emotions as the weather. The atmosphere is constant, while the weather is ever-changing. In mindful acceptance, you simply observe and accept changing weather, without reacting, while you as the observer remain constant.

There are many benefits to using mindful acceptance when you are emotionally triggered:

- Practicing mindful acceptance can help you tolerate pain without acting on it.

- Practicing mindful acceptance can help you recover more quickly from the distress of the trigger.

- Practicing mindful acceptance can help you find the space you need to thoughtfully and consciously choose how you will respond to the pain.

Mindful acceptance is practiced by learning to observe and accept the four parts of emotion: sensations, feelings, thoughts, and urges. Following is a simple description for practicing mindful acceptance you can use as you do your skills practice outside of session. Try to practice for at least 10 minutes a day when you are resting or when you get emotionally triggered.

1. Sensation Acceptance

   Scan your body for sensations with the intention of observing and accepting them instead of reacting to them. Just notice all the details of the sensations: size, shape, temperature, tension, and movement. See if you can soften to the sensation and make space for it, without trying to change it…just allowing it to be exactly as it is.

2. Feeling Labeling

   Try to identify the feeling that goes with the emotion. Name it and allow it to be exactly as it is, without judging it.

3. Thought Watching

   Clear your mind, and then wait and watch for each thought as it arises; let the thought go without getting involved in it. Come back to the present moment and wait for the next thought to show up. When a thought arises, you might say to yourself, "There's a thought," and then just let it go. If you find yourself struggling to let the thought go, you might just acknowledge it as a "sticky thought," and then let it go.

4. Urge Noticing

   Notice if the emotion comes with an urge to do or not do something. Allow yourself to sit with the urge, without acting on it or judging it. Then notice what it's like not to act on it.

The more you practice these mindful acceptance skills, the bigger your emotion efficacy muscle will grow. It will get easier and easier to observe and accept your emotions instead of acting on them. Practicing mindful acceptance will also prepare you to use the other skills you will learn in EET.

Emotion Efficacy Therapy (EET) © 2016

Script for Guided Mindful Acceptance

For the next ten minutes I'm going to lead you through a mindful acceptance practice exercise. You will practice observing and accepting your emotional experience in the present moment. Practicing mindful acceptance in a neutral state will build your emotion efficacy muscle and make it easier for you to use this skill when you are triggered.

First, just sit comfortably, and either close your eyes or relax your gaze and pick a spot to focus on in front of you.

Now, take a few minutes to notice any sensations in your body. Scan your body until you find a sensation and rest your attention on it. See if you can let it be just as it is and get curious about it. Notice its size and shape; whether it's moving or staying the same; if there's any temperature or tension to it. See if you can soften to it, or even lean into the sensation…

Now, see if you can identify a feeling label that goes with the sensation…just name it and allow it to be as it is without judgment or reacting to it.

Next, we'll spend a few minutes just noticing and watching our thoughts. Our brains produce different kinds of thoughts all the time, and the key is not to get involved with them. Instead, as each thought arises, you can simply say, "There's a thought," and then let the thought go. Then, just return to the present moment, and wait for the next thought to arise. For the next few minutes, notice your thoughts until I say stop…

Okay, now stop. Next, see if there's an urge that goes with your sensations, feelings, or thoughts. It could be an urge to do something or not do something. Try to just sit with the urge. Notice what it's like not to act on the urge, to just surf it.

[Allow the client to sit with the urge for 30 seconds. Then repeat the sequence one more time.]

Before you come out of this exercise, take a few deep breaths and slowly open your eyes as you bring your attention back to the room.

Consequences of Emotion Avoidance

There are at least five types of emotion avoidance that researchers believe are at the root of many emotion problems.

Situational: people, places, things, and activities

Cognitive: thoughts, images, and memories

Somatic: internal sensations such as racing heart, palpitations, breathlessness, overheating, fatigue, or unwanted sexual arousal

Protective: avoiding uncertainty through checking, cleaning, perfectionism, procrastination, or reassurance seeking

Substitution: avoiding painful emotions with replacement emotions, numbing out, alcohol, drugs, bingeing, or gambling

Why not just keep on avoiding? Because the consequences of emotion avoidance are usually worse than the experience of what we try to avoid.

- Since distress, discomfort, and anxiety are all a guaranteed part of life, emotion avoidance is often only a temporary and superficial "solution."

- Emotion avoidance reinforces the idea that discomfort/distress/anxiety is "bad" or "dangerous." It reduces your ability to face and tolerate necessary pain.

- Emotion avoidance often requires effort and energy. It's exhausting and time-consuming.

- Emotion avoidance limits your ability to fully experience the present.

- Emotion avoidance can keep you from moving toward important, valued aspects of life.

- Emotion avoidance often doesn't work. When you tell yourself not to think about something, you have to think about not thinking about it. When you try to avoid an emotion, you often end up feeling it anyway.

- Emotion avoidance often leads to suffering: addiction, helplessness, hopelessness, depression, damaged relationships, and lost opportunities.

By allowing yourself to experience fears—and difficult thoughts, feelings, sensations, and urges—you can learn to decrease your suffering.

Emotion Avoidance Consequences Worksheet

Emotion	Pros of Avoiding	Cons of Avoiding	Cons of Experiencing	Pros of Experiencing

Script for Guided Emotion Surfing

After the provoking scene is "shut off," a typical emotion surfing exercise might look like this:

What do you notice in your body right now? Can you describe the sensations? [Client responds.]

What are the feelings that go with that? [Client responds.]

If there are thoughts, can you just watch them and let them go? Any time a thought shows up, just say so. Any thoughts now? [Client responds.] See if you can just let go of any thoughts that arise.

Where are you on the wave? [Client responds.] SUDS? [Client responds.]

Any urges? Does the emotion make you want to do something? [Client responds.] Notice how you can just observe the urge. You don't have to act on it.

What's happening in your body right now? [Client responds.]

Can you label your feelings? [Client responds.] See if you can just allow the feelings without reacting to them.

Remember to watch and let go of any thoughts. Are thoughts showing up? [Client responds.]

Urges? Something the emotion wants you to do? [Client responds.] See what it's like to just notice the urge without acting on it.

Where are you on the wave? SUDS? [Client responds.]

What are you experiencing in your body right now? [Client responds.] Can you make room for that and just allow that sensation?

Your feelings? [Client responds.] Can you just allow that feeling? Can you let it be there without trying to control or stop it?

Watch the thoughts and let them go. [Client responds.]

Urges? [Client responds.]

Check the wave. Where are you? [Client responds.] SUDS? [Client responds.]

Emotion Efficacy Therapy (EET) © 2016

6. Psychoeducation on exposure and practice

Using the Introduction to Exposure handout, orient clients to exposure and how it will be used to enhance skills training. If you have a group where multiple members have a history of severe trauma, you may consider adopting guidelines to prevent clients from triggering each other. For example, you may want to ask that no details of the situations they choose for imaginal exposure be shared during feedback. Rather, they can just share the course of their emotion wave and SUDS level at the beginning, middle, and end of exposure practice.

Setting up exposure in a group setting requires some extra time and attunement. Some people—such as those with high anxiety, a severe trauma history, or panic disorder—may need to set their target SUDS levels lower in the beginning, while others can target the recommended 5 to 6 range.

You'll easily identify clients struggling with imaginal exposure during the group practice. After having clients close their eyes and locate themselves in the triggering scene, ask them to raise their hands when they get to their SUDs level. This will allow you to know when to proceed to the next phase of exposure. Often, the clients who struggle to become activated will not raise their hand, and you'll want to check in with them during the exposure feedback or after session. They can still practice exposure in the group, but the research shows the best outcomes occur when clients' SUDS are elevated, so you'll want to work with clients to find a way to do skills practice in an activated state.

Following is a script and the Introduction to Exposure handout you can use to help clients figure out how to find the right "stretch" with exposure.

Therapist-Client Dialogue Example: Setting Up Exposure in a Group

Therapist:	So we've talked about how it's important to practice skills in the same emotional state as you'll be in outside of group. It's important to choose situations that you know can activate you emotionally, but they shouldn't be so upsetting that you can't recover after the exercise.
Client A:	Yeah… I'm afraid if I choose the wrong scene I'll get totally overwhelmed.
Therapist:	Right, so I'm going to give you some suggestions about how to choose a situation that works for you. Has anyone heard of the SUDS? It's an acronym for a fancy scale you can use to rate how upset you are. It stands for the subjective units of distress scale: S-U-D-S [draws a continuum on the white board with 0 on the far left, 5 in the middle, and 10 on the far right].

Therapist:	Basically, if you were in no distress you would rate your SUDS as a 0; if you are in the most distress you can imagine you would rate yourself at 10. For our exposure exercises, you want to try to pick scenes to work with that will activate you somewhere between a 5 or 6 SUDS.
Client B:	So how do we predict that?
Therapist:	Great question. It can take some practice to get good at predicting. Everyone is different, and some people can get activated at a high SUDS level very quickly, and others may have a hard time getting activated at all. The best way to figure it out is to start with something that's not too distressing when you think about it, but immediately activates emotion. In others words, you don't want to pick something that will leave you feeling too exposed or inside out. Does that make sense?
Client C:	So like if I think about the fight I just had with my partner, and I immediately start to feel tense?
Therapist:	Exactly. And do you have some idea about how upsetting it might make you to revisit that scene?
Client C:	Well, it's not horrible or anything…not like the car accident I had last year…that would be like a 10 on the SUDS!
Therapist:	Right. So where do you predict your SUDS might be if you use the fight with your partner?
Client C:	Probably around a 6. I was pretty upset and have been for the last few days.
Therapist:	That sounds like a good scene to work with. It's likely you'll have a sense of what you can handle. The important thing is that you want to stretch yourself enough to get the benefit of the exposure. If you're not very activated, you won't experience the shift in distress tolerance that exposure can provide.
Therapist:	[To Client A] Do you feel like you can find a scene to work with that's in the 5 to 6 SUDS range?
Client A:	I'm not sure… I understand what you're saying, but sometimes I can't predict how I'm going to feel. I can go straight to panic and down the rabbit hole.

Therapist:	I'm glad you brought that up. It may help you to start by choosing a scene you don't predict is too activating. If it ends up being too low—under a 5—you can always switch it for the next practice.
Client A:	Okay. But what if I end up getting really upset during the exercise and start to panic?
Therapist:	Any time you start to sense you may be getting too distressed to recover, you can just come out of the exercise, open your eyes, and ground yourself by counting your breaths or focusing on feeling your feet on the floor. If you still feel too distressed, you can leave the room.
Client A:	Well, that might be embarrassing.
Therapist:	It sounds like you're concerned about drawing attention to yourself?
Client A:	Yeah, and I don't want to mess it up for the rest of the group.
Therapist:	I appreciate that. But it's really important that you know how to take care of yourself during the treatment. If you need to come out of the exposure or leave the room, please do that. Everyone here is on his or her own path, and each person has different challenges with their emotions.
Client A:	I get it. I'll try.
Therapist:	Great. After each exposure, we will have time to check in and share feedback. If you still feel distressed after the exposure and feedback time, I'd like you to check in with me once the session has concluded. Does that work for everyone? Any questions?

While it might seem daunting to conduct an exposure-based treatment in a group setting with clients struggling with emotions, using exposure in a group format, as compared to individual, showed no treatment difference (Barrera, Mott, Hofstein, & Teng, 2013). In fact, there are many benefits from doing EET in a group format. Having multiple treatment participants normalizes the struggle with emotions, allows the group members to learn from each other's challenges, and can provide a supportive context for treatment.

Introduction to Exposure

In this treatment we'll be doing some skills practice we'll call "exposure exercises." The exercises are intended to help you "expose" yourself to the experience of difficult emotions so you can learn how to recover from distress as well as learn new ways of responding that enrich your life. Research shows that when you face distress instead of avoiding it, you can not only increase your tolerance of the distress but also recover more quickly.

Here's how it works. First pick a situation or scene that is distressing to you. For example, try to recall the last time you got upset, and see if you can feel yourself getting activated when you think about it. Then, assess whether it is activating enough to use for your exposure using the following SUDS tool.

The SUDS Rating

The SUDS rating stands for *subjective units of distress scale*. In plain terms, this just means how much distress you experience when you think about the situation on a scale of 1 to 10, with 1 being no distress and 10 being the most distress you can imagine. For each situation, you want to predict how upset you might become if you expose yourself fully to the emotion of the situation. Ideally, your distress will be in the 5 to 7 range. If your distress is too low, the exercise is unlikely to be effective, and if it's too high, you may become distracted and unable to stay engaged.

1 = no distress

3 = noticeable distress

5 = moderate distress

7 = distressing and uncomfortable

10 = worst distress imaginable

If at any point in the exposure exercise you begin to feel too distressed to stay with it, you should let the therapist know and stop the exercise. You are in the driver's seat. Once you have done a few exposures, you may want to try to use situations that you predict will take you higher, to an 8 or 9.

Emotion Efficacy Therapy (EET) © 2016

7. Session 2 skills assignment

Use the following handout (available in downloadable format at http://www.newhar binger.com/34039) to review the skills practice for the week and to give clients a reminder of what they should practice.

Session 2 Skills Practice

_____ Practice mindful acceptance for at least 10 minutes a day by observing and accepting the four components of emotion when you get emotionally triggered, or using emotion exposure to a difficult event, situation, or emotion. Observe all four parts of the emotion, and surf the emotion wave. Record your mindful acceptance skills practice in the first row of your Skills Practice Record.

_____ Using the Emotion Surfing Practice handout, practice emotion surfing using emotion exposure. First, find something to intentionally activate your emotions (e.g., recall a recent difficult situation or a distressing memory) that gets your SUDS up in the 5 to 7 range. Practice observing and accepting the parts of emotion. Notice and record your SUDS level at the end of your exercise. Record your skills practice in the second row on your Skills Practice Record.

_____ Review the Values Clarification Worksheet and select (circle) the 10 values that most closely reflect your core values.

_____ Record any events that trigger you during the week at the bottom of your Skills Practice Record.

_____ Bring all of these materials to review in your next session.

Emotion Efficacy Therapy (EET) © 2016

Skills Practice Record

Emotion Efficacy Therapy

Directions: Place a check mark next to the skill you practice each day. Record any triggers at the bottom. Bring this record to your next session.

	Day 1	Day 2	Day 3	Day 4	Day 5	Day 6	Day 7
Observe the four parts of an emotion: sensations, feelings, thoughts, and urges.							
Observe, accept, and surf your emotion wave, with SUDS.							
Observe, accept, and choose a values-based action.							
Observe, accept, and choose a relaxation skill.							
Observe, accept, and choose a self-soothing skill.							
Observe, accept, and choose a coping thought.							
Observe, accept, and choose to practice radical acceptance.							
Observe, accept, and choose a distraction task or activity.							
Observe, accept, and choose a time-out.							

Emotional triggers: Record any events or emotions that are distressing during this week.

_____

_____

_____

Emotion Efficacy Therapy (EET) © 2016

Emotion Surfing Practice

Once you're emotionally activated, take note of your SUDS level and then begin to practice emotion surfing following the sequence below:

1. Ask yourself, "What sensations do I notice in my body?"

2. Ask yourself, "What's the feeling that goes with it?"

3. Watch and let go of thoughts.

4. Notice urges. Locate the moment of choice instead of acting on the urges.

5. Ask yourself, "Where am I on the wave?" Determine your SUDS rating.

6. Ask yourself, "What's happening in my body?" Try to allow that sensation.

7. Ask yourself, "What's happening to the feeling?" Try to allow and make room for that feeling.

8. Watch thoughts and notice urges. Try not to get involved with them.

9. Ask yourself, "Where am I on the wave?"

10. Ask yourself, "What's the sensation in my body?" Try to accept that sensation.

11. Ask yourself, "What's my feeling?" Try to allow and make room for that feeling.

12. Watch thoughts and notice urges. Try not to get involved with them.

13. Ask yourself, "Where am I on the wave?"

Keep going until the distress improves or the emotion shifts. Record your SUDS level when finished.

Emotion Efficacy Therapy (EET) © 2016

EET Session 3: O + A + Choose VBA

Components Covered: Values-Based Action Part 1 and
Exposure-Based Skills Practice (Chapter 5)

Session 3 begins the first of two sessions focused on values-based action (VBA). Group members will learn the key skill for choosing alternatives to emotion-driven behaviors: locating the moment of choice. In addition, they begin to clarify values in each of their life domains and to identify how they can express these values when they are emotionally triggered. Finally, clients begin working with VBA using imaginal exposure both in session and between sessions.

Materials

- Script for Guided Mindful Acceptance

- Moment of Choice handout

- Values Domains Worksheet

- Filled-Out Values Domains Worksheet

- Benefits of Values-Based Action Worksheet

- Session 3 Skills Practice handout

- Skills Practice Record

Overview

1. Mindful acceptance practice and feedback

2. Skills practice review

3. Psychoeducation on the moment of choice

4. Introduction to values-based action

5. Whiteboard exercise with values and emotional barriers

6. VBA using imaginal exposure and feedback

7. Skills practice assignment

Procedures

1. Mindful acceptance practice and feedback

For the first ten minutes of session, lead group members through mindful acceptance practice using the Script for Guided Mindful Acceptance. Ask clients to provide feedback about their experience as an opportunity for learning and troubleshooting.

2. Skills practice review

Briefly review Session 2 skills and ask clients to share feedback about their weekly practice using their Skills Practice Record.

3. Psychoeducation on the moment of choice

Using the Moment of Choice handout, introduce clients to the moment of choice. Emphasize that finding this "pause" is critical for being able to make choices that are effective and that will help them create lives that reflect their values.

4. Introduction to values-based action

Give clients the sample Values Domain Worksheet, as well as the blank Values Domains Worksheet, and ask them to complete it using their Values Clarification Worksheet from Session 2.

5. Whiteboard exercise with values and emotional barriers

Lead a whiteboard exercise using client examples. First, list a core value. Second, identify a recent situation when a client was emotionally triggered. Third, identify the values-based action he or she could have chosen to reflect the core value. Do at least two to three examples to reinforce how VBA works and to prepare clients for the group exercise, Monsters on the Bus.

Next, have clients complete the Benefits of Values-Based Action worksheet. Then solicit feedback.

6. VBA using imaginal exposure and feedback

Following is a guide to helping your clients practice using VBA with imaginal exposure. Be sure to explain that this is the way they will practice VBA using imaginal exposure outside of session during the week. You may also encourage clients to try to use VBA in vivo when any triggers arise.

Step 1: Select a distressing situation. Ask clients to describe a recent distressing event in which they became emotionally triggered and responded with experiential avoidance or other emotion-driven behavior. Check in to be sure each client has identified a situation to work with before moving forward.

Step 2: Identify the value and the VBA. Explore which of the clients' values relate to the situation they have chosen. Then prompt clients to identify a specific VBA that they would have preferred to enact. You'll want to get the clients to articulate exactly what this alternative behavior would look like—everything the clients say and do, including tone of voice and body language.

Step 3: Visualize enacting the VBA. Have the clients briefly visualize using the values-based action, mentally rehearsing the scene several times until they are clear about what they will do.

Step 4: O+A+C. Begin the exposure by having clients form a clear image of the triggering scene. Encourage them to notice the environment where the trigger occurred: watch the action in the scene, hear what's said, feel whatever physical sensations are part of the scene, notice if there's an urge to do something or not to do something. As the clients become emotionally activated, ask them to continue to describe the sensations, thoughts, feelings, and urges that come up. Encourage an accepting attitude whereby the client "makes room" for the emotion, allowing it to be what it is with no effort at controlling or avoiding it.

While still visualizing the triggering event, have the clients observe any action urges that arise. Is there a desire to be verbally aggressive, to withdraw, to stonewall, to be defensive? Have the clients describe such urges and notice that the urges don't have to become action. This is the moment of choice, and it's important for the clients to stay with it for several minutes: observing the emotional pain, accepting and allowing the pain to be there without avoidance, and choosing not to act on emotion-driven urges.

Step 5: Imaginal exposure with VBA. Now that your clients have identified the moment of choice, check for SUDS and introduce the values-based action as a guided visualization. Ask your clients to continue the distressing scene, and, instead of imagining the emotion-driven behavior that accompanied the actual scene, have them visualize the alternative VBA they rehearsed earlier. As noted before, encourage clients to watch themselves saying and/or doing the new behavior, with tone of voice and posture matching the VBA. For the next three to five minutes, have clients repeat this visualization, moving from the triggering scene (and the moment of choice) through the new values-based responses several times.

Ask clients to rate their SUDS at the end. The entire exposure sequence—O+A+C + values-based action—should last eight to ten minutes.

Step 6: Consolidating what was learned. Consolidate what the clients have learned through a brief conversation. Did observing and accepting the target emotion decrease their distress? What did they observe about the moment of choice? How did visualizing an alternate response (VBA) impact them? Did it reduce their distress? Increase their distress tolerance? Did it increase confidence that the client could choose VBAs in distressing situations?

7. Session 3 skills assignment

Use the following handout to review the skills practice for the week and to give clients a reminder of what they should practice.

Script for Guided Mindful Acceptance

For the next ten minutes I'm going to lead you through a mindful acceptance practice exercise. You will practice observing and accepting your emotional experience in the present moment. Practicing mindful acceptance in a neutral state will build your emotion efficacy muscle and make it easier for you to use this skill when you are triggered.

First, just sit comfortably, and either close your eyes or relax your gaze and pick a spot to focus on in front of you.

Now, take a few minutes to notice any sensations in your body. Scan your body until you find a sensation and rest your attention on it. See if you can let it be just as it is and get curious about it. Notice its size and shape; whether it's moving or staying the same; if there's any temperature or tension to it. See if you can soften to it, or even lean into the sensation…

Now, see if you can identify a feeling label that goes with the sensation…just name it and allow it to be as it is without judgment or reacting to it.

Next, we'll spend a few minutes just noticing and watching our thoughts. Our brains produce different kinds of thoughts all the time, and the key is not to get involved with them. Instead, as each thought arises, you can simply say, "There's a thought," and then let the thought go. Then, just return to the present moment, and wait for the next thought to arise. For the next few minutes, notice your thoughts until I say stop…

Okay, now stop. Next, see if there's an urge that goes with your sensations or thoughts. It could be an urge to do something or not do something. Try to just sit with the urge. Notice what it's like not to act on the urge, to just surf it.

[Allow the client to sit with the urge for 30 seconds. Then repeat the sequence one more time.]

Before you come out of this exercise, take a few deep breaths and slowly open your eyes as you bring your attention back to the room.

Moment of Choice

As humans, we don't have control over whether or not we have emotions. Emotions will arise naturally in response to what's happening inside us and around us. But we can control how we respond to our emotions, and that's where we find true emotion efficacy.

This concept was illuminated by neurologist and psychiatrist Victor Frankl as follows:

Between stimulus and response there is space.

In that space lies our freedom and power to choose our response.

In those choices lie our growth and happiness. (n.d.)

How effectively we respond to difficult emotions depends on being able to locate this "moment of choice." This moment is the time when you realize that you're emotionally triggered, and you realize you have the power to choose how to respond. You might think of it as a "sacred pause" when you can either react, avoid, or try to control it—or you can choose a response that is life enriching.

In EET, you'll learn a variety of skills you can choose to use in your moment of choice to help you respond to your emotions in a way that brings you close to what you want to create in the moment.

EET Model = Observe + Accept Emotions > Locate Moment of Choice > Choose EET Skill

Values Domains Worksheet

1. Intimate relationships   Value: _____ I = _____ A = _____

     Values-Based Action:

_____

2. Parenting   Value: _____ I = _____ A = _____

     Values-Based Action:

_____

3. Education/learning   Value: _____ I = _____ A = _____

     Values-Based Action:

_____

4. Friends/social life   Value: _____ I = _____ A = _____

     Values-Based Action:

_____

5. Physical self-care/health   Value: _____ I = _____ A = _____

     Values-Based Action:

_____

6. Family of origin   Value: _____ I = _____ A = _____

     Values-Based Action:

_____

I = Importance

Rate:

0 = unimportant

1 = moderately important

2 = very important

A = Action: How much action did you take in the last seven days toward your value?

Rate:

0 = no action

1 = one or two actions

2 = three or four actions

3 = five or more actions

7. Spirituality   Value: _____ I = _____ A = _____

Values-Based Action:

_____

8. Community life/citizenship   Value: _____ I = _____ A = _____

Values-Based Action:

_____

9. Recreation   Value: _____ I = _____ A = _____

Values-Based Action:

_____

10. Work/career   Value: _____ I = _____ A = _____

Values-Based Action:

_____

11. _____ Value: _____ I = _____ A = _____

Values-Based Action:

_____

12. _____ Value: _____ I = _____ A = _____

Values-Based Action:

_____

I = Importance

Rate:

0 = unimportant

1 = moderately important

2 = very important

A = Action: How much action did you take in the last seven days toward your value?

Rate:

0 = no action

1 = one or two actions

2 = three or four actions

3 = five or more actions

Values Domain Worksheet

(Client Sample)

1. Intimate relationships   Value: _Caring_   I = _2_   A = _0_

                                     Values-Based Action:

Express concern, interest re: difficulty getting organized

2. Parenting   Value: _Supportive_   I = _2_   A = _0_

                                       Values-Based Action:

Talk with gentleness/love when they didn't listen or are sassy

3. Education/learning   Value: _Learn how to write_   I = _1_   A = _0_

                                       Values-Based Action:

Enroll in community college class

4. Friends/social life   Value: _Listen_   I = _1_   A = _2_

                                       Values-Based Action:

Ask about what's going on, be interested. Don't interrupt or judge.

5. Physical self-care/health   Value: _Healthy stamina_   I = _1_   A = _1_

                                       Values-Based Action:

Cardio exercise 3x week

6. Family of origin   Value: _____   I = _0_   A = _0_

                                       Values-Based Action:

7. Spirituality   Value: _____   I = _0_   A = _0_

                                       Values-Based Action:

8. Community life/citizenship   Value: _Volunteering_____   I = __1__ A = __0__

   Values-Based Action:

_Help at children's school_____

9. Recreation   Value: _____   I = __0__ A = __0__

   Values-Based Action:

_____

10. Work/career   Value: _Support co-workers____   I = __2__ A = __2__

   Values-Based Action:

_Ask how their projects are going_____

_____

Emotion Efficacy Therapy (EET) © 2016

Benefits of Values-Based Action Worksheet

Now that you've identified your values—and you understand that the moment of choice presents an opportunity to make a helpful decision about how to respond in an emotion-filled situation—let's explore possible reactions. Answer the following questions about your values, your intentions, and your actions around your values.

How does values-based action affect my relationships with friends and family?

_____

How does values-based action affect my relationship with my spouse or partner, or my living situation?

_____

How does values-based action affect my relationships when I am emotionally triggered?

_____

How does values-based action affect my work or school?

_____

How does values-based action affect my financial situation?

_____

How does values-based action affect my health?

_____

How does values-based action affect my long-term goals?

_____

How does values-based action affect my safety and security?

_____

_____

Emotion Efficacy Therapy (EET) © 2016

Session 3 Skills Practice

_____ Practice mindful acceptance for at least 10 minutes a day by observing and accepting the four components of emotion when you get emotionally triggered, or using emotion exposure to a difficult event, situation, or emotion. Observe all four parts of the emotion, and surf the emotion wave. (Refer to the mindful acceptance directions from Session 2 Skills Practice, if needed.) Record your mindful acceptance skills practice in the first row of your Skills Practice Record.

_____ Practice using values-based action with imaginal exposure by taking the following five steps:

Step 1: Identify the value and the VBA for the distressing situation you want to work with.

Step 2: Imagine the distressing situation and describe it to yourself until you are activated and you have reached your target SUDS level.

Step 3: Practice mindful acceptance (observe + accept all parts of the emotion: thoughts, feelings, sensations, and urges), and locate the moment of choice.

Step 4: Note your SUDS level, and visualize enacting your VBA for 3 to 5 minutes.

Step 5: Record your SUDS level at the end of your exercise. Record your skills practice on the third row of your Skills Practice Record.

_____ Record any events that trigger you during the week at the bottom of your Skills Practice Record.

_____ Bring all of these materials to review in your next session.

Skills Practice Record

Emotion Efficacy Therapy

Directions: Place a check mark next to the skill you practice each day. Record any triggers at the bottom. Bring this record to your next session.

	Day 1	Day 2	Day 3	Day 4	Day 5	Day 6	Day 7
Observe the four parts of an emotion: sensations, feelings, thoughts, and urges.							
Observe, accept, and surf your emotion wave, with SUDS.							
Observe, accept, and choose a values-based action.							
Observe, accept, and choose a relaxation skill.							
Observe, accept, and choose a self-soothing skill.							
Observe, accept, and choose a coping thought.							
Observe, accept, and choose to practice radical acceptance.							
Observe, accept, and choose a distraction task or activity.							
Observe, accept, and choose a time-out.							

Emotional triggers: Record any events or emotions that are distressing during this week.

_____

_____

_____

EET Session 4: O + A + Choose VBA

Components Covered: Values-Based Action Part 2 and Exposure-Based Skills Training (Chapter 6)

Session 4 is the second of two sessions focused on values-based action. Using a group experiential exposure, Monsters on the Bus, clients drill down further on the experience of accepting difficult emotions and tolerating their distress in order to choose values-based action. The consequences of choosing to avoid painful emotions are highlighted to increase willingness and motivation for clients to choose VBAs in the moment of choice. Group members continue working with VBA using imaginal exposure as well as in vivo.

Materials

- Script for Guided Mindful Acceptance

- Session 4 Skills Practice handout

- Skills Practice Record

Overview

1. Mindful acceptance practice and feedback

2. Skills practice review

3. Monsters on the Bus exercise

4. VBA using imaginal exposure and feedback

5. Session 4 skills assignment

Procedures

1. Mindful acceptance practice and feedback

For the first ten minutes of session, lead group members through mindful acceptance practice using the guided script. Ask clients to provide feedback about their experience as an opportunity for learning and troubleshooting.

2. Skills practice review

Briefly review Session 3 skills and ask group members to share feedback about their weekly practice using their Skills Practice Record.

3. Monsters on the Bus exercise

First, ask a group member to volunteer for the exercise; the client will be working with values-based action and the barriers that show up when trying to choose VBA.

Next, ask the volunteer to choose a situation from one of his or her life domains that is distressing. Then have the volunteer identify what value he or she would like to express in the situation. Make sure that the value is rated as very important to ensure the likelihood that group members will be motivated to try a new behavior.

Ask the volunteer to identify the values-based action that could be enacted to move in the direction of his or her value in that particular domain, and help the volunteer be very specific about how the VBA would be enacted in the situation.

Ask the volunteer what emotional barriers come up when he or she visualizes enacting a VBA. Make a list of all the barriers—thoughts, feelings, sensations, and urges—writing each one on its own piece of paper. These pieces of paper will represent the "monsters" for the exercise. If you have time and are so inclined, you can even draw a picture of the monster for each emotional barrier.

Instruct the volunteer to stand up at one end of the room. Place a sheet of paper with the VBA written on it at the other end, so that it's visible to the volunteer. Place the pieces of paper with the emotional components, which serve as the "monsters," in any order in a row between the volunteer and the VBA.

Tell the volunteer that you will be going on the journey as his or her guide toward the VBA. Explain that the volunteer will be driving a bus in the direction of his or her VBA, and along the way he or she will encounter "monsters"—the barriers to reaching his or her VBA. Let the volunteer know that, while you are guiding him or her, he or she is in complete control of what he or she chooses to do along the way.

Ask for more volunteers from the group to act as the barriers, or "monsters." Explain to them that, when you cue them, they should come and stand in front of the volunteer driving the bus and say their line. For example, if the barrier identified was the thought "I will never be good enough," have a volunteer say that. Or if the barrier is a feeling of anxiety, have another volunteer say, "You're feeling anxious." If the barrier is a sensation, have an additional volunteer say what it is, for example, "tingling in the fingers" or "hot flashes."

Take the first volunteer—now the bus driver—on the journey, and when he or she encounters a monster, ask the bus driver how he or she can get past the monster. The rule is that the monster will not let the bus by, and the only choices are: veer off the path and onto the road to emotion avoidance, or let the monster on the bus and keep driving.

At each barrier, or monster, ask the driver if he or she wants to stay on the path to his or her VBA or veer off and onto the road to emotion avoidance. At least once, if the driver doesn't choose it, suggest to the client that he or she might take the path to emotion avoidance to see what it's like.

When the driver does choose the path to emotion avoidance, guide the driver to the side and ask him or her to take a moment to experience the pros and cons of emotion avoidance. If the client is able to recognize the consequences of avoiding, he or she will choose to get back on the values-based path.

Once the client has successfully made it to his or her value, take a moment to review how being able to choose values-based action means being clear on what it is for that situation, and then being willing to experience all the uncomfortable emotions while moving in a valued direction.

For a more detailed therapist-client dialogue, refer to the Therapist-Client Dialogue Example: Monsters on the Bus, in chapter 6.

If you have time, repeat the Monsters on the Bus exercise a second or third time, trying to involve each group member in either the bus driver or monster roles. After each experiential, ask if group members learned anything about their relationship with their emotions from the exercise.

4. VBA using imaginal exposure and feedback

For the session exposure practice, repeat imaginal exposure + VBA using the following guide:

Step 1: Select a distressing situation. Ask clients to describe a recent distressing event in which they became emotionally triggered and responded with experiential avoidance or other emotion-driven behavior. Check in to be sure each client has identified a situation to work with before moving forward.

Step 2: Identify the value and the VBA. Explore which of the clients' values relate to the situation they have chosen. Then prompt clients to identify a specific VBA that they would have preferred to enact. You'll want to get the clients to articulate exactly what this alternative behavior would look like—everything the clients say and do, including tone of voice and body language.

Step 3: Visualize enacting the VBA. Have the clients briefly visualize using the values-based action, mentally rehearsing the scene several times until they are clear about what they will do.

Step 4: O+A+C. Begin the exposure by having clients form a clear image of the triggering scene. Encourage them to notice the environment where the trigger occurred: watch the action in the scene, hear what's said, feel whatever physical sensations are part of the scene, notice if there's an urge to do something or not to do something. As the clients become emotionally activated, ask them to continue to describe the sensations, thoughts, feelings, and urges that come up. Encourage an accepting attitude whereby the client "makes room" for the emotion, allowing it to be what it is with no effort at controlling or avoiding it.

While still visualizing the triggering event, have the clients observe any action urges that arise. Is there a desire to be verbally aggressive, to withdraw, to stonewall, to be defensive? Have the clients describe such urges and notice that the urges don't have to become action. This is the moment of choice, and it's important for the clients to stay with it for several minutes: observing the emotional pain, accepting and allowing the pain to be there without avoidance, and choosing not to act on emotion-driven urges.

Step 5: Imaginal exposure with VBA. Now that your clients have identified the moment of choice, check for SUDS and introduce the values-based action as a guided visualization. Ask your clients to continue the distressing scene, and, instead of imagining the emotion-driven behavior that accompanied the actual scene, have them visualize the alternative VBA they rehearsed earlier. As noted before, encourage clients to watch themselves saying and/or doing the new behavior, with tone of voice and posture matching the VBA. For the next three to five minutes, have clients repeat this visualization, moving from the triggering scene (and the moment of choice) through the new values-based responses several times. Ask clients to rate their SUDS at the end. The entire exposure sequence— O+A+C + values-based action—should last eight to ten minutes.

Step 6: Learning consolidation. Consolidate what the clients have learned through a brief conversation. Did observing and accepting the target emotion decrease their distress? What did they observe about the moment of choice? How did visualizing an alternate response (VBA) impact them? Did it reduce their distress? Increase their distress tolerance? Did it increase confidence that the client could choose VBAs in distressing situations?

5. Session 4 skills assignment

Your clients have now had two sessions on values-based action and may be ready to practice in vivo. Invite them to think of a situation that is going to present itself in the week ahead. Ask them to consider practicing mindful acceptance and then choosing a VBA when they get triggered.

Remind clients that they have the Exposure with Values-Based Action handout to help them practice this skill again between sessions.

Script for Guided Mindful Acceptance

For the next ten minutes I'm going to lead you through a mindful acceptance practice exercise. You will practice observing and accepting your emotional experience in the present moment. Practicing mindful acceptance in a neutral state will build your emotion efficacy muscle and make it easier for you to use this skill when you are triggered.

First, just sit comfortably, and either close your eyes or relax your gaze and pick a spot to focus on in front of you.

Now, take a few minutes to notice any sensations in your body. Scan your body until you find a sensation and rest your attention on it. See if you can let it be just as it is and get curious about it. Notice its size and shape; whether it's moving or staying the same; if there's any temperature or tension to it. See if you can soften to it, or even lean into the sensation...

Now, see if you can identify a feeling label that goes with the sensation... just name it and allow it to be as it is without judgment or reacting to it.

Next, we'll spend a few minutes just noticing and watching our thoughts. Our brains produce different kinds of thoughts all the time, and the key is not to get involved with them. Instead, as each thought arises, you can simply say, "There's a thought," and then let the thought go. Then, just return to the present moment, and wait for the next thought to arise. For the next few minutes, notice your thoughts until I say stop...

Okay, now stop. Next, see if there's an urge that goes with your sensations or thoughts. It could be an urge to do something or not do something. Try to just sit with the urge. Notice what it's like not to act on the urge, to just surf it.

[Allow the client to sit with the urge for 30 seconds. Then repeat the sequence one more time.]

Before you come out of this exercise, take a few deep breaths and slowly open your eyes as you bring your attention back to the room.

Session 4 Skills Practice

_____ Practice mindful acceptance for at least 10 minutes a day by observing and accepting the four components of emotion when you get emotionally triggered, or using emotion exposure to a difficult event, situation, or emotion. Observe all four parts of the emotion, and surf the emotion wave. (Refer to the mindful acceptance directions from Session 2 Skills Practice, if needed.) Record your mindful acceptance skills practice in the first row of your Skills Practice Record.

_____ Using the Exposure with Values-Based Action handout, practice using VBA with imaginal exposure or in vivo by taking the following steps:

Step 1: Identify the value and the VBA for the distressing situation you want to work with.

Step 2: Imagine the distressing situation and describe it to yourself until you are activated and you have reached your target SUDS level.

Step 3: Practice mindful acceptance (observe + accept all parts of the emotion: thoughts, feelings, sensations, and urges), and locate the moment of choice.

Step 4: Note your SUDS level, and visualize enacting your VBA for 3 to 5 minutes.

Step 5: Record your SUDS level at the end of your exercise. Record your skills practice on the third row of your Skills Practice Record.

_____ Record any events that trigger you during the week at the bottom of your Skills Practice Record.

_____ Bring all of these materials to review in your next session.

Skills Practice Record

Emotion Efficacy Therapy

Directions: Place a check mark next to the skill you practice each day. Record any triggers at the bottom. Bring this record to your next session.

	Day 1	Day 2	Day 3	Day 4	Day 5	Day 6	Day 7
Observe the four parts of an emotion: sensations, feelings, thoughts, and urges.							
Observe, accept, and surf your emotion wave, with SUDS.							
Observe, accept, and choose a values-based action.							
Observe, accept, and choose a relaxation skill.							
Observe, accept, and choose a self-soothing skill.							
Observe, accept, and choose a coping thought.							
Observe, accept, and choose to practice radical acceptance.							
Observe, accept, and choose a distraction task or activity.							
Observe, accept, and choose a time-out.							

Emotional triggers: Record any events or emotions that are distressing during this week.

_____

_____

_____

Emotion Efficacy Therapy (EET) © 2016

EET Session 5: O + A + Choose Mindful Coping

Components Covered: Mindful Coping Through Relaxation, Self-Soothing, and Exposure-Based Skills Practice (Chapter 7)

Session 5 introduces the last EET component, mindful coping. Unlike mindful acceptance and values-based action, mindful coping is only used when clients have tried to observe and accept painful emotions (mindful acceptance), and/or have attempted to choose a values-based action, but are too overwhelmed to execute them effectively. Instead, mindful coping skills are intended to facilitate a decrease in emotion activation. In this session, clients learn how to use relaxation and self-soothing to downregulate emotion. These mindful coping skills are practiced using emotion exposure in session, with time for feedback and troubleshooting.

Materials

- Script for Guided Mindful Acceptance

- Mindful Coping Through Relaxation handout

- Mindful Coping Through Self-Soothing handout

- Session 5 Skills Practice handout

- Skills Practice Record

Overview

1. Mindful acceptance practice and feedback

2. Skills practice review

3. Psychoeducation on mindful coping

4. Introduction to relaxation and self-soothing

5. Relaxation skills practice with emotion exposure and feedback

6. Self-soothing skills practice with emotion exposure and feedback

7. Skills practice assignment

Procedures

1. Mindful acceptance practice and feedback

For the first ten minutes of session, lead group members through mindful acceptance practice using the guided script. Ask clients to provide feedback about their experience as an opportunity for learning and troubleshooting.

2. Skills practice review

Briefly review Session 4 skills and ask clients to share feedback about their weekly practice using their Skills Practice Record.

3. Psychoeducation on mindful coping

Mindful coping skills are used in combination with mindful acceptance and only when necessary—when clients are unable to choose a VBA or recover through the practice of mindful acceptance alone. Emphasize to clients that the goal of EET is to help them be more powerful when facing and tolerating difficult emotions and still move in the direction of their values; mindful coping skills are used only in crisis situations to help regulate their emotions when they are flooded, so they can recover enough to choose a VBA.

4. Introduction to relaxation and self-soothing

Relaxation and self-soothing skills work by using somatic stimulation and intention to decrease emotional activation. By learning how to intentionally let go of tension, and/or create pleasurable sensations in the body, clients learn to use relaxation and self-soothing to downshift emotion.

5. Relaxation skills practice with emotion exposure and feedback

Lead your clients through emotion exposure by selecting one of the relaxation skills on the Mindful Coping Through Relaxation handout, and then follow the step-by-step guide below. Be sure to leave at least ten minutes for feedback and troubleshooting after the exposure.

Step 1: Identify the relaxation skill. Prompt clients to identify the relaxation skill they want to use in the moment of choice.

Step 2: Select a distressing situation. Ask clients to identify a recent distressing event in which they became emotionally triggered and responded with experiential avoidance or other emotion-driven behavior. Check in to be sure each client has identified a situation to work with before moving forward.

Step 3: Initiate emotion exposure. Prompt clients to close their eyes or pick a spot to focus on in front of them while visualizing the triggering scene they have chosen, noticing the environment where the trigger occurred: watch the action in the scene; hear what's said. After a few minutes, have clients rate their SUDS and indicate emotional activation by raising their hand.

Step 4: Initiate the practice of mindful acceptance. Instruct clients to practice observing and accepting the emotion, "making room" for any thoughts, sensations, feelings, or urges, allowing the emotion to be what it is with no effort at controlling or avoiding them. Have clients rate their SUDS before you move into the next step.

Step 5: Guide clients through the skill. Now ask clients to locate their moment of choice. Then instruct them to use the relaxation skill they've chosen for the next five minutes.

Step 6: Close the exposure and consolidate learning. Ask clients to rate their final SUDS, and check in with each client to confirm that either their activation has come down or that they are able to tolerate any remaining levels of activation. Ask clients for feedback about their exposure experience, and troubleshoot what obstacles got in the way, if any, of them being able to practice mindful acceptance or using their EET skill.

6. Self-soothing skills practice with emotion exposure and feedback

Next, lead your group through emotion exposure by selecting one of the self-soothing skills on the Mindful Coping Through Self-Soothing handout and then following the step-by-step guide below. Be sure to leave at least ten minutes for feedback and troubleshooting after the exposure.

Step 1: Identify the self-soothing skill. Prompt clients to identify the self-soothing skill they want to use in the moment of choice.

Step 2: Select a distressing situation. Ask clients to identify a recent distressing event in which they became emotionally triggered and responded with experiential avoidance or other emotion-driven behavior. Check in to be sure each client has identified a situation to work with before moving forward.

Step 3: Initiate emotion exposure. Prompt clients to close their eyes or pick a spot to focus on in front of them while visualizing the triggering scene they have chosen, noticing the environment where the trigger occurred: watch the action in the scene; hear what's said. After a few minutes, have clients rate their SUDS and indicate emotional activation by raising their hand.

Step 4: Initiate the practice of mindful acceptance. Instruct clients to practice observing and accepting the emotion, "making room" for any thoughts, sensations, feelings, or urges, allowing the emotion to be what it is with no effort at controlling or avoiding them. Have clients rate their SUDS before you move into the next step.

Step 5: Guide clients through the skill. Now ask clients to locate their moment of choice. Then instruct them to use the self-soothing skill they've chosen for the next five minutes.

Step 6: Close the exposure and consolidate learning. Ask clients to rate their final SUDS, and check in with each client to confirm that either their activation has come down, or that they are able to tolerate any remaining levels of activation. Ask clients for feedback about their exposure experience, and troubleshoot what obstacles got in the way, if any, of them being able to practice mindful acceptance or using their EET skill.

7. Session 5 skills assignment

Your clients have now had their first session combining mindful acceptance and mindful coping skills. While they can still practice mindful acceptance with values-based action, invite them to try using relaxation and self-soothing skills—even if they don't feel flooded—to help them begin to internalize how to use mindful coping. This way, when they are too triggered to choose VBA, they will have had practice in an activated state.

Script for Guided Mindful Acceptance

For the next ten minutes I'm going to lead you through a mindful acceptance practice exercise. You will practice observing and accepting your emotional experience in the present moment. Practicing mindful acceptance in a neutral state will build your emotion efficacy muscle and make it easier for you to use this skill when you are triggered.

First, just sit comfortably, and either close your eyes or relax your gaze and pick a spot to focus on in front of you.

Now, take a few minutes to notice any sensations in your body. Scan your body until you find a sensation and rest your attention on it. See if you can let it be just as it is and get curious about it. Notice its size and shape; whether it's moving or staying the same; if there's any temperature or tension to it. See if you can soften to it, or even lean into the sensation…

Now, see if you can identify a feeling label that goes with the sensation…just name it and allow it to be as it is without judgment or reacting to it.

Next, we'll spend a few minutes just noticing and watching our thoughts. Our brains produce different kinds of thoughts all the time, and the key is not to get involved with them. Instead, as each thought arises, you can simply say, "There's a thought," and then let the thought go. Then, just return to the present moment, and wait for the next thought to arise. For the next few minutes, notice your thoughts until I say stop…

Okay, now stop. Next, see if there's an urge that goes with your sensations or thoughts. It could be an urge to do something or not do something. Try to just sit with the urge. Notice what it's like not to act on the urge, to just surf it.

[Allow the client to sit with the urge for 30 seconds. Then repeat the sequence one more time.]

Before you come out of this exercise, take a few deep breaths and slowly open your eyes as you bring your attention back to the room.

Emotion Efficacy Therapy (EET) © 2016

Mindful Coping Through Relaxation

When a powerful emotion has been triggered and you are suddenly facing your moment of choice, a mindful coping skill can help downregulate your emotions before you decide on a values-based action. Practice these relaxation techniques daily so that you can rely on them in your moment of choice.

Diaphragmatic Breathing

Place one hand on your abdomen, just above the belt line, and the other on your chest.

Take a slow, deep breath into the abdomen. The hand on the abdomen should move but not the hand on the chest.

If you are having difficulty pushing the breath into your abdomen (and the hand on your chest is moving), you can do one of two things:

- Press your hand into your abdomen, and then inhale so that the breath pushes your hand out.

- Lie down and put a phone book over your abdomen. Breathe so that your inhale pushes the phone book up.

Practice 15 diaphragmatic breaths three times a day.

Relaxation Without Tension

Choose a cue word. Identify a word or phrase that you associate with relaxation. This could be a color (golden light, sea blue), a place that calms you (Tuolumne, Shenandoah), a command ("relax now"), or a spiritual mantra (*om, peace on earth, I let go*). This cue word will become associated with, and soon trigger, deep relaxation.

Observe a muscle group (see next paragraph) and notice any tension. Take a deep, diaphragmatic breath. At the top of the breath, say to yourself the cue word. Now, as you exhale, relax away any tension in the target muscle group. Do this process twice with each muscle group, in any order.

The five muscle groups you will relax are:

- Face (forehead and jaw)

- Neck and shoulders

- Arms and hands

- Chest, back, abdomen

- Legs (buttocks, thighs, calves, feet)

Practice this skill three times a day.

Cue-Controlled Breathing

Use the same cue word you established with Relaxation Without Tension.

Take a deep, diaphragmatic breath. At the top of the breath, say to yourself the cue word. Now, as you exhale, relax away any tension throughout your body at once. Let your body slump forward slightly as you exhale and release all tension.

Take 15 cue-controlled breaths three times a day to practice this new skill.

Five-Senses Exercise

For 30 seconds, focus on every sound you can hear: voices, traffic noise, machinery noise such as the hum of an air conditioner, sounds of movement, sounds your body makes. Try to keep your attention fully on these sounds. If your mind wanders, gently bring it back to focusing on what you hear.

For 30 seconds focus on what you can smell: fragrances, odors, scents from your own body or the environment. Try to keep attention on what you smell; return to this focus when your mind wanders.

For 30 seconds focus on your sense of touch, including temperature and texture, noticing the pressure where your body touches the floor or chair. Return to your sense of touch when your mind wanders.

For 30 seconds focus on visual sensations, observing color and shapes, and noticing the objects in your environment. When you get distracted, bring your attention back to what you see.

For 30 seconds focus on your sense of taste. What residual tastes do you notice in your mouth—bitter, sweet, sour, salty? Are there more-subtle tastes? If you get distracted, bring your attention back to taste.

Practice this exercise twice daily as a way to focus attention away from negative thoughts and onto present-moment experience.

Emotion Efficacy Therapy (EET) © 2016

Mindful Coping Through Self-Soothing

This worksheet will help you identify some ways to soothe yourself using each of your five senses.

Sense of Smell

Using your sense of smell can activate specific thoughts, memories, or sensations that can be calming. If you identify smells that make you feel good in advance, you will be prepared to use them when triggered. Following are some examples, and feel free to add your own ideas:

_____ Burn scented candles or incense that you like.

_____ Wear scented oils, perfume, or cologne that makes you feel happy, confident, or sexy.

_____ Carry perfumed cards from magazines, or ones that you make, in your purse, wallet, or car.

_____ Go someplace where you know the scent is pleasing to you, such as a bakery or coffee shop.

_____ Lie down in a park where you can smell grass, flowers, or other outdoor smells.

_____ Buy flowers or find flowers in your neighborhood.

_____ Hug someone whose smell makes you feel calm.

_____ Other ideas: _____

Sense of Sight

Sight is an important sense for humans in that a large portion of our brain is devoted to what we see. What we look at can have powerful effects on our emotions, for better or for worse. If you identify images that make you feel good in advance, you will be prepared to use them when upset. Following are some examples, and a place for you to add your own ideas:

_____ Look online, through magazines, and in books to select pictures you like. Make a collage of them to hang on your wall, add as a screensaver on your computer, or keep with you in your purse or wallet to look at throughout the day.

_____ Find a physical place that's soothing for you to look at, like a park, a lake, a museum, or other landmark. Or take a picture of that place.

_____ Go online or to the bookstore and find a collection of photographs or paintings that you find relaxing, such as the nature photographs by Ansel Adams.

_____ Draw or paint a picture that's pleasing to you.

_____ Carry a picture of someone you love, someone you find attractive, or someone you admire.

_____ Other ideas: _____

Sense of Hearing

Certain sounds can be very soothing. For example, everyone has his or her own tastes or preferences in music. By identifying in advance songs or sounds you know are soothing for you, you will be prepared to use them to help calm down. Following are some examples, and a place for you to add your own ideas:

_____ Listen to soothing music: classical, opera, oldies, new age, Motown, jazz, emo, whatever works for you. It might be instrumental or music with singing. Go online to iTunes and listen to a variety of music to determine what helps you relax. Look for preselected compilations for relaxation and meditation.

_____ Listen to audiobooks or CDs. Many public libraries will let you check out audiobooks. Try some to see if they help you relax. You don't even have to pay attention to the story line; sometimes just listening to the sound of someone's voice can be relaxing.

_____ Watch TV or stream shows on your computer. Find a show that's boring or sedate, not anything activating, like reality TV, or that would make you angry, like the news. Keep the volume at a low level.

_____ Listen to a gentle talk-show podcast, like a gardening or music show.

_____ Listen to white noise, a fan, or sound machine. White noise is a blend of sounds that blocks out other distracting sounds. A sound machine has recorded sounds such as birds, waterfalls, wind, rain, and waves. Many people find these machines very relaxing.

_____ Listen to the sounds of rushing or trickling water. Find a personal electronic water fountain or a nearby fountain in a park or a mall.

_____ Listen to a relaxation or meditation exercise. Exercises like these help you imagine yourself relaxing in different ways.

_____ Other ideas: _____

Sense of Taste

Our tongues have distinct regions on them that use taste buds to differentiate flavors and tastes of food. These sensations can also trigger memories and feelings. By identifying tastes you know are soothing for you in advance, you will be prepared to use them to deal with upsets. Following are some examples, and a place for you to add your own ideas:

_____ Enjoy your favorite meal. Eat it slowly and mindfully so you can savor all of its various flavors.

_____ Carry gum, mints, mouth spray, or other tasty treats with you to taste when you're feeling upset.

_____ Eat a "comfort" food that's soothing to you.

_____ Drink something you find soothing, such as tea, coffee, or hot chocolate.

_____ Suck on a popsicle or ice cube, especially if you're feeling warm.

_____ Find a piece of ripe, juicy fruit and eat it slowly.

_____ Other ideas: _____

Sense of Touch

Our skin is the largest organ in the body, and it's completely covered with nerves that carry sensations to our brain. This makes skin a powerful emotional messenger. By identifying tactile sensations you know are soothing for you in advance, you will be prepared to use them to quiet your emotions. Following are some examples, and a place for you to add your own ideas:

_____ Work in the garden, touching the cool earth.

_____ Carry something soft or velvety in your pocket to touch when you're upset.

_____ Take a hot or cold shower and observe the sensations of water on your skin.

_____ Take a warm bath with bubbles or scented oil.

_____ Get a massage. If you're not comfortable taking your clothes off, look for massage types such as Shiatsu, which simply requires you to wear loose-fitting clothes. Or find a seated chair massage for a shoulder and neck rub.

_____ Massage yourself.

_____ Play with a pet—yours or someone else's. Stroking an animal's fur or skin can provide a soothing tactile experience. In fact, having a pet can have many health benefits, such as lower blood pressure, lower cholesterol levels, and reduced risk for heart disease. If you can't find a pet, visit your local animal shelter, where you can play with the rescued animals.

_____ Wear your most comfortable clothes, for instance a worn-in T-shirt, baggy sweats, and so on.

_____ Other ideas: _____

Emotion Efficacy Therapy (EET) © 2016

Session 5 Skills Practice

_____ Practice mindful acceptance for at least 10 minutes a day by observing and accepting the four components of emotion when you get emotionally triggered, or using emotion exposure to a difficult event, situation, or emotion. Observe all four parts of the emotion, and surf the emotion wave. (Refer to the mindful acceptance directions from Session 2 Skills Practice, if needed.) Record your mindful acceptance skills practice in the first row of your Skills Practice Record.

_____ Practice using relaxation or self-soothing skills with exposure, or in vivo if a situation presents itself, by taking the following steps:

Step 1: Identify a relaxation or self-soothing skill you want to practice ahead of time.

Step 2: Either find something to intentionally activate your emotions (e.g., recall a recent difficult situation or a distressing memory) or engage in a situation you know will be triggering. Pick something that you believe will take your SUDS up into the 5 to 7 range.

Step 3: Get into the scene or triggering situation until you reach your target SUDS, or until at least 5 minutes have passed.

Step 4: Practice mindful acceptance of the painful emotion (observe + accept all parts of the emotion: thoughts, feelings, sensations, and urges). Stay here for 5 minutes, if possible.

Step 5: Identify the moment of choice and apply the relaxation or self-soothing skill you've chosen. Do this for at least 5 minutes.

Step 6: Notice and record your SUDS level at the end of your exercise.

Step 7: Record your skills practice on the fourth row of your Skills Practice Record.

_____ Record any events that trigger you during the week at the bottom of your Skills Practice Record.

_____ Bring all of these materials to review in your next session.

Skills Practice Record

Emotion Efficacy Therapy

Directions: Place a check mark next to the skill you practice each day. Record any triggers at the bottom. Bring this record to your next session.

	Day 1	Day 2	Day 3	Day 4	Day 5	Day 6	Day 7
Observe the four parts of an emotion: sensations, feelings, thoughts, and urges.							
Observe, accept, and surf your emotion wave, with SUDS.							
Observe, accept, and choose a values-based action.							
Observe, accept, and choose a relaxation skill.							
Observe, accept, and choose a self-soothing skill.							
Observe, accept, and choose a coping thought.							
Observe, accept, and choose to practice radical acceptance.							
Observe, accept, and choose a distraction task or activity.							
Observe, accept, and choose a time-out.							

Emotional triggers: Record any events or emotions that are distressing during this week.

_____

_____

_____

EET Session 6: O + A + Choose Mindful Coping

Components Covered: Mindful Coping Through Coping Thoughts, Radical Acceptance, and Exposure-Based Skills Practice (Chapter 8)

Session 6 continues with mindful coping skills, to be used only when clients have tried to observe and accept painful emotions (mindful acceptance), and/or have attempted to choose a values-based action, but are too overwhelmed to execute them effectively. While the skills in Session 5 are focused on using sensations to downregulate emotion, Session 6 skills focus on using cognition to decrease emotional activation through coping thoughts and radical acceptance. These mindful coping skills are practiced using emotion exposure in session, with time for feedback and troubleshooting.

Materials

- Script for Guided Mindful Acceptance

- Client Coping Thoughts handout

- Replacing Automatic Thoughts with Coping Thoughts worksheet (blank)

- Replacing Automatic Thoughts with Coping Thoughts worksheet (Filled-Out Sample)

- The Art of Radical Acceptance handout

- Radical Acceptance worksheet

- Session 6 Skills Practice handout

- Skills Practice Record

Overview

1. Mindful acceptance practice and feedback

2. Skills practice review

3. Psychoeducation on coping thoughts

4. Coping thoughts practice with emotion exposure and feedback

5. Psychoeducation on radical acceptance

6. Radical acceptance practice with emotion exposure and feedback

7. Session 6 skills assignment

Procedures

1. Mindful acceptance practice and feedback

For the first ten minutes of session, lead group members through mindful acceptance practice using the guided script. Ask clients to provide feedback about their experience as an opportunity for learning and troubleshooting.

2. Skills practice review

Briefly review Session 5 skills and ask clients to share feedback about their weekly practice using their Skills Practice Record.

3. Psychoeducation on coping thoughts

Use the Client Coping Thoughts handout to introduce your clients to coping thoughts. Tell them how coping thoughts can be helpful in the moment of choice. Then use the worksheets to let clients create their own coping thoughts as alternatives to automatic thoughts.

4. Coping thoughts practice with emotion exposure and feedback

Lead your clients through emotion exposure with a coping thought using the following step-by-step guide. Be sure to leave at least ten minutes for feedback and troubleshooting after the exposure.

Step 1: Identify the coping thought. Prompt clients to use their Client Coping Thoughts handout to identify one they want to use in the moment of choice.

Step 2: Select a distressing situation. Ask clients to identify a recent distressing event in which they became emotionally triggered and responded with experiential avoidance or other emotion-driven behavior. Check in to be sure each client has identified a situation to work with before moving forward.

Step 3: Initiate emotion exposure. Prompt clients to close their eyes or pick a spot to focus on in front of them while visualizing the triggering scene they have chosen, noticing the environment where the trigger occurred: watch the action in the scene; hear what's said. After a few minutes, have clients rate their SUDS and indicate emotional activation by raising their hand.

Step 4: Initiate the practice of mindful acceptance. Instruct clients to practice observing and accepting the emotion, "making room" for any thoughts, sensations, feelings, or urges, allowing the emotion to be what it is with no effort at controlling or avoiding them. Have clients rate their SUDS before you move into the next step.

Step 5: Guide clients through the skill. Now ask clients to locate their moment of choice. Then instruct them to use the coping thought they've chosen for the next five minutes.

Step 6: Close the exposure and consolidate learning. Ask clients to rate their final SUDS, and check in with each client to confirm that either their activation has come down or that they are able to tolerate any remaining levels of activation. Ask clients for feedback about their exposure experience, and troubleshoot what obstacles got in the way, if any, of them being able to practice mindful acceptance or using their EET skill.

5. Psychoeducation on radical acceptance

Use the following handout to introduce your clients to radical acceptance and how it can be helpful in the moment of choice. Then have clients complete the worksheet to help them use radical acceptance with a specific situation or reality they are resisting and that is emotionally triggering for them.

6. Radical acceptance practice with emotion exposure and feedback

Lead your clients through emotion exposure with radical acceptance using the following step-by-step guide. Be sure to leave at least ten minutes for feedback and troubleshooting after the exposure.

Step 1: Identify a radical acceptance statement. Prompt clients to use the Art of Radical Acceptance handout to identify one radical acceptance statement to use in the moment of choice.

Step 2: Select a distressing situation. Ask clients to identify a recent distressing event in which they became emotionally triggered and responded with experiential avoidance or other emotion-driven behavior. Check in to be sure each client has identified a situation to work with before moving forward.

Step 3: Initiate emotion exposure. Prompt clients to close their eyes or pick a spot to focus on in front of them while visualizing the triggering scene they have chosen, noticing the environment where the trigger occurred: watch the action in the scene; hear what's said. After a few minutes, have clients rate their SUDS and indicate emotional activation by raising their hand.

Step 4: Initiate the practice of mindful acceptance. Instruct clients to practice observing and accepting the emotion, "making room" for any thoughts, sensations, feelings, or urges, allowing the emotion to be what it is with no effort at controlling or avoiding them. Have clients rate their SUDS before you move into the next step.

Step 5: Guide clients through the skill. Now ask clients to locate their moment of choice. Then instruct them to use the radical acceptance statement they've chosen for the next five minutes.

Step 6: Close the exposure and consolidate learning. Ask clients to rate their final SUDS, and check in with each client to confirm that either their activation has come down or that they are able to tolerate any remaining levels of activation. Ask clients for feedback about their exposure experience, and troubleshoot what obstacles got in the way, if any, of them being able to practice mindful acceptance or use their EET skill.

7. Session 6 skills assignment

Your clients' focus this week should be on practicing mindful acceptance with coping thoughts and radical acceptance. Again, they can still practice mindful acceptance with values-based action, but invite them to try using coping thoughts and radical acceptance—even if they don't feel flooded—to help them begin to internalize how to use mindful coping.

Script for Guided Mindful Acceptance

For the next ten minutes I'm going to lead you through a mindful acceptance practice exercise. You will practice observing and accepting your emotional experience in the present moment. Practicing mindful acceptance in a neutral state will build your emotion efficacy muscle and make it easier for you to use this skill when you are triggered.

First, just sit comfortably, and either close your eyes or relax your gaze and pick a spot to focus on in front of you.

Now, take a few minutes to notice any sensations in your body. Scan your body until you find a sensation and rest your attention on it. See if you can let it be just as it is and get curious about it. Notice its size and shape; whether it's moving or staying the same; if there's any temperature or tension to it. See if you can soften to it, or even lean into the sensation…

Now, see if you can identify a feeling label that goes with the sensation…just name it and allow it to be as it is without judgment or reacting to it.

Next, we'll spend a few minutes just noticing and watching our thoughts. Our brains produce different kinds of thoughts all the time, and the key is not to get involved with them. Instead, as each thought arises, you can simply say, "There's a thought," and then let the thought go. Then, just return to the present moment, and wait for the next thought to arise. For the next few minutes, notice your thoughts until I say stop…

Okay, now stop. Next, see if there's an urge that goes with your sensations or thoughts. It could be an urge to do something or not do something. Try to just sit with the urge. Notice what it's like not to act on the urge, to just surf it.

[Allow the client to sit with the urge for 30 seconds. Then repeat the sequence one more time.]

Before you come out of this exercise, take a few deep breaths and slowly open your eyes as you bring your attention back to the room.

Emotion Efficacy Therapy (EET) © 2016

Client Coping Thoughts

Coping thoughts can be used when you are facing a difficult emotion. They may be especially helpful after you've practiced observing and accepting the difficult emotion, and you're still struggling with specific ruminations, or a repetitive automatic thought is fueling your emotion wave.

You now know that your emotions will follow whatever you pay attention to. If you're triggered, you're likely to have negative automatic thoughts. One way to tolerate the distress and shift your emotion is to replace the negative automatic thought with a coping thought. The key with a coping thought is that you believe it to be true and realistic. If you don't believe the thought, it's unlikely to be effective.

Following are some examples of coping thoughts:

"This situation won't last forever."

"I can feel anxious/sad/angry without reacting."

"I can tolerate this emotion until the wave goes down."

"This emotion won't kill me, it just doesn't feel good right now."

"I've dealt with this situation before, and I can do it again."

"I can take all the time I need to just let go and relax."

"I can let this emotion run the show, or I can use values-based action."

"Just because I feel this emotion, doesn't mean I have to act on it."

"I am not my emotions… I can choose my next action."

Replacing Automatic Thoughts with Coping Thoughts

Use this worksheet to record specific triggers, the automatic thoughts that go with them, and alternative coping thoughts with which you can replace them.

Trigger	Automatic Thought	Coping Thought
1.	1.	1.
2.	2.	2.
3.	3.	3.
4.	4.	4.
5.	5.	5.

Replacing Automatic Thoughts with Coping Thoughts

(Client Sample)

Trigger	Automatic Thought	Coping Thought
1. Turning in a project to my boss.	1. My work isn't as good as it should be.	1. I'm doing my best, which is all I can do.
2. Being at a party with people I don't know.	2. If I don't say the right thing at this party, people are going to think I'm a loser.	2. I can have this thought without acting on it.
3. My wife comes home and goes straight to the bedroom.	3. My wife doesn't love me anymore.	3. My defectiveness schema is talking, but I'm not listening.
4. Anytime…… …	4. Something's wrong with me.	4. I have strengths and weaknesses, just like everybody else.
5. My boss doesn't talk to me at the office-wide lunch.	5. My boss doesn't like me.	5. It's not my job to be liked. It's my job to do my job.

The Art of Radical Acceptance

What It Is

Part of successfully navigating intense emotions is knowing when it's time to try to improve your situation and when it's time to accept it. *Radical acceptance* is another mindful coping skill that allows you to accept "what is" and stop suffering from rejecting the reality in front of you. We have a choice in every moment: to reject the reality of what is or to accept it. The choice we make will determine whether we continue to suffer or create space for something else to exist.

Our natural response to distressing emotions is to fight against the reality that we think caused them. In doing this, we can make ourselves and others miserable. Choosing radical acceptance—to accept "what is"—is a huge shift for most people. It feels like the opposite of what your emotions urge you to do when you encounter pain.

What It's Not

Radical acceptance does not mean you like or condone what happened. It just means that you accept the reality that it happened. In other words, some situations in life are simply unjust or unfair. In other situations, you may share responsibility for what happened. Either way, just because you accept that it happened doesn't mean you're condoning it.

The more you practice radical acceptance, the easier it will become to stop resisting what you cannot change.

Following are a few examples of radical acceptance:

"My girlfriend broke up with me, but it doesn't mean I have to retaliate or try to win her love back."

"I have suicidal thoughts all the time, but that doesn't mean I like having them or that I will act on them."

"I didn't set a reminder to pay that phone bill, so I will have to take responsibility for the consequences."

Radical acceptance requires a willingness to look at things differently. Sometimes our disappointments and moments of frustration were preventable. We can also practice radical acceptance by accepting what we might have done differently, and taking responsibility for how we didn't. For example, could you have prevented being late to an appointment, forgetting to do work assignments, or behaving in a way that was less than stellar? Moreover, could you have prevented lying to hurt someone or allowing yourself to be motivated by hate? Many times we have culpability in "what is." Accepting that is key to practicing radical acceptance.

While the outcomes of these situations may have serious consequences, they can also be opportunities for growth if you can view them as moments of learning. Often people who struggle with intense emotions believe that life is something that "happens" to them, instead of recognizing their own power in creating their experience.

The good news is that if we have responsibility in the things happening, we also have the power to make different choices—choices that can alleviate suffering and bring us closer to living the life we want in accordance with our values.

Radical Acceptance

Assessing the Situation

Think of a situation you have no control over, but about which you struggle to accept. Then answer the following questions:

Describe briefly the distressing situation:

What past events led to the situation?

What role, if any, did you play in creating the situation?

What roles, if any, did others play in the situation?

What do you have control of in this situation?

What do you *not* have control of in this situation?

What was your response to this situation?

How did your response affect your own thoughts and feelings?

How did your response affect the thoughts and feelings of others?

How could you have changed your response to this situation so that it led to less suffering for yourself and others?

How could the situation have occurred differently if you had chosen to radically accept the situation?

How to Practice Radical Acceptance

Once you've identified the situation and have a clear understanding of it, you can use these steps to practice radical acceptance during imaginal exposure or when you get upset.

1. Recognize your resistance to the reality of "what is."

2. Practice mindful acceptance of the emotion that goes with the situation or reality. Using the four components of emotion, make room for all your thoughts, feelings, sensations, and urges, allowing them to be there without reacting or acting on them.

3. Stop resisting by reminding yourself of the facts, such as: "This is just the way it is, I can't change it" or "I have to accept the consequences of my actions."

Emotion Efficacy Therapy (EET) © 2016

Session 6 Skills Practice

_____ Practice mindful acceptance for at least 10 minutes a day by observing and accepting the four components of emotion when you get emotionally triggered, or using emotion exposure to a difficult event, situation, or emotion. Observe all four parts of the emotion, and surf the emotion wave. (Refer to the mindful acceptance directions from Session 2 Skills Practice, if needed.) Record your mindful acceptance skills practice in the first row of your Skills Practice Record.

_____ Practice using coping thoughts or radical acceptance with exposure or in vivo by taking the following steps:

Step 1: Identify a coping thought or a radical acceptance skill you want to practice ahead of time.

Step 2: Either find something to intentionally activate your emotions (e.g., recall a recent difficult situation or a distressing memory) or engage in a situation you know will be triggering. Pick something that you believe will take your SUDS up into the 5 to 7 range.

Step 3: Get into the scene or triggering situation until you reach your target SUDS, or until at least 5 minutes have passed.

Step 4: Practice mindful acceptance of the painful emotion (observe + accept all parts of the emotion: thoughts, feelings, sensations, and urges). Stay here for 5 minutes, if possible.

Step 5: Identify the moment of choice and apply the coping thought or radical acceptance skill you've chosen. Do this for at least 5 minutes.

Step 6: Notice and record your SUDS level at the end of your exercise.

Step 7: Record your skills practice on the fourth row of your Skills Practice Record.

_____ Record any events that trigger you during the week at the bottom of your Skills Practice Record.

_____ Bring all of these materials to review in your next session.

Skills Practice Record

Emotion Efficacy Therapy

Directions: Place a check mark next to the skill you practice each day. Record any triggers at the bottom. Bring this record to your next session.

	Day 1	Day 2	Day 3	Day 4	Day 5	Day 6	Day 7
Observe the four parts of an emotion: sensations, feelings, thoughts, and urges.							
Observe, accept, and surf your emotion wave, with SUDS.							
Observe, accept, and choose a values-based action.							
Observe, accept, and choose a relaxation skill.							
Observe, accept, and choose a self-soothing skill.							
Observe, accept, and choose a coping thought.							
Observe, accept, and choose to practice radical acceptance.							
Observe, accept, and choose a distraction task or activity.							
Observe, accept, and choose a time-out.							

Emotional triggers: Record any events or emotions that are distressing during this week.

_____

_____

_____

Emotion Efficacy Therapy (EET) © 2016

EET Session 7: O + A + Choose Mindful Coping

Components Covered: Mindful Coping Through Distraction and Exposure-Based Skills Practice (Chapter 9)

Session 7 completes mindful coping skills with the final skills: distraction and time-out. Distraction focuses on shifting attention of present-moment awareness away from the distressing stimulus or emotion to something that has more positive affect to downregulate emotion. Distraction is practiced using imaginal exposure in session, as well as in vivo, with time for feedback and troubleshooting.

Materials

- Script for Guided Mindful Acceptance

- Before You Act, Distract handout

- Distraction Strategies worksheet

- Take a Time-Out handout

- Emotion Efficacy Therapy Skills handout

- Personalized Emotion Efficacy Plan worksheet

- Session 7 skills practice handout

- Skills Practice Record

Overview

1. Mindful acceptance practice and feedback

2. Skills practice review

3. Psychoeducation on distraction and time-out

4. Distraction with imaginal or emotion exposure and feedback

5. Introduction to personalized emotion efficacy plan

6. Skills practice assignments

Procedures

1. Mindful acceptance practice and feedback

For the first ten minutes of session, lead clients through mindful acceptance practice using the guided script. Ask clients to provide feedback about their experience as an opportunity for learning and troubleshooting.

2. Skills practice review

Briefly review Session 6 skills and ask clients to share feedback about their weekly practice using their Skills Practice Record.

3. Psychoeducation on distraction and time-out

Use the following handouts to introduce clients to the mindful coping skills of distraction and time-out.

4. Distraction with imaginal or emotion exposure and feedback

Lead your clients through emotion exposure with distraction using the following step-by-step guide. Be sure to leave at least ten minutes for feedback and troubleshooting after the exposure.

Step 1: Identify a distraction. Prompt clients to use the Distraction Strategies handout to identify one task or activity they want to use in the moment of choice.

Step 2: Select a distressing situation. Ask clients to identify a recent distressing event in which they became emotionally triggered and responded with experiential avoidance or other emotion-driven behavior. Check in to be sure each client has identified a situation to work with before moving forward.

Step 3: Initiate emotion exposure. Prompt clients to close their eyes or pick a spot to focus on in front of them while visualizing the triggering scene they have chosen, noticing the environment where the trigger occurred: watch the action in the scene; hear what's said. After a few minutes, have clients rate their SUDS and indicate emotional activation by raising their hand.

Step 4: Initiate the practice of mindful acceptance. Instruct clients to practice observing and accepting the emotion, "making room" for any thoughts, sensations, feelings, or urges, allowing the emotion to be what it is with no effort at controlling or avoiding them. Have clients rate their SUDS before you move into the next step.

Step 5: Guide clients through the skill. Now ask clients to locate their moment of choice. Then instruct them to use the distraction skill they've chosen for the next five minutes.

Step 6: Close the exposure and consolidate learning. Ask clients to rate their final SUDS, and check in with each client to confirm that either their activation has come down or that they are able to tolerate any remaining levels of activation. Ask clients for feedback about their exposure experience, and troubleshoot what obstacles got in the way, if any, of them being able to practice mindful acceptance or using their EET skill.

5. Introduction to Personalized Emotion Efficacy Plan

The Personalized Emotion Efficacy Plan is intended to help clients review and consolidate what they've learned. Having a plan written down will assist with this, giving them something to refer to after treatment has ended to practice and to prevent relapse. Encourage clients to take time to think about what has worked for them and what they want to continue to work on, as well as any questions they have about skills that were more difficult for them.

6. Session 7 skills assignment

Clients will practice mindful acceptance with distraction. As with previous weeks, invite them to try using distraction—even if they don't feel flooded—to help them begin to internalize how to use mindful coping.

Clients will also review all the EET skills they've learned and complete the Personalized Emotion Efficacy Plan worksheet, which you'll review in Session 8.

Script for Guided Mindful Acceptance

For the next ten minutes I'm going to lead you through a mindful acceptance practice exercise. You will practice observing and accepting your emotional experience in the present moment. Practicing mindful acceptance in a neutral state will build your emotion efficacy muscle and make it easier for you to use this skill when you are triggered.

First, just sit comfortably, and either close your eyes or relax your gaze and pick a spot to focus on in front of you.

Now, take a few minutes to notice any sensations in your body. Scan your body until you find a sensation and rest your attention on it. See if you can let it be just as it is and get curious about it. Notice its size and shape; whether it's moving or staying the same; if there's any temperature or tension to it. See if you can soften to it, or even lean into the sensation…

Now, see if you can identify a feeling label that goes with the sensation…just name it and allow it to be as it is without judgment or reacting to it.

Next, we'll spend a few minutes just noticing and watching our thoughts. Our brains produce different kinds of thoughts all the time, and the key is not to get involved with them. Instead, as each thought arises, you can simply say, "There's a thought," and then let the thought go. Then, just return to the present moment, and wait for the next thought to arise. For the next few minutes, notice your thoughts until I say stop…

Okay, now stop. Next, see if there's an urge that goes with your sensations or thoughts. It could be an urge to do something or not do something. Try to just sit with the urge. Notice what it's like not to act on the urge, to just surf it.

[Allow the client to sit with the urge for 30 seconds. Then repeat the sequence one more time.]

Before you come out of this exercise, take a few deep breaths and slowly open your eyes as you bring your attention back to the room.

Before You Act, Distract

Emotions mirror what we pay attention to. If we pay attention to people, things, or situations that anger or upset us, our feelings will reflect that. And the intensity of those emotions can make it hard to act on our values. If we switch attention to something else, our feelings will reflect the new experience we've chosen. We have the power to shift how we feel by shifting our attention. There are several benefits from using distraction:

You're less likely to be swept into destructive, emotion-driven behaviors.

Your upset is likely to subside more quickly than if you act on your emotion.

You're more likely to feel able to act on your values.

Avoiding Avoidance

Sometimes it's hard to tell if you're using mindful coping to avoid your emotions or to move in the direction of your values. If you're not sure, you can ask yourself this basic question: "Am I using this skill to move toward my values or to avoid my emotion?" Using distraction after you observe and accept your emotional experience can be a life-improving, values-consistent choice in situations when you're getting overwhelmed and need to "downshift" an emotion wave.

Mindful Coping with Distraction

Follow these steps for mindful distraction:

Step 1: **Select a triggering event.** Visualize an upsetting event until you are at the target level of arousal (usually 5 to 6 SUDS).

Step 2: **Observe and accept.** Observe and accept the sensations, emotions, and urges that come up for at least 5 minutes. Make room for all the experience.

Step 3: **Choose distraction.** Begin using a distraction technique of your choice for at least 5 minutes. You may also choose additional distraction strategies, if you want.

Remember, if you experience a strong, painful emotion in the course of daily life, you can do one of two things: You can stay with the feeling, noticing the moment of choice, and responding with a values-based action. Or, if the pain is pushing you hard toward emotion-driven behavior and you can't muster a values-based response, you can mindfully choose distraction (or any of the other mindful coping skills).

Distraction Strategies

The following handout will help you identify mindful coping ideas to distract yourself when you have already tried to use mindful acceptance and/or values-based action and are still feeling triggered.

Pay Attention to Someone Else

One effective way to shift your attention when you are emotionally triggered is to place your attention on someone else. Following are some examples of how you might do this, as well as a space for your own ideas:

_____ Call your friends and ask if they need help doing something, such as a chore, grocery shopping, or housecleaning.

_____ Ask any family members who live nearby if you can assist them with something: running errands, yard work, babysitting, walking the dog, etc.

_____ Call your local soup kitchen, homeless shelter, volunteer organization, or advocacy group and sign up to help.

_____ Bake cookies for a neighbor or coworker.

_____ Send a "just because" card to someone you haven't talked to in a while.

_____ Write a thank-you email to someone who did something kind for you.

_____ Write a handwritten letter to someone who has changed your life for the better and tell him or her why.

_____ Make a list of people you admire and want to be like and write down why.

_____ People-watch. Go to a local store, shopping center, bookstore, or park and notice what other people do, how they dress. Listen to their conversations. Observe as many details about other people as you can.

_____ Play counting games while people-watching, for example, count the number of blue-eyed people versus brown-eyed people you see.

_____ Think about someone you care about. What do you imagine he or she is doing right now?

_____ Keep a picture of those you love in your wallet or purse. These people can range from family members to friends to public figures you admire. Look at the photo whenever you need comfort.

_____ Imagine having a healing, peaceful conversation with someone you deeply care about or admire. What would he or she say to you that would help you feel better? Imagine him or her saying this to you.

_____ Other ideas: _____

Pay Attention to Something Else

Our brains are amazing thinking machines. They produce millions of thoughts every day. Our emotions follow what we think about, and you can intentionally shift your thoughts when you're triggered to decrease your emotional activation. Following are some examples of how you might do this, as well as a space for your own ideas:

_____ Pay attention to the natural world around you. Observe the flowers, trees, sky, and landscape as closely as possible. Observe any animals that are around. Listen to all the sounds around you. Or, if you live in a city without much nature, observe what you can see and hear.

_____ Keep a copy of your favorite prayer or saying with you. When you feel distressed, read it to yourself. Imagine the words calming and soothing you. Use imagery (such as white light coming down from the sky) to soothe you as you read the words.

_____ Walk around your neighborhood or a park and notice the scenery, the colors, the textures of your surroundings.

_____ Listen to music that's pleasing to you. Also try listening to new music: from a different genre or from another country.

_____ Listen to an engaging audiobook. Close your eyes and really try to pay attention.

_____ Watch a TV show or movie you know will hold your attention and take your focus off yourself. Think about whether you would have written a different plot or ending.

_____ Learn a new language.

_____ Learn how to play a musical instrument.

_____ Write a letter to God or your higher power.

_____ Write in your journal.

_____ Other ideas: _____

Be Productive

Many people don't schedule time to take care of themselves or their living environments. Doing tasks and chores can be an effective way to shift your attention away from your distress. Following are some examples, and a place for you to add your own ideas:

_____ Make a to-do list.

_____ Wash the dishes.

_____ Make phone calls to people with whom you are not angry and want to catch up with.

_____ Clear your room or house.

_____ Clean out your closet and donate old clothes.

_____ Redecorate a room in your house.

_____ Organize your books, files, drawers, etc.

_____ Make a plan of action for finding a job, or for finding a better job if you already have one.

_____ Make appointments with various people—doctor, dentist, optometrist, accountant, etc.—and arrive on time.

_____ Get a new hairstyle or haircut.

_____ Get a manicure or pedicure.

_____ Get a massage.

_____ Wash your car.

_____ Plan something: a party, event, your next vacation.

_____ Mow the lawn.

_____ Plant a garden, or do gardening work in your own space or in a community garden.

_____ Clean out your garage.

_____ Do homework or other work.

_____ Clean your bathtub and take a bath.

_____ Go grocery shopping and cook a nice dinner for yourself.

_____ Pay bills.

_____ Other ideas: _____

Do a Pleasurable Activity

_____ Call or text a friend.

_____ Visit a friend or invite a friend to come over.

_____ Exercise: lift weights; do yoga, tai chi, or Pilates, or take classes to learn how; stretch your muscles; ride your bike; go swimming or hiking; play something you can do by yourself, such as basketball, bowling, handball, miniature golf, billiards.

_____ Get out of your house and go for a drive in your car, or ride public transportation.

_____ Plan a daytrip to somewhere you've always wanted to go.

_____ Sleep or take a nap.

_____ Eat something you really like.

_____ Cook your favorite meal.

_____ Watch TV or stream shows on the Internet.

_____ Go to a sporting event.

_____ Play video games.

_____ Join an Internet dating service.

_____ Create your own blog or website.

_____ Go shopping.

_____ Go to a bookstore and read.

_____ Go to your place of worship.

_____ Sing or learn how to sing.

_____ Take pictures.

_____ Join a club or attend a meet-up group.

_____ Make a movie or video with your phone.

_____ Go to a flower shop and smell your favorite flowers.

_____ Knit, crochet, or sew, or learn how.

_____ Make a scrapbook.

_____ Write a loving letter to yourself when you're feeling good, and read it when you're feeling upset.

_____ Draw or paint a picture, or learn how.

_____ Make a bucket list of things you want to do before you die.

_____ Make a list of 10 things you're good at or that you like about yourself.

_____ Masturbate or have sex with someone you care about.

_____ Join a public-speaking group and write a speech.

_____ Pray or meditate.

_____ Other ideas: _____

Alternatives to Self-Destructive Behaviors

Some people who struggle with overwhelming emotions use self-destructive behaviors to temporarily relieve their distress. Instead of continuing to hurt yourself, consider using some tools to help shift your emotions rather than acting on them. Following are some examples, and a place for you to add your own ideas:

_____ Instead of hurting yourself, hold an ice cube in one hand and squeeze it. The sensation from the cold ice will be numbing and distracting.

_____ Write on yourself with a red felt-tip marker instead of cutting. Draw exactly where you would cut. Use red paint or nail polish to make it look like you're bleeding. Then draw stitches with a black marker. If you need more distraction, squeeze an ice cube in the other hand at the same time.

_____ Snap a rubber band on your wrist each time you feel like hurting yourself. This is very painful, but it causes less permanent damage than cutting, burning, or otherwise mutilating yourself.

_____ Dig your fingernails into your arm without breaking the skin.

_____ Throw foam balls, rolled up socks, or pillows against the wall as hard as you can.

_____ Scream as loud as you can into a pillow or scream someplace where you won't draw attention, like your car or at a loud concert.

_____ Cry. Sometimes people don't cry because they're afraid that if they start they'll never stop. This never happens. In fact, the truth is that crying can make you feel better because it releases stress hormones.

_____ Other ideas: _____

Take a Time-Out

Sometimes when you get emotionally triggered, the best thing you can do is leave, or take a "time-out." If you find yourself in an extremely distressing situation with someone or something, and, after trying to practice mindful acceptance or enact a values-based action, you're still very upset, it's often best to distance yourself and shift your attention away from the trigger to a more positive present-moment experience.

Try to remember that if you're already overwhelmed by your emotions, it will be more difficult to resolve your problem in a healthy way. If you stay in the situation, you may make it worse than it is already. If you can put some distance between you and the situation, and give yourself time to calm your emotions, you can better think about what to do next.

It may be helpful to rehearse doing this, or to write a short script ahead of time, so that you'll know exactly how you want to excuse yourself from the situation. If you don't feel you have time to excuse yourself, sometimes just walking away is the best you can do to keep from making a difficult situation worse.

Emotion Efficacy Therapy (EET) © 2016

Emotion Efficacy Therapy Skills

You now have a whole new set of skills to use to help you make choices that are effective and consistent with your values when you get triggered. Use the following list to review the EET skills you've learned and to complete the Personalized Emotion Efficacy Plan worksheet.

Mindful Acceptance

_____ Sensation Acceptance

_____ Feeling Labeling

_____ Thought Watching

_____ Urge Noticing

_____ Emotion Surfing

Mindful Coping

_____ Relaxation

_____ Self-Soothing

_____ Pleasurable Activities

_____ Coping Thoughts

_____ Distraction

_____ Time-Out

Values-Based Action

_____ Identify your value and the corresponding action in the moment of choice

Emotion Efficacy Therapy (EET) © 2016

Personalized Emotion Efficacy Plan

Use this list of EET skills to remember what works for you when you get emotionally triggered. In addition, there is space for you to write down what else you have learned or want to remember about your relationship with your emotions.

Mindful Acceptance Skills (O + A)

When I am triggered, I can practice the following mindful acceptance skills:

_____ **Sensation acceptance:** Identify any sensations, describe them to myself, make room for them to be exactly as they are, without reacting or judging.

_____ **Feeling labeling:** Identify any feeling labels, sit with the feeling, allow it to be exactly as it is without reacting or judging.

_____ **Thought watching:** Watch my thoughts as they arise, and then let them go. Notice any "sticky" thoughts and let them be exactly as they are, without reacting or judging.

_____ **Urge noticing:** Notice any urges to do something or not to do something. Notice what it's like not to act on the urge.

Values-Based Action (O + A + Choose Values-Based Action)

When I've practiced mindful acceptance (observe + accept) and want to choose to move toward my values, I can choose the following values-based actions:

Situation   VBA

_____   _____

Situation   VBA

_____   _____

Situation   VBA

_____   _____

Situation   VBA

_____   _____

Situation   VBA

_____   _____

Mindful Coping (**O** + **A** + **C**hoose Mindful Coping)

When I have practiced mindful acceptance and/or have tried to use values-based action and still feel at risk of acting on destructive urges, I can choose the following skills:

_____ **Relaxation:** Use diaphragmatic breathing, relaxation without tension, cue-controlled breathing, or the five-senses exercise to downshift emotion.

_____ **Self-soothing:** Stimulate each of my five senses to downshift emotion.

_____ **Coping thoughts:** Use a coping thought to reframe the situation and downshift emotion.

_____ **Radical acceptance:** Practice radical acceptance to allow difficult situations instead of resisting them, to downshift emotion.

_____ **Distraction:** Shift my attention to alternative present-moment experiences to downshift emotion.

_____ **Time-out:** Remove yourself from situations that are triggering where you risk making a difficult situation worse.

_____ **Other:** I want to remember the following about my relationship with my emotions:

_____

_____

_____

_____

_____

_____

_____

Emotion Efficacy Therapy (EET) © 2016

Session 7 Skills Practice

_____ Practice mindful acceptance for at least 10 minutes a day by observing and accepting the four components of emotion when you get emotionally triggered, or using emotion exposure to a difficult event, situation, or emotion. Observe all four parts of the emotion, and surf the emotion wave. (Refer to the mindful acceptance directions from Session 2 Skills Practice, if needed.) Record your mindful acceptance skills practice in the first row of your Skills Practice Record.

_____ Practice using distraction with exposure or in vivo by taking the following steps:

Step 1: Identify a distraction skill you want to practice ahead of time.

Step 2: Either find something to intentionally activate your emotions (e.g., recall a recent difficult situation or a distressing memory) or engage in a situation you know will be triggering. Pick something that you believe will take your SUDS up into the 5 to 7 range.

Step 3: Get into the scene or triggering situation until you reach your target SUDS, or until at least 5 minutes have passed.

Step 4: Practice mindful acceptance of the painful emotion (observe + accept all parts of the emotion: thoughts, feelings, sensations, and urges). Stay here for 5 minutes, if possible.

Step 5: Identify the moment of choice and apply the distraction skill you've chosen. Do this for at least 5 minutes.

Step 6: Notice and record your SUDS level at the end of your exercise.

Step 7: Record your skills practice on the fourth row of your Skills Practice Record.

_____ Practice using time-out when an appropriate triggering situation arises.

_____ Record any events that trigger you during the week at the bottom of your Skills Practice Record.

_____ Bring all of these materials to review in your next session.

Skills Practice Record

Emotion Efficacy Therapy

Directions: Place a check mark next to the skill you practice each day. Record any triggers at the bottom. Bring this record to your next session.

	Day 1	Day 2	Day 3	Day 4	Day 5	Day 6	Day 7
Observe the four parts of an emotion: sensations, feelings, thoughts, and urges.							
Observe, accept, and surf your emotion wave, with SUDS.							
Observe, accept, and choose a values-based action.							
Observe, accept, and choose a relaxation skill.							
Observe, accept, and choose a self-soothing skill.							
Observe, accept, and choose a coping thought.							
Observe, accept, and choose to practice radical acceptance.							
Observe, accept, and choose a distraction task or activity.							
Observe, accept, and choose a time-out.							

Emotional triggers: Record any events or emotions that are distressing during this week.

_____

_____

_____

Emotion Efficacy Therapy (EET) © 2016

EET Session 8

Components Covered: Emotion Awareness, Mindful Acceptance, Values-Based Action, Mindful Coping, and Exposure-Based Skills Practice (chapters 2–9)

Session 8 attempts to pull together and consolidate everything clients have learned during EET treatment. The session begins with a review of the Personalized Emotion Efficacy Plans with ample time for feedback and troubleshooting. Clients will get to choose from their skills to do a final exposure using either emotion or imaginal exposure and an EET skill of their choice. Next, group members will rate their emotion efficacy and share how they think they can continue to increase it. Finally, clients receive validation for participating in treatment, especially for their willingness to learn and try new behaviors. Outcome measures would ideally be administered before clients leave session.

Materials

None

Overview

1. Mindful acceptance practice and feedback

2. Skills practice review

3. Review of Personalized Emotion Efficacy Plans, feedback, and troubleshooting

4. Imaginal or emotion exposure with EET skill and feedback

5. Rate emotion efficacy

6. Closing remarks and appreciations

7. Administration of any posttreatment questionnaires

Procedures

1. Mindful acceptance practice and feedback

For the first ten minutes of session, lead clients through mindful acceptance practice using the guided script. Ask clients to provide feedback about their experience as an opportunity for learning and troubleshooting.

2. Skills practice review

Briefly review Session 7 skills and ask clients to share feedback about their weekly practice using their Skills Practice record.

3. Review of Personalized Emotion Efficacy Plans, feedback, and troubleshooting

Using the completed PEEPs, ask each client to share what he or she recorded. Solicit any questions they have about the skills. Emphasize that treatment is only eight weeks and that skills that are more difficult will become easier the more they are practiced.

4. Imaginal or emotion exposure with EET skill and feedback

Lead your clients through a final exposure using a situation and skill of their choosing. Be sure to leave at least fifteen minutes for feedback.

Step 1: Identify the EET skill. Ask group participants to identify what skill they want to choose in the moment of choice. Be sure you have the list of EET skills for reference.

Step 2: Select a distressing situation. Instruct clients to identify a recent distressing event in which they became emotionally triggered and responded with experiential avoidance or other emotion-driven behavior.

Step 3: Initiate emotion exposure. Tell group participants to visualize the triggering scene, noticing the environment where the trigger occurred: watch the action in the scene; hear what's said. Then instruct them to practice observing and accepting the emotion, "making room" for any thoughts, sensations, feelings, or urges, allowing the emotion to be what it is with no effort at controlling or avoiding them. Have clients rate their SUDS and record it.

Step 4: Initiate the practice of mindful acceptance. Instruct clients to practice mindful acceptance by observing and accepting any thoughts, feelings, sensations, or urges, without resisting or reacting to them. Have clients rate their SUDS and record it.

Step 5: Guide clients through the skill. Now ask clients to locate their moment of choice. Then lead them through the EET skill of their choice for the next five minutes or until their SUDS have dropped below a 2. Ask group participants to rate their SUDS at the end and record it.

5. Rate emotion efficacy

Now that treatment is coming to an end, you'll want to ask clients to informally rate their emotion efficacy when they began treatment and now, at the end. You can use the Emotion Efficacy Scale as a brief measure pretreatment and posttreatment. Or, you can conduct an informal assessment by asking them to rate their emotion efficacy using a scale from 0 to 10, with 1 being no emotion efficacy, 5 being able to use skills about 50 percent of the time, and 10 being able to use skills every time they are emotionally triggered to choose a VBA. You might also ask group members what they think will help them increase their emotion efficacy.

6. Closing remarks and appreciations

As noted in chapter 1, changing behavior is difficult when people have been hardwired for survival, have a negativity bias, and—since these clients are seeking treatment for emotion problems—are usually highly reactive. Validate clients for being willing and flexible enough to try new behaviors and make choices that will often feel unnatural when they are first used. Remind them that they can continue to improve their emotion efficacy through practice, especially in an emotionally activated state.

This is also a time to speak to any specific challenges that were shared and overcome in the group, how the group may have supported each of its members, and what they were able to learn from each other.

7. Administer any posttreatment questionnaires

If you are using posttreatment measures, administer them at the end of this session. A list of recommended questionnaires is provided in chapter 10, and full versions are available in Appendix A: Outcome Measures.

Script for Guided Mindful Acceptance

For the next ten minutes I'm going to lead you through a mindful acceptance practice exercise. You will practice observing and accepting your emotional experience in the present moment. Practicing mindful acceptance in a neutral state will build your emotion efficacy muscle and make it easier for you to use this skill when you are triggered.

First, just sit comfortably, and either close your eyes or relax your gaze and pick a spot to focus on in front of you.

Now, take a few minutes to notice any sensations in your body. Scan your body until you find a sensation and rest your attention on it. See if you can let it be just as it is and get curious about it. Notice its size and shape; whether it's moving or staying the same; if there's any temperature or tension to it. See if you can soften to it, or even lean into the sensation…

Now, see if you can identify a feeling label that goes with the sensation…just name it and allow it to be as it is without judgment or reacting to it.

Next, we'll spend a few minutes just noticing and watching our thoughts. Our brains produce different kinds of thoughts all the time, and the key is not to get involved with them. Instead, as each thought arises, you can simply say, "There's a thought," and then let the thought go. Then, just return to the present moment, and wait for the next thought to arise. For the next few minutes, notice your thoughts until I say stop…

Okay, now stop. Next, see if there's an urge that goes with your sensations or thoughts. It could be an urge to do something or not do something. Try to just sit with the urge. Notice what it's like not to act on the urge, to just surf it.

[Allow the client to sit with the urge for 30 seconds. Then repeat the sequence one more time.]

Before you come out of this exercise, take a few deep breaths and slowly open your eyes as you bring your attention back to the room.

Emotion Efficacy Therapy (EET) © 2016

EET References

Allen, L. B., McHugh, R. K., and Barlow, D. B. (2008). Emotional disorders: A unified protocol. In D. B. Barlow (Ed.), *Clinical handbook of psychological disorders* (pp. 216–249). New York: Guilford Press.

Barrera, T. L., Mott, J. M., Hofstein, R. F., & Teng, E. J. (2013). A meta-analytic review of exposure in group cognitive behavioral therapy for post-traumatic stress disorder. *Clinical Psychology Review, 1*, 24–32

Berking, M., Margraf, M., Ebert, D., Wupperman, P., Hofmann, S. G., & Junghanns, K. (2011). Deficits in emotion-regulation skills predict alcohol use during and after cognitive-behavioral therapy for alcohol dependence. *Journal of Consulting in Clinical Psychology, 79*(3), 307–318.

Brach, T. (2003). *Radical Acceptance: Embracing Your Life With the Heart of a Buddha.* New York: Bantam.

Bond, F. W., Hayes, S. C., Baer, R. A., Carpenter, K. M., Guenole, N., Orcutt, H. K., ... & Zettle, R. D. (2011). Preliminary psychometric properties of the Acceptance and Action Questionnaire–II: A revised measure of psychological flexibility and experiential avoidance. *Behavior Therapy, 42*, 676–688.

Caprara, G. V., Di Giunta, L., Eisenberg, N., Gerbino, M., Pastorelli, C., & Tramontano, C. (2008). Assessing regulatory emotional self-efficacy in three countries. *Psychological Assessment, 20*(3), 227–237. http://doi.org/10.1037/1040–3590.20.3.227.

Carver, C. S., Johnson, S. L., & Joormann, J. (2008). Serotonergic function, two-mode models of self-regulation, and vulnerability to depression: What depression has in common with impulsive aggression. *Psychological Bulletin, 134*(6), 912–943.

Craske, M. G., Treanor, M., Conway, C., Zbozinek, T., & Vervliet, B. (2014). Maximizing exposure therapy: an inhibitory learning approach. *Behaviour Research and Therapy, 58*, 10–23. http://doi.org/10.1016/j.brat.2014.04.006.

Eisenberg, N., Fabes, R. A., Guthrie, I. V., & Reiser, M. (2000). Dispositional emotionality and regulation: Their role in predicting quality of social functioning. *Journal of Personality and Social Psychology, 78*(1), 136–157.

Ekman, P. (1994). All emotions are basic. In P. Ekman and R. Davidson (Eds.), *The Nature of Emotion: Fundamental Questions* (pp. 15–19). New York: Oxford University Press.

Frank, S., & Davison, J. (2014). *The transdiagnostic roadmap for case formulation and treatment planning.* Oakland, CA: New Harbinger Publications Inc.

Frankl, Victor. (n.d.). Retrieved from http://izquotes.com/quote/65260. Accessed on November 1, 2015.

Garnefski, N., & Kraaij, V. (2007). The cognitive emotion regulation questionnaire: Psychometric features and prospective relationships with depression and anxiety in adults. *European Journal of Psychological Assessment, 23*(3), 141–149.

Gratz, K., & Roemer, L. (2004). Multidimensional assessment of emotion regulation and dysregulation: Development, factor structure, and initial validation of the Difficulties in Emotion Regulation Scale. *Journal of Psychopathology and Behavioral Assessment, 26*(1), 41–54.

Hanson, R. (2009). *Buddha's brain: The practical neuroscience of happiness, love & wisdom.* Oakland, CA: New Harbinger Publications.

Hayes, S. C., Luoma, J., Bond, F., Masuda, A., & Lillis, J. (2006). Acceptance and commitment therapy: Model, processes, and outcomes. *Behaviour Research and Therapy, 44*(1), 1–25.

Hayes, S. C., Strosahl, K., & Wilson, K. G. (1999). *Acceptance and commitment therapy: An experiential approach to behavior change.* New York: The Guilford Press.

Kleiman, E. M., & Riskind, J. H. (2012). Cognitive vulnerability to comorbidity: Looming cognitive style and depressive cognitive style as synergistic predictors of anxiety and depression symptoms. *Journal of Behavior Therapy and Experimental Psychiatry, 43,* 1,109–1,114.

Kliem, S., Kroger, C., & Kosfelder, J. (2010). Dialectical behavior therapy for borderline personality disorder: A meta-analysis using mixed-effects modeling. *Journal of Consulting and Clinical Psychology, 78*(6), 936–951.

Kring, A. M. (2010). The future of emotion research in the study of psychopathology. *Emotion Review, 2*(3), 225–228.

Kring, A. M., & Sloan, A. M. (2010). *Emotion regulation and psychopathology.* New York: The Guilford Press.

Lauterbach, D. L., & Gloster, A. T. (2007). Description, mechanisms of action, and assessment. In D. C. S. Richard & D. L. Lauterbach, (Eds.), *Handbook of exposure therapies.* Burlington, MA: Elsevier.

Linehan, M. M. (1993). *Cognitive-behavioral treatment for borderline personality disorder.* New York: Guilford Press.

Lovibond, P. F., & Lovibond, S. H. (1995). The structure of negative emotional states: Comparison of the Depression Anxiety Stress Scales (DASS) with the Beck Depression and Anxiety Inventories. *Behaviour Research and Therapy, 33*(3), 335–343.

Lovibond, S. H., & Lovibond, P. F. (1995). *Manual for the Depression Anxiety Stress Scales.* (2nd. Ed.) Sydney: Psychology Foundation. http:// www.psy.unsw.edu.au/dass/.

Marx , B. P., & Sloan, D. M. (2002). The role of emotion in the psychological functioning of adult survivors of childhood sexual abuse. *Behavior Therapy, 33*, 563–577.

McCracken, L. M., Spertus, I. L., Janeck, A. S., Sinclair, D., & Wetzel, F. T. (1999). Behavioral dimensions of adjustment in persons with chronic pain: Pain-related anxiety and acceptance. *Pain, 80*, 283–289.

McEvoy, P. M., Nathan, P., & Norton, P. J. (2009). Efficacy of transdiagnostic treatments: The review of published outcome studies and future research directions. *Journal of Cognitive Psychotherapy: An International Quarterly, 23*(1), 20–33.

McKay, M., Rogers, P. D., & McKay, J. (2003). *When anger hurts.* Oakland, CA: New Harbinger Publications.

McKay, M., Wood, J. C., & Brantley, J. (2007). *The dialectical behavior therapy skills workbook.* Oakland, CA: New Harbinger Publications.

Ost, L-G. (1987). Applied relaxation: Description of a coping technique and review of controlled studies. *Behavior Research Therapy, 25*, 397–409.

Persons, J., & Miranda, J. (1992). Cognitive theories of vulnerability to depression: Reconciling negative evidence. *Cognitive Therapy and Research, 16*(4), 485–502.

Rafaeli, E., Bernstein, D. P., & Young, J. E. (2011). *Schema therapy: Distinctive features.* Hove, East Sussex: Routledge.

Richards, J. M., & Gross, J. J. (2000). Emotion regulation and memory: The cognitive costs of keeping one's cool. *Journal of Personality and Social Psychology, 79*, 410–424.

Ruiz, F. J. (2010). A review of acceptance and commitment therapy (ACT) empirical evidence: Correlational, experimental psychopathology, component and outcome studies. *International Journal of Psychology and Psychological Therapy, 10*(1), 125–162.

Simons, J. S., & Gaher, R. M. (2005). The distress tolerance scale: Development and validation of a self-report measure. *Motivation and Emotion, 29*(2), 83–102.

Szymanski, J., & O'Donohue, W. (1995). The potential role of state-dependent learning in cognitive therapy with spider phobics. *Journal of Rational-Emotive & Cognitive-Behavior Therapy, 13*(2), 131–150.

Tryon, W. W. (2005). Possible mechanisms for why desensitization and exposure therapy work. *Clinical Psychology Review, 25,* 67–95.

Wilamoska, Z. A., Thompson-Hollands, J., Fairholme, C. P., Ellard, K. K., Farchione, T.J., & Barlow, D. H. (2010). Conceptual background, development and preliminary data from the unified protocol for transdiagnostic treatment of emotional disorders. *Depression and Anxiety, 27,* 882–890.

Wilson, K. G., Sandoz, E. K., Kitchens, J., & Roberts, M. E. (2010). The Valued Living Questionnaire: Defining and measuring valued action within a behavioral framework. *The Psychological Record, 60,* 249–272.

Zettel, R. D. (2007). *ACT for depression.* Oakland, CA: New Harbinger Publications.

Matthew McKay, PhD, is a professor at the Wright Institute in Berkeley, CA. He has authored and coauthored numerous books, including *The Relaxation and Stress Reduction Workbook, Self-Esteem, Thoughts and Feelings, When Anger Hurts*, and *ACT on Life Not on Anger*. McKay received his PhD in clinical psychology from the California School of Professional Psychology, and specializes in the cognitive behavioral treatment of anxiety and depression. He lives and works in the greater San Francisco Bay Area.

Aprilia West, PsyD, MT, is a psychotherapist and emotion researcher based in the San Francisco Bay Area, where she specializes in treating anxiety disorders, mood disorders, and trauma. She became interested in the concept of emotion efficacy working as a former advisor, organizational consultant, mediator, and executive coach to members of Congress, Fortune 500 companies, entertainment industry professionals, and international advocacy campaigns. West holds a PsyD in clinical psychology from the Wright Institute in Berkeley, CA, and a master's degree in teaching from the University of Virginia.

Index

A

about this book, 10–11
Acceptance and Action Questionnaire (AAQ-2), 145, 158
acceptance and commitment therapy (ACT), 3
acceptance of emotions. *See* mindful acceptance
acceptance of reality. *See* radical acceptance
Anatomy of an Emotion handout, 20, 173
Art of Radical Acceptance handout, 113–114, 234–235
assessment: emotion efficacy, 259; importance of ongoing, 145; outcome measures for, 145, 149–158; symptom inventories and, 145–146; values, 60–69
attention, shifting, 124, 125–126, 130
automatic negative thoughts, 103; identified by clients, 104; replacing with coping thoughts, 104–105, 107–108, 232–233
avoidance of emotions. *See* emotion avoidance
awareness of emotions. *See* emotion awareness

B

Before You Act, Distract handout, 133–134, 244
behavior dysregulation, 2

behaviors

behaviors: emotion-driven, 43, 51–52; self-destructive, 124, 129–130
Benefits of Values-Based Action Worksheet, 72, 203
Brach, Tara, 17
breathing: cue-controlled, 93, 96, 219; diaphragmatic, 92, 95, 218

C

choice. *See* moment of choice
chronic pain, 143, 146
Client Coping Thoughts handout, 106, 231
clients: assessment process for, 145–146; orienting to treatment, 13–14; providing ongoing support to, 146–147; self-assessment of emotion efficacy, 259; tailoring treatment for, 144
cognitive emotion avoidance, 44
confidentiality in groups, 167
Consequences of Emotion Avoidance handout, 44–45, 183
consolidating learning, 139–142, 196, 209, 257–260
coping thoughts, 103–112; examples of, 106, 108; exposure and, 105, 109–112, 227–228; guiding the creation of, 104–105; handout and worksheet on, 106–108, 231–233; introducing clients to, 104–105; O+A+C model and, 105; psychoeducation on, 227; replacing automatic thoughts with, 104–105, 107–108, 232–233; summary points

about, 121; therapy dialogue example, 109–112. *See also* mindful coping

cue-controlled breathing, 93, 96, 219

D

defusion, 29

demoralization, 143–144

Depression, Anxiety, and Stress Scale–21 (DASS–21), 145, 156–157

dialectical behavior therapy (DBT), 3, 112

diaphragmatic breathing, 92, 95, 218

Difficulties in Emotion Regulation Scale (DERS), 145, 151–152

disclosure in groups, 167

distraction, 123–134; benefits of, 133; emotion exposure and, 241–242; explanation of, 123–124; handout on using, 133–134, 244; O+A+C model and, 131; psychoeducation on, 130, 241; steps for mindful, 133–134, 244; strategies for, 124–130, 245–250; summary points about, 138; therapy dialogue example, 131–133

Distraction Strategies handout, 124–130, 245–250

distress intolerance, 1, 4

distress tolerance, 7, 9, 89, 160, 163

Distress Tolerance Scale (DTS), 145, 150

distressing situations: accessing values during, 69–70, 75–76, 83–87; imaginal exposure using, 83–87

E

EET. *See* emotion efficacy therapy

eight-session protocol for EET, 142–143, 165–260. *See also specific EET sessions*

emotion activation, 144–145

emotion avoidance, 43, 44–49; consequences of, 45, 46–47; emotion efficacy and, 1, 4; mindful coping and, 133; pros and cons of, 46–47; strategies

related to, 44, 45; therapy dialogue example, 48–49

Emotion Avoidance Consequences Worksheet, 47, 184

emotion awareness, 6, 13–25; components of emotion and, 19–25; demoralization related to, 143–144; feelings word list for, 24; handout explaining, 17–18, 171–172; introducing to clients, 16–19; psychoeducation on, 168; session protocol for, 165–177; summary points about, 27; therapy dialogue examples, 18–19, 21–22; worksheet for practicing, 23, 174

Emotion Awareness handout, 17–18, 171–172

emotion dysregulation, 2, 7, 9, 30, 33

emotion efficacy: client self-assessment of, 259; definition of, 1, 11, 15; explaining to clients, 14–16; impact of low, 2

Emotion Efficacy Scale (EES), 145, 155

emotion efficacy therapy (EET): assessment in, 145–146; components of, 5–8, 15–16; conceptualization of, 1–2; consolidating learning about, 139–142; eight-session protocol for, 142–143, 165–260; exposure used in, 33–37; foundational elements of, 3–5; moment of choice in, 37–41; orienting clients to, 13–14; outcome measures used in, 145, 149–158; providing ongoing support in, 146–147; reasons for using, 2–3; research results on, 159–163; session structure for, 10–11, 25; Skills Practice Record, 25–26, 168, 177; summary points about, 11, 147; treatment challenges in, 143–145; uniqueness of, 8–9. *See also specific EET sessions*

Emotion Efficacy Therapy Skills handout, 139–140, 252

emotion exposure, 8, 33, 258; coping thoughts and, 227–228; distraction and, 241–242; final session exercise on, 258;

mindful acceptance and, 34–37; radical acceptance and, 228–229; relaxation skills and, 214–215; self-soothing skills and, 215–216. *See also* exposure-based skills practice; imaginal exposure

emotion regulation: mindful coping and, 8, 104; research results on EET for, 159, 161–162

emotion surfing, 43–58; emotion avoidance vs., 44–49; emotion-driven behavior vs., 51–52; exposure-based practice and, 54–56; handouts for practicing, 53, 57, 192; key abilities required for, 43–44; mindful acceptance and, 52; psychoeducation on, 179; rumination vs., 50–51; script for guided, 55, 185; summary points about, 58; therapy dialogue examples, 53–54, 56

Emotion Surfing Practice handout, 57, 192

Emotion Watching Worksheet, 23, 174

emotion wave metaphor, 43

emotional triggers: imaginal exposure using, 83–87; values-based action and, 69–70, 75–76, 83–87

emotion-driven behavior, 43, 51–52; emotion intensified by, 51; talking with clients about, 52

emotions: activation of, 144–145; anatomy of, 20, 173; components of, 19–25; explaining to clients, 16, 17–18; psychoeducation on, 168; reasons people struggle with, 18

experiential avoidance, 1, 9, 160, 163

experiential exercises: five-senses relaxation, 93, 96–97, 219; Monsters on the Bus, 75–82, 207–208. *See also* guided practices

explanations, 50, 51

exposure therapy, 5

exposure-based skills practice, 5, 8, 33–37; coping thoughts and, 105, 109–112, 227–228; distraction and, 131; emotion surfing and, 54–56; final session exercise on, 258; handout for introducing, 34, 189; imaginal vs. emotion exposure in, 8, 33; mindful acceptance and, 34–37, 186–188; psychoeducation on, 186–188; radical acceptance and, 228–229; relaxation and, 214–215; self-soothing and, 215–216; values-based action and, 83–87, 194–196, 208–209

F

feelings: emotional experience and, 20; labeling without judging, 31, 180; list of words describing, 24, 175

Feelings Word List, 24, 175

five-senses exercise, 93, 96–97, 219

Frankl, Victor, 38

G

group dynamics, 167, 186, 188

guided practices: emotion surfing, 55; mindful acceptance, 32–33, 182. *See also* experiential exercises

H

handouts: Anatomy of an Emotion, 20, 173; Art of Radical Acceptance, 113–114, 234–235; Before You Act, Distract, 133–134, 244; Client Coping Thoughts, 106, 231; Consequences of Emotion Avoidance, 44–45, 183; Distraction Strategies, 124–130, 245–250; Emotion Awareness, 17–18, 171–172; Emotion Efficacy Therapy Skills, 139–140, 252; Emotion Surfing Practice, 57, 192; Feelings Word List, 24, 175; How to Surf an Emotion Wave, 53; Introduction to Exposure, 34, 189; Mindful Acceptance | Observe + Accept, 31–32, 180–181; Mindful Coping Through Relaxation, 95–97, 218–219; Moment of Choice, 37–38, 198; Rumination, 51; Take a Time-Out, 134, 251; What Is Emotion

Efficacy?, 15, 170; What You Can Expect from Emotion Efficacy Therapy, 14, 169. *See also* worksheets

Hayes, Steven, 3

hearing, sense of, 98–99, 221–222

high emotion efficacy, 3, 15

How to Surf an Emotion Wave handout, 53

I

imaginal exposure, 8, 33; coping thoughts and, 105, 109–112; emotion surfing and, 54, 58; final session exercise on, 258; mindful acceptance and, 34–37, 186–188; psychoeducation on, 186–188; values-based action and, 83–87, 194–196, 208–209. *See also* emotion exposure; exposure-based skills practice

Introduction to Exposure handout, 34, 189

J

judgments, 50, 51

K

Kabat-Zinn, Jon, 30

L

learning: consolidating, 139–142, 196, 209, 257–260; state-dependent, 5, 57, 90; transemotional, 4–5

Linehan, Marsha, 3, 112

low emotion efficacy: characteristics of, 1–2; transdiagnostic treatment for, 3–4

M

maladaptive behavioral responses, 1

metaphors: emotion wave, 43; monsters on the bus, 75

mindful acceptance, 6–7, 29–42; benefits to using, 31; consolidating learning about, 140–141; emotion surfing and, 52; exposure-based practice and, 33–37;

handout for introducing, 31–32, 180–181; moment of choice and, 37–41; psychoeducation on, 29–33, 179; script for guided, 32–33, 182; session protocol for, 178–192; summary points about, 42; therapy dialogue examples, 34–37, 38–41, 186–188. *See also* radical acceptance

Mindful Acceptance | Observe + Accept handout, 31–32, 180–181

mindful coping, 7–8, 89–138; advantages of, 90; consolidating learning about, 140, 141–142; coping thoughts and, 103–112, 231–233; criteria for using, 137; in daily life, 137–138; distraction and, 123–134, 244–250; explanation of, 89–90; introducing to clients, 90–91; O+A+C model and, 92, 101–102; outside-of-session use of, 101–102; psychoeducation on, 214; radical acceptance and, 112–120, 234–237; relaxation skills and, 92–97, 218–219; self-soothing techniques and, 97–101, 220–223; session protocols for, 213–256; steps for guiding practice of, 91; summary points about, 102, 121, 138; therapy dialogue examples, 91, 93–95, 101, 137–138; time-out and, 134–137

Mindful Coping Through Relaxation handout, 95–97, 218–219

Mindful Coping Through Self-Soothing worksheet, 97–100, 220–223

mindfulness: mindful acceptance derived from, 29, 31; videos for introducing, 30

moment of choice: client identification of, 7, 15; handout for introducing, 37–38, 198; mindful acceptance and, 29, 37–41; psychoeducation on, 194; therapy dialogue example, 38–41; values-based action and, 71, 88

Moment of Choice handout, 37–38, 198

Monsters on the Bus exercise, 75–82; in-session use of, 207–208; preparing clients for, 76; therapy dialogue example, 77–82

motivation, 60, 71, 74, 75–76, 88

N

negative thoughts. *See* automatic negative thoughts

negativity bias, 17

O

O+A+C (observe + accept + choose) model, 83; coping thoughts and, 105; distraction and, 131; imaginal exposure with VBA and, 83–84, 195, 208–209; mindful coping and, 92, 101–102; time-out and, 135

outcome measures, 145, 149–158; Acceptance and Action Questionnaire, 158; Depression, Anxiety, and Stress Scale–21, 156–157; Difficulties in Emotion Regulation Scale, 151–152; Distress Tolerance Scale, 150; Emotion Efficacy Scale, 155; Valued Living Questionnaire, 153–154

P

panic disorder, 143

Personalized Emotion Efficacy Plan, 140–142, 253–254

perspective taking, 29

pleasurable activities, 124, 128–129

posttreatment measures, 259

predictions, 50, 51

pretreatment measures, 166

productivity, focusing on, 124, 126–127

protective emotion avoidance, 44

psychoeducation: on coping thoughts, 227; on distraction, 130; on emotion awareness, 168; on emotion surfing, 179; on mindful acceptance, 29–33, 179; on mindful coping, 214; on moment of

choice, 194; on radical acceptance, 228; on time-out, 135

R

radical acceptance, 112–120; emotion exposure and, 228–229; examples of, 113; explanation of, 112, 113–114; handout on art of, 113–114, 234–235; practice worksheet, 118–120, 236–237; psychoeducation on, 228; situational assessment, 118–120; steps for practicing, 120, 237; summary points about, 121; therapy dialogue example, 114–118. *See also* mindful acceptance

Radical Acceptance worksheet, 118–120, 236–237

relaxation, 92–97; emotion exposure and, 214–215; techniques used for, 92–93, 95–97, 218–219; therapy dialogue example, 93–95

relaxation without tension practice, 92–93, 96, 218

Replacing Automatic Thoughts with Coping Thoughts worksheet, 107–108

research results on EET, 159–163

rumination, 43, 50–51; handout about, 51; skill difficulties related to, 143; three main forms of, 50

Rumination handout, 51

S

sacred pause, 38

safe space in groups, 167

scripts: Guided Emotion Surfing, 55, 185; Guided Mindful Acceptance, 32–33, 182. *See also* experiential exercises

self-destructive behaviors, 124, 129–130

self-report scales, 145

self-soothing, 97–101; emotion exposure and, 215–216; five senses used for, 97–100, 220–223; therapy dialogue example, 101 sensations: emotional experience and, 20; mindful acceptance of, 31, 143, 180

senses: five-senses relaxation exercise, 93, 96–97; self-soothing using each of, 97–100, 220–223

session 1 of EET (Emotion Awareness), 165–177; description, 165; group dynamics, 167; handouts and worksheets, 169–175; materials list, 166; pretreatment measures, 166; procedures overview, 166–168; skills practice, 176–177

session 2 of EET (Mindful Acceptance), 178–192; description, 178; exposure exercise, 186–188; group dynamics, 186, 188; handouts and worksheets, 180–185, 189; materials list, 178; procedures overview, 179; scripts, 182, 185; skills practice, 190–191

session 3 of EET (Values-Based Action), 193–205; description, 193; handouts and worksheets, 197–203; imaginal exposure, 194–196; materials list, 193; procedures overview, 194–196; skills practice, 204–205

session 4 of EET (Values-Based Action), 206–212; description, 206; handouts and worksheets, 210–211; imaginal exposure, 208–209; materials list, 206; Monsters on the Bus exercise, 207–208; procedures overview, 206–209; skills practice, 211–212

session 5 of EET (Mindful Coping), 213–225; description, 213; emotion exposure, 214–216; handouts and worksheets, 217–223; materials list, 213; procedures overview, 214–216; relaxation practice, 214–215, 218–219; self-soothing practice, 215–216, 220–223; skills practice, 224–225

session 6 of EET (Mindful Coping), 226–239; coping thoughts practice, 227–228, 231–233; description, 226; emotion exposure, 227–229; handouts and worksheets, 230–237; materials list, 226; procedures overview, 227–229; radical acceptance practice, 228–229, 234–237; skills practice, 238–239

session 7 of EET (Mindful Coping), 240–256; description, 240; distraction practice, 241–242, 244–250; EET skills review, 252; emotion exposure, 241–242; handouts and worksheets, 243–254; materials list, 240; Personalized Emotion Efficacy Plan, 242, 253–254; procedures overview, 241–242; skills practice, 255–256; time-out practice, 251

session 8 of EET (Consolidation), 257–260; description, 257; emotion efficacy rating, 259; exposure exercise, 258; posttreatment measures, 259; procedures overview, 257–259; validation and closing remarks, 259

shifting attention, 124, 125–126, 130

sight, sense of, 98, 220–221

situational emotion avoidance, 44

skills: difficulty with specific, 143; importance of practicing, 168

Skills Practice Record, 25–26, 168, 177

smell, sense of, 97–98, 220

somatic emotion avoidance, 44

state-dependent learning, 5, 57, 90

"stretch" in EET, 144

Strosahl, Kirk, 3

substitution emotion avoidance, 44

SUDS rating, 34, 189

surfing emotions. See emotion surfing

symptom inventories, 145–146

T

Take a Time-Out handout, 134, 251

taste, sense of, 99–100, 222

thoughts: automatic negative, 103, 104; coping, 103–112; emotional experience and, 20; mindful watching of, 32, 50, 143, 181 time-out, 134–136; explanation of, 134; handout on taking, 134, 251; introducing to clients, 135; psychoeducation about, 135, 241; summary points about, 138; therapy dialogue example, 136

touch, sense of, 100, 222–223

transdiagnostic treatments, 3–4

transemotional learning, 4–5

triggering situations: coping thoughts and, 104; imaginal exposure using, 83–87; values-based action and, 69–70, 75–76, 83–87

U

urges: emotional experience and, 20; mindful noticing of, 32, 181; problem with acting on, 51

V

Valued Living Questionnaire (VLQ), 145, 153–154

values: accessing during distress, 69–70; barriers to acting on, 70–71; client assessment of, 60–69

values assessment, 60–69; by life domain, 63–69; therapy dialogue example, 66–67; worksheets for, 61–62, 64, 68–69

Values Clarification Worksheet, 61–62

Values Domains worksheet, 64–65, 68–69, 199–202

values-based action (VBA), 7, 59–88; assessing values for, 60–69; barriers to, 70–71; benefits of, 60, 72, 73; consolidating learning about, 140, 141; distressing situations and, 69–70, 75–76, 83–87; explanation of, 59–60; imaginal exposure and, 83–87, 194–196, 208–209; life domains and, 63–69; moment of choice and, 71, 88; Monsters on the Bus exercise and, 75–82; motivation and, 60, 71, 74, 75–76, 88; session protocols for, 193–212; summary points about, 73–74, 88; therapy dialogue examples, 66–67, 73, 77–82, 84–87

videos on mindfulness, 30

W

watching thoughts, 32, 50, 143, 181

What Is Emotion Efficacy? handout, 15, 170

What You Can Expect from Emotion Efficacy Therapy handout, 14, 169

Wilson, Kelly, 3

worksheets: Benefits of Values-Based Action, 72, 203; Emotion Avoidance Consequences, 47, 184; Emotion Watching, 23, 174; Mindful Coping Through Self-Soothing, 97–100, 220–223; Personalized Emotion Efficacy Plan, 140–142, 253–254; Radical Acceptance, 118–120, 236–237; Replacing Automatic Thoughts with Coping Thoughts, 107–108; Skills Practice Record, 25–26, 168, 177; Values Clarification, 61–62; Values Domains, 64–65, 68–69, 199–202. *See also* handouts

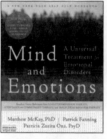

Register your **new harbinger** titles for additional benefits!

When you register your **new harbinger** title—purchased in any format, from any source—you get access to benefits like the following:

- Downloadable accessories like printable worksheets and extra content

- Instructional videos and audio files

- Information about updates, corrections, and new editions

Not every title has accessories, but we're adding new material all the time.

Access free accessories in 3 easy steps:

1. Sign in at NewHarbinger.com (or **register** to create an account).

2. Click on **register a book**. Search for your title and click the **register** button when it appears.

3. Click on the **book cover or title** to go to its details page. Click on **accessories** to view and access files.

That's all there is to it!

If you need help, visit:

NewHarbinger.com/accessories

new harbinger
CELEBRATING
40 YEARS